Maryland
REAL ESTATE
Practice & Law
FOURTEENTH EDITION

Donald A. White

Dearborn
Real Estate Education

President: Dr. Andrew Temte
Chief Learning Officer: Dr. Tim Smaby
Executive Director, Real Estate Education: Melissa Kleeman-Moy
Development Editor: Adam Bissen

MARYLAND REAL ESTATE PRACTICE & LAW FOURTEENTH EDITION
©2014 Kaplan, Inc.
Published by DF Institute, Inc., d/b/a Dearborn Real Estate Education
332 Front St. S., Suite 501
La Crosse, WI 54601

Printed in the United States of America

ISBN: 978-1-4754-2181-1 / 1-4754-2181-8
PPN: 1510-0814

Contents

Preface

As a student entering a real estate prelicensing course, you face exciting challenges. You must learn a large body of theory and understand how it applies to real estate practice. You will want to know legal principles and real estate theory so well that when you get your license, you will be able to do the right thing almost automatically.

If you fail to understand and appreciate law and theory, you can suffer devastating financial and legal consequences. On the other hand, if you build your educational foundation in real estate carefully, you should be able to make the money you want and not lose the money you've made through costly mistakes.

The purpose of this book is to present, as clearly as possible, many of the laws and operating requirements for real estate brokerage in the State of Maryland. It builds on basic information presented in Dearborn™ Real Estate Education's real estate principles texts. The author has been careful to avoid duplicating information presented in the principles texts. Therefore, you should study each subject area in *both* the basic text and in this book (see Figure P.1 under "How to Use This Book"). Additional information can be accessed online using the web addresses found throughout the text and in Appendix D.

When you have studied each chapter, be certain that you can both *answer* every question and *understand* the explanations given in the answer keys found at the end of the book.

You will want to make frequent use of Appendix D, "Maryland Real Estate-Related Websites." It contains several carefully chosen "hub" sites that give you access to multiple official sources for real estate law and regulation at various levels of government.

While the author has exercised care in providing information pertaining to the laws governing the practice of real estate in Maryland, the reader is urged to consult with legal counsel regarding any statutory enactment and should not rely solely on this publication as legal authority for compliance with any statute.

Throughout your real estate course, you'll be studying and taking practice tests in preparation for the Maryland Real Estate Licensing Examination. That examination is prepared and administered for the State Real Estate Commission by an independent testing service, PSI Examination Services Inc., Las Vegas, Nevada. *Maryland Real Estate Practice & Law* is designed to familiarize you with the Maryland-specific subject matter you will find on that examination. The questions at the end of each chapter are prepared in a multiple-choice format similar to the one used in the licensing examination.

The statutes and regulations discussed in this book are those enacted at the time of its publication.

About the Author

Maryland Real Estate Practice & Law (14th edition) is written by Donald A. White, who was licensed as a Maryland real estate salesperson in 1967 and as an associate broker in 1972. He holds degrees in music (BS MusEd), religious education (MRE), and business (MA). He is professor emeritus in the Department of Business at Prince George's Community College, where he taught real estate licensing courses continuously from 1972 to 2013. He served several terms as chair of the Education Committee of the Prince George's Association of REALTORS®. A past president of the Maryland Real Estate Educators Association, he also served on the Educational Advisory Committee to the Education Committee of the Maryland Real Estate Commission.

The author, a charter member of the Real Estate Educators Association, taught frequently in REALTORS'® continuing education seminars. He also was the principal author of *Questions and Answers on Maryland Real Estate* and coauthor, with Maurice Boren, of the *Study Guide to Maryland Real Estate License Examinations*.

Mr. White lives with his wife, Elizabeth Gill White—a concert pianist—at Riderwood Village, a senior living community in Silver Spring.

Acknowledgments

The author appreciates constructive suggestions on the updating and revision of this text provided by the following reviewers: William B. Frost, GRI, Frost and Associates; Sharyn J. Kotrosa, instructor, Long and Foster Real Estate Inc.; Colin McGowan, CDEI, The Frederick Academy of Real Estate; Pam Nunzio, professional development trainer and senior instructor, Weichert Institute of Real Estate; Marie S. Spodek, DREI, Professional Real Estate Services; and Linda L. Wise, Coldwell Banker Residential Brokerage/Southern Maryland Association of REALTORS®.

He also extends thanks to his wife, Elizabeth, for her keen eye and constant encouragement.

How to Use This Book

The chapter conversion, Figure P.1, provides a ready reference for using *Maryland Real Estate Practice & Law* in conjunction with various principles books. For instance, *Maryland Real Estate Practice & Law's* Chapter 16, "Closing the Real Estate Transaction," may be read in conjunction with Chapter 22 in *Modern Real Estate Practice*, Chapter 17 in *Real Estate Fundamentals*, or Chapter 12 in *Mastering Real Estate Principles*.

FIGURE P.1

Chapter Conversion Table

Maryland Real Estate Practice & Law (14th edition)	Modern Real Estate Practice, 19th Edition	Modern Real Estate Practice, 18th Edition	Real Estate Fundamentals, 8th Edition	Mastering Real Estate Principles, 6th Edition
1. Maryland Real Estate License Law and Regulations	—	—	—	16
2. Real Estate Agency	9	4	7	13
3. Real Estate Brokerage	10	5	7	13
4. Listing and Buyer Representation Agreements	11	6	7, 8	15
5. Interests in Real Estate	4	7	3	4, 7
6. How Ownership Is Held	5	8	5	9
7. Legal Descriptions	6	9	2	6
8. Real Estate Taxes and Other Liens	13	10	3, 10	5, 25
9. Real Estate Contracts	12	11	8	14
10. Transfer of Title	7	12	4	10
11. Title Records	8	13	6	11
12. Real Estate Financing	14, 15	14, 15	12, 13	Unit VII
13. Leases	18	16	9	8
14. Environmental Issues and the Real Estate Transaction	21	21	16	3
15. Fair Housing	3	20	15	17
16. Closing the Real Estate Transaction	17	22	17	12

CHAPTER 1

Maryland Real Estate License Law and Related Regulations

■ KEY TERMS

administrative law

affiliates

associate brokers

clock hours

Code of Maryland Regulations (COMAR)

common law

irrevocable consent

jointly and severally liable

judicial activism

latent defects

natural persons

nonresidential property

precedent

real estate

real estate broker

real estate brokerage services

red flags

salespersons

statutes

strict construction

■ OVERVIEW

In this chapter, you will learn some of the history of brokerage regulation in Maryland; learn which Maryland statutes and regulations govern the industry today; come to understand the structure, duties, and powers of the Maryland Real Estate Commission; and begin to appreciate the mechanics of obtaining, maintaining, and upgrading a brokerage license. You will also be introduced to various requirements and prohibitions that guide the everyday life of a real estate licensee.

■ HISTORY AND SOURCES OF MARYLAND LICENSE LAW

The Maryland Real Estate Brokers Act, a law designed to protect the public interest, became effective June 1, 1939. Since then, there have been frequent revisions. All the work of real estate licensees is affected by this important statute. It is, therefore, the basis of much of this chapter.

The Maryland Real Estate Brokers Act appears as Title (Chapter) 17 in the *Business Occupations and Professions* Article of the Annotated Code of Maryland. This textbook refers to that statute as the "Brokers Act" and as "Title 17." It is helpful to note that each book that contains Maryland law is called an *Article*; each article is divided into chapter-like *titles*.

Real estate brokerage is governed both by statutory law, such as the Brokers Act mentioned above, and by administrative law, found in the Code of Maryland Regulations (COMAR). Regulations governing the practice of real estate brokerage are enacted and enforced by the Maryland Real Estate Commission—a body within the executive branch of government. The Maryland Real Estate Brokers Act was enacted by the legislative branch of Maryland government: the General Assembly. Therefore, it is an example of legislative (statutory) law, while COMAR is administrative law.

In addition to statutes and regulations, some aspects of common law apply to real estate brokerage in Maryland. Common law is called the *unwritten law* because it is not written by a legislative body; it is found in numerous volumes of decisions from courts of appeal. That's where the unwritten law is written. Such court decisions are needed in situations for which no relevant statute exists or when an existing statute is challenged as unconstitutional. They also arise in cases of ambiguity where uncertainty of language or intent makes a statute difficult to apply.

On occasion, older laws no longer seem to make sense to the courts called on to give their opinions. Judges may then "modernize" the law. This is in contrast to strict construction, which takes statutes at their face value and defers to the original intention of their writers. For example, in 1965, the U.S. Supreme Court held that the Civil Rights Act of 1866 still applied literally—word for word—and was still the law of the land almost a century after it was written. Their decision was an example of strict construction and greatly advanced the cause of civil rights.

Statutes are voted into law by legislative bodies, but common law is handed down by judges. Decisions made by courts of appeal become binding on lower courts within their judicial area. The higher the court of appeal making a decision, the more numerous the lower courts in which that decision becomes the standard—the precedent—for their decisions.

The Maryland Real Estate Commission, one of the largest licensing boards within the Department of Labor, Licensing, and Regulation, adopts and enforces regulations to implement the Brokers Act. These regulations are administrative law. Regulations apply statutes to the details of particular situations. The Code of Maryland Regulations (COMAR) contains regulations adopted by all 18 of Maryland's licensing boards.

The Brokers Act and regulations from COMAR relating to real estate can be found in many college and public libraries in bound volumes in the legal reference section. They are also available to the public through the Real Estate Commission website: www.dllr.state.md.us/license/law/mreclaw.shtml.

■ DEFINITIONS OF TERMS [§17-101]

As used in Title 17, certain terms have specific definitions that apply to either a section of the law or the entire statute. For example, a real estate broker is defined as an individual who provides real estate brokerage services. *Consideration* in this section refers to *compensation* (payment) for brokerage services, defined as any of the following acts:

- For consideration and for another person—selling, buying, exchanging, or leasing any real estate or collecting rent for its use
- For consideration, assisting another person to locate or obtain for purchase or lease any residential real estate
- Engaging regularly in a business of dealing in real estate or leases or options on real estate
- Engaging in a business, the primary purpose of which is promoting the sale of real estate through a listing in a publication issued primarily for promotion of real estate sales
- Engaging in a business that subdivides land located in any state into lots and then selling those subdivided lots
- For consideration, serving as a consultant for any of the activities in this list

Although Maryland law generally defines *persons* as "individuals, receivers, trustees, guardians, personal representatives, fiduciaries, or representatives of any kind and any partnership, firm, association, or other entity," only natural persons (individuals) may hold Maryland real estate licenses. However, a broker's license, rather than showing the broker's actual name, may show the name under which the broker is operating—typically a company name. This is called the broker's designated name. Branch offices are issued certificates rather than licenses. Time-share licenses are issued to brokerage firms that deal in time-shares.

In the statute and in this book, *Commission* refers to the State Real Estate Commission. When the term *licensed* is used, it refers to the status of an individual licensed by that Commission.

■ LICENSES AND CERTIFICATES ISSUED BY THE COMMISSION (TITLE 17, SUBTITLE III)

The Commission issues three levels of license for individuals delivering real estate brokerage services: broker, associate broker, and salesperson. It issues branch office certificates. It also registers time-share developers. Currently, there are over 38,000 active licensees, including more than 4,400 brokers, 3,000 associate brokers, and almost 30,000 salespersons; these totals do not include the 2,000 plus inactive licenses. Licenses may be kept on inactive status no longer than three years, after which they expire. Expired licenses are then held three years from the date of their expiration, during which time they may be reinstated as discussed later in this chapter. Persons named on inactive or expired licenses may not perform acts of real estate brokerage. For instance, they may not receive compensation from participation in referral companies.

In addition to the three basic levels of license, each level has subtypes. Broker licenses may be resident, nonresident, reciprocal, or temporary/for commercial only. Associate broker and salesperson licenses include resident, nonresident, and reciprocal. (Maryland has reciprocal licensing agreements only with Pennsylvania and Oklahoma.) In addition to being licensed, some associate brokers and salespersons may also be *registered* to manage branch offices.

To have an active license, a salesperson or an associate broker must be affiliated with and under the authority of a licensed broker. Individuals affiliate with brokers either as employees or nonemployees of their broker. Currently, the vast majority of Maryland real estate brokerage affiliates are in a nonemployee relationship with their brokers. Affiliates, although fully subject to supervision and control by their brokers, can still meet Internal Revenue Service (IRS) requirements for qualified real estate agent—also called statutory nonemployees—and be treated as self-employed from the point of view of reporting income for taxation.

Affiliates meet the IRS requirements for statutory nonemployee (self-employed) status when their broker does not withhold federal or state income taxes or pay their Social Security or Medicare assessments. Affiliates' paychecks are "net" to them, leaving them responsible for paying all of their own taxes. Section 3508 of the IRS Code specifies that such Qualified Real Estate Agents may report their income as "self-employed" persons using Schedule 1040C. To be recognized as a qualified real estate agent, affiliates must:

■ be licensed real estate agents (hold an active real estate license);
■ receive "substantially all"—meaning at least 90%—of their brokerage remuneration for production rather than for hours worked; and
■ act pursuant to written contracts with their brokerage firms, which state that, for federal tax purposes, the affiliates will not be treated as employees.

Throughout this book, *affiliate* (the noun) refers either to a licensed associate broker or a licensed salesperson. Associate brokers are individuals who have met the educational, experience, and testing requirements for becoming real estate brokers but who request licenses that authorize them to provide real estate brokerage services only under a broker with whom they affiliate as associate brokers. Despite their education and experience, their duties and authority are no greater than those of salespersons. Salespersons and associate brokers are individuals who aid brokers, with whom they are affiliated, in providing real estate brokerage services. Salespersons and associate brokers are *general agents* of their broker. Note, however, that brokers are *special agents* of their clients.

Real estate, as used in the Brokers Act, is defined as any interest in real property anywhere. It even includes interests in condominiums, time-share estates, and time-share licenses, as those terms are defined in the *Real Property* Article, as well as fee estates and life estates.

In the Brokers Act, the term *state* refers to any state in the United States, its territories, possessions, or the District of Columbia. In this book, when *State* is capitalized, it refers to the State of Maryland. In the statute, *Department* refers to the Department of Labor, Licensing, and Regulation under whose authority the Commission operates. *Secretary* refers to the chief executive of that department.

Persons not Subject to the Brokers Act When Performing Acts of Real Estate Brokerage [§17102]

Certain persons are permitted to perform real estate brokerage activities without being licensed or governed by the provisions of the Brokers Act. However, like all persons in the State, they are governed in their real estate dealings by other Maryland laws, such as those in the *Real Property* Article. Examples are:

- persons acting under a judgment or order of a court,
- public officers performing the duties of their office,
- landlords or owners of any real estate, unless their primary business is providing real estate brokerage services,
- persons engaging in a single transaction selling or leasing real estate, if they are acting under a power of attorney executed by the owner of that real estate,
- auctioneers, licensed by various jurisdictions within Maryland, to sell real estate at public auction, and
- persons acting as receivers, trustees, personal representatives, or guardians.

Persons who Must Conform to the Brokers Act When Performing Acts of Real Estate Brokerage Although They are not Required to Hold Brokerage Licenses [§17-301(b)]

In contrast, other persons, when performing acts of real estate brokerage, are governed by and must still conform to the relevant requirements of the Brokers Act, although they need not hold real estate licenses. They are:

- financial institutions in the leasing or selling of property they have acquired through foreclosure or by receiving a deed or an assignment in lieu of foreclosure;
- lawyers who are not regularly engaged in the business of providing real estate services and who do not advertise that they conduct such business;
- homebuilders in the rental or initial sale of homes they have constructed (although homebuilders and their salespersons must be registered with the Home Builder and Home Builder Sales Representative Registration Unit of the Consumer Affairs Division in the Office of the Attorney General);
- agents of a licensed real estate broker or of an owner of real estate, while managing or leasing that real estate for that broker or for the property's owner;
- persons who negotiate the sale, lease, or transfer of businesses when the sale does not include any interest in real property other than the lease for the property where the business operates; and
- owners who subdivide and sell not more than six lots of their own unimproved property in any one calendar year. (Note that if they or their family have owned the property for 10 years or more, there is no limit on the number of the lots they may sell.)

■ THE MARYLAND REAL ESTATE COMMISSION [§17-201–§17-214]

The Maryland Real Estate Commission is one of several commissions within the Department of Labor, Licensing, and Regulation. It consists of nine members; five of which hold real estate licenses and are chosen—one each—from the Eastern Shore, Baltimore Metropolitan Area, Baltimore City, Southern Maryland, and Western Maryland. These five members must have held Maryland real estate licenses for at least 10 years and have resided in the areas from which they are appointed for at least five years, both immediately prior to their appointment. The other four members are consumer members who shall not have had an ownership interest in or received compensation from an entity regulated by the Commission in the year just before their appointment. They shall not be licensees or otherwise be subject to regulation by the Commission.

Members are appointed by the Governor with the advice of the Secretary and the advice and consent of the Senate. Membership terms, which are staggered to ensure regulatory continuity, begin on June 1, and end four years later, either with reappointment or on the appointment of a qualified replacement. Members may be removed before the end of their terms by the Governor in cases of incompetence or misconduct.

Each year, members of the Commission elect, from among themselves, a chairperson to preside at their meetings. This officer is covered by a surety bond. The Commission meets each month with a majority of the members then under appointment constituting a quorum. Meetings are open to the public.

The Commission has adopted bylaws for the conduct of its meetings and regulations for the conduct of hearings and for issuance of licensing applications. With 10 days' advance written notice, a member of the public may speak before the Commission.

The Commission's Executive Director, who is appointed by and serves at the pleasure of the Secretary, is not a member of the Commission. Neither is the Executive Director the chairperson of the Commission. The Executive Director, a State employee who is also covered by a surety bond, attends and participates in the monthly meetings, directs the day-to-day operations of the Commission, and supervises its office staff and field inspectors between monthly meetings.

Duties and Powers [§17-209, §17-212]

The Commission's primary duties are administration and enforcement of the Brokers Act through the licensing process. To carry out this duty, the Commission is empowered to

- investigate complaints of unlicensed brokerage activity,
- investigate complaints about licensee behavior,
- conduct hearings and administer oaths,
- issue subpoenas for attendance of witnesses or production of evidence,
- take depositions, and
- seek injunctions (in certain circumstances).

The Commission adopts, maintains, and enforces General Regulations and a Code of Ethics that set forth standards of conduct for all individuals who are under the authority of the Brokers Act. The General Regulations (09.11.01) and the Code of Ethics (09.11.02) are found in COMAR under 09.11. Such subsections of COMAR are called "Chapters." The Code of Ethics addresses licensees' relations with the client, the public, and with other licensees; it is separate and distinct from the Code of Ethics of the National Association of REALTORS®. However, the two codes are complementary in that neither contradicts the other. Other portions of COMAR relating to the work of the Commission are Chapter 3, Hearing Regulations; Chapter 4, Time Share Regulations; Chapter 5, Supervision; Chapter 6, Continuing Education; Chapter 7, Residential Property Disclosure/Disclaimer; Chapter 8, Agency Relationship Disclosure/Dual Agency Consent; and Chapter 9, Fees.

The Commission must investigate any written, sworn complaint alleging that an unauthorized person has provided real estate brokerage services. The Commission has statutory authority to hold hearings on alleged violations and to impose penalties not to exceed

- $5,000 for the first proven violation of any Title 17 provision,
- $15,000 and/or two years' imprisonment for the second violation, and
- $25,000, and/or three years' imprisonment for the third or subsequent violation.

(An "unauthorized person" is one who neither holds a required license nor is exempt from the requirement to have one.)

Other Powers and Duties [§17-208–§17-214]

The Commission has many powers and duties. In the course of its operation, it routinely:

- issues, renews, suspends, or revokes licenses;
- orders investigations and holds hearings as needed;
- after hearings, reprimands and/or fines licensees who are found to have violated laws or regulations;
- forwards the license fees it collects to the Comptroller, who distributes such funds to the State Real Estate Commission Fund;
- collects fines and forwards them to the General Fund of the State;
- submits an annual report of its activities to the Secretary;
- certifies, on request of any person and payment of the required fee, the licensing status and qualifications of any person who is the subject of the request;
- approves the content of educational courses for licensing and for continuing education;
- adopts regulations and a code of ethics to implement Title 17;
- convenes hearing boards (panels) of three members, at least one of whom must be a consumer member and one a professional member (licensee) from among the commissioners; and
- maintains and administers a Guaranty Fund to reimburse members of the public as much as $50,000 for actual losses caused by licensees and their employees.

■ REQUIREMENTS FOR LICENSURE

Before providing real estate brokerage services in the State, individuals generally must be licensed by the Commission either as real estate brokers or as associate brokers or salespersons affiliated with and working under the authority of a licensed broker. Licenses are granted for a two-year term beginning on the date they are issued.

Brokers [§17-305]

To qualify for the real estate broker license, applicants must

- be of good character and reputation and at least 18 years of age;
- have completed a 135-hour course in real estate—including three clock hours of real estate ethics—approved by the Commission;

■ have been licensed as real estate salespersons actively and lawfully for at least three years; and

■ have passed the broker prelicensing examination.

For applicants who are qualified to practice law in this State, the Commission waives the education and experience requirements but not the examination requirement. Broker education requirements for all others persons are in addition to the salesperson (60-hour) requirements they may have previously met. However, an individual who has been engaged in real estate practice as a licensed real estate broker in another state for at least three of the five years immediately preceding submission of application is considered to have satisfied the broker educational requirements.

Associate Brokers [§17-304]

To qualify for the associate real estate broker license, an applicant must meet the education and experience requirements for a broker license. The applicant must also obtain written commitment from a licensed real estate broker to accept the applicant as an associate broker of the firm when all other associate broker requirements have been satisfied.

Salespersons [§17-303]

To qualify for issuance of the salesperson license, an applicant must

■ be of good character and reputation;

■ be at least 18 years of age;

■ successfully complete a basic (60-hour) course in real estate—including three clock hours of real estate ethics—approved by the Commission;

■ pass the required examination; and

■ obtain written commitment from a licensed real estate broker to accept the applicant as a salesperson of the firm when all other salesperson licensing requirements have been satisfied.

General Rules [§17-307]

The usual steps leading to a license are education, examination, and application. Applicants must successfully complete prelicensing education requirements before taking salesperson or broker examinations. The specific time limits for salesperson and broker are presented in Figure 1.1. The Commission's application forms must be used, and the required fees, shown in Figure 1.2, paid.

FIGURE 1.1

Deadlines for Testing and Licensure

Deadlines for Testing and Licensure	Time Requirement	Consequences of Failing to Meet the Requirement	Authority
Deadline for candidate to pass the salesperson licensing exam	Not more than one year after completing education requirements	Any prior or partial test results become invalid. Candidate must complete a new salesperson prelicensing course before taking (or re-taking) licensing exam.	Gen Reg .11-F Gen Reg .11-G (1)
Deadline for candidate to apply for salesperson license	Not more than one year after passing both portions of the salesperson exam	Complete a new salesperson prelicensing course.	Gen Reg .11-G (1)
Deadline for candidate to pass the broker licensing exam	Not more than one year after satisfying education requirements	Any prior or partial test results become invalid. Candidate must complete a new broker prelicensing course before taking (or re-taking) licensing exam.	Gen Reg .14-H(1)
Deadline for candidate to apply for broker license	Not more than one year after passing both portions of the broker exam	Complete a new broker prelicensing course.	Gen Reg .14-I

FIGURE 1.2

Usual License Fees

	Original License Fee	Guaranty Fund Assessment*	Total Original Fees	Renewal or Exchange of License Fee
Broker	$210	$20	$210	$190
Associate Broker	$150	$20	$150	$130
Salesperson	$110	$20	$110	$90

The proper fees must accompany every application. These fees are set and subject to annual change by the Commission. Applicants are also required to pay the testing service a $66 examination fee to register, take, or retake all or part of either real estate examination. Standard examination registration fees, which are neither refundable nor transferable, may be paid by check, money order, company check, or cashier's check. Cash is not accepted.

Fees for other services:

Certificate of License History (5-yr.)	$25	Reactivate Inactive License	$50
Certificate of License History (full)	$75	Reinstatement of License/Late Fee	$150
Broker Business Address Change	$5	Transfer to Another Broker	$25
Broker Business Name Change	$25	Time-share Registration	$100
Branch Office License	$25	Duplicate License or Pocket Card	$25
Personal Name Change	$25	Dishonored Check	$25

* The Guaranty Fund initial assessment, paid on issuance of the first license to an applicant, is not paid on renewals unless needed to replenish the Guaranty Fund. This has happened only once in the past 35 years.

Requirements for Nonresidents [§17-514]

Salesperson, associate broker, and broker applicants who are not residents of the State must submit to the Commission their irrevocable consent, which allows them to be served with official documents without the server having to travel to a foreign (out-of-state) jurisdiction to present them. Applicants are required to submit any additional documentation that the Commission requires to determine their professional competence, good character, and reputation. Broker applicants must also submit or pay for a credit report.

Licenses for Nonresidents to Perform Commercial Brokerage [§17-536–§17-540]

In the previous sections, a "nonresident real estate broker" is a person licensed by a jurisdiction other than Maryland to provide real estate brokerage services there. That broker may either be an individual, a partnership, joint venture, limited liability company, limited liability partnership, or corporation depending on the jurisdiction. "Nonresident real estate salespersons" (and associate brokers) are individuals who are licensed, not by the Commission but by another state, to provide real estate brokerage services under a nonresident real estate broker—in this context, a broker who has complied with the Commission's detailed requirements for a temporary license to perform acts of brokerage involving Maryland commercial property. Nonresident brokers may qualify for such a license only if their own state grants similar privileges to Maryland licensees. The nonresident broker may deal with commercial property only through and under a licensed Maryland real estate broker with whom the nonresident has a written agreement detailing their entire relationship for specific proposed transactions. Nonresident commercial licenses are rarely issued: only two have been issued in the past 11 years.

Waiver of Requirements for Licensure [§17-308]

The Commission may waive any requirement for individual licenses for applicants who hold comparable or equivalent licenses granted by another state if those applicants pay the required application fees, meet the relevant requirements, and submit certification of license history from the other state. If applicants are seeking broker licenses based on their comparable licenses in another state, they must provide adequate evidence of actively maintaining brokerage offices there.

Reciprocity [§17-3A-01–§17-3A-10]

To facilitate transactions involving parties from other states seeking to buy, rent, or sell property in Maryland and Maryland residents seeking to buy, rent, or sell in other states, the 2006 legislative session made provisions for reciprocal real estate brokerage licensing. Under the terms of any reciprocal licensing agreement, the Brokers Act requires the following:

■ That each state recognize the previous education, experience, and examination of applicants for any of the licensure classes authorized in the applicants' home state as satisfying the requirements for licensure in the reciprocal state

■ That applicants submit consent to service of process, in a form required by the Commission (similar to the irrevocable consent required of traditional nonresident applicants by §17-514)

■ That applicants verify they have read and agree to comply with all laws of the state for which they are seeking reciprocal licensure

■ That applicants, other than brokers, provide certification from their broker that the broker is currently licensed and will actively and personally supervise the applicants performing real estate brokerage services in the state where they would be receiving the reciprocal licensure

■ That neither state requires additional continuing education to renew reciprocal licenses

■ That applicants furnish to Maryland, Certificates of Licensure or Records of Good Standing from the state from which the applicants are applying. (Such statements must contain the applicants' names, addresses, licensure classifications, and history of past or present disciplinary proceedings. Applicants themselves must give written statements as to whether they are subjects of any disciplinary proceedings or criminal investigations anywhere and whether they have been convicted in the United States of any felony or certain misdemeanors or of any crimes that violate the Maryland Brokers Act.)

■ That each state requires that brokers holding reciprocal licenses, who later open principal places of business in the state that granted them reciprocal licenses, promptly notify that state and obtain a standard nonresident license within 90 days after establishing those principal places of business

■ That applicants for standard nonresident licenses may be required to pass the state portion of a licensure examination required by the state granting the reciprocal licenses.

■ That states have the right, for cause, to deny applications for reciprocal licensure

Maryland has signed reciprocity agreements with only Pennsylvania and Oklahoma but is negotiating with other states. Many states have multiple reciprocity agreements, often found on each state's website. In each situation, the details of the reciprocity may be very different from those of the Maryland program. The Maryland Real Estate Commission appears to be proceeding with great care to establish the reciprocity authorized by the 2006 legislation. Barriers to agreement between states sometimes include unwillingness to renew without the reciprocal license holder completing the host state's continuing education requirements, passing a host state's law exam, or taking the same number of prelicensure hours as required by the host state. Maryland law requires mutual concession in all these areas. In January 2014, there were 81 reciprocal brokers, 23 reciprocal associate brokers, and 155 reciprocal salespersons.

Pocket Cards and License Certificates [§17-309]

License certificates and pocket cards issued by the Commission show

■ the name of the licensee,
■ the designated name of the licensed real estate broker with whom a salesperson or associate broker is affiliated,
■ the date the license will expire, and
■ the licensing registration number of the licensee.

License certificate and pocket card images issued for affiliates are downloaded digitally by their brokers. Pocket card images are detached and given to affiliates to sign and carry. Affiliates also sign their license certificate images. Each signed license certificate image is retained in the office out of which each licensee operates. Although no such requirement is explicitly stated anywhere in the Brokers Act or in any regulation, the Commission states that licensees are expected to carry their pocket cards whenever they engage in real estate brokerage activity.

Unlicensed Activity: A Violation of Title 17 [§17-613 (d)]

Real estate broker licenses authorize their holders to provide real estate brokerage services to the public. Persons who hold associate broker and salesperson licenses may never provide real estate brokerage services in their own name or in the name of any broker with whom they are not affiliated. They may only provide brokerage services in the name of the broker under whom they are licensed.

Salespersons and associate brokers on inactive status have no broker. Therefore, they have no one under whom they are authorized to provide brokerage services. Their licenses and pocket cards have been returned to the Commission. Performing any act of real estate brokerage while on inactive status is a violation of law, which is a misdemeanor punishable initially by a fine as much as $5,000 and by as much as two years' imprisonment and a fine of $15,000 for a second conviction for the same offense. Any person found guilty of a third or subsequent violation of any provision of the sections listed in subsection (a) of 17-613 is subject to a fine not exceeding $25,000 or three years' imprisonment or both.

Exchange of Licenses and Additional Licenses and Affiliations [§17-311–§17-313]

A licensed real estate broker may also hold licenses as a real estate salesperson or associate broker, affiliated under another licensed real estate broker. This requires submission of additional proper applications to the Commission and payment of additional license fees. A broker in one company who works at the same time for the broker of another company as an affiliate must obtain a commitment for such affiliation from that other broker and must inform that broker of the other license. A broker may operate more than one real estate company, but for each additional real estate brokerage company, the broker must obtain a separate real estate broker's license. Therefore, it is legally possible for an individual to hold two or more broker licenses simultaneously. For example, an individual may hold one license for a broker's residential resale company in town and another license for the broker's vacation rental property firm at the shore.

Licensees who hold salesperson, associate broker, or broker licenses may exchange those licenses for other levels of license by complying with procedures established by the Commission and paying the required additional fees. Affiliates may obtain additional licenses and become affiliated with additional Maryland brokers by obtaining a commitment from each additional broker, paying the required additional licensing fees, and giving notice of such multiple relationships to all their brokers.

Reinstatement after Nonrenewal [§17-314]

Reinstatement of a license that has expired due to nonrenewal is possible within the three-year period following the date of its expiration. Reinstatement requires that applicants show proof of having met all applicable continuing education requirements for the period(s) since expiration, having paid all past-due renewal fees, and having paid a $150 reinstatement fee. They must also meet the requirement of good character and reputation. Neither timely nor late renewal of a license affects the power of the Commission to bring charges for prior acts or conduct.

Transfer of Affiliation [§17-311]

Affiliates may apply to the Commission to transfer their affiliation from one broker to another after obtaining, from the new broker, a commitment stating that, upon termination of the current affiliation and issuance of new license certificates and pocket cards, they will become affiliated with the new broker. They shall also submit to the Commission, either from their former brokers or from themselves, a statement confirming termination of their prior relationship with their transfer applications. It is advisable in every case, although not clearly required by law or regulation, that the former broker be informed of the details of the transfer.

Dishonored Checks [§17-521]

In the event of a dishonored check, licensees are not considered to have properly renewed their licenses until they pay both the original amount of the renewal fees and a collection fee of $25 for each dishonored check.

■ LICENSE TERM, TRANSFER, AND RENEWAL [§17-314]

If the Commission has the brokers' current email addresses, license expiration date reminders and renewal application forms for brokers and their affiliates are emailed no less than 30 days before the licenses expire. The notices state:

- the dates on which the current licenses expire,
- the dates by which the Commission must receive the renewal applications, if licensees use hard copy (paper) applications for renewal, and
- the amount of the renewal fees (see Figure 1.2).

Although the usual mode of application for renewal is online—a method that enables instantaneous and less expensive processing—the Commission continues to accept and process hard-copy renewal and upgrade applications.

Continuing Education Requirements [§17-315]

Continuing education for license renewal is measured in clock hours, with credit allowed only for approved, individual courses of not less than one and a half and not more than six hours in length. A *clock hour* is defined in COMAR 09.11.06.01 B(3) as 50 minutes of actual instruction per 60-minute hour [§1-101].

Completion of the specified number of continuing education hours, including some in specific subjects, is required for renewal of any level of license (see Figure 1.3). The standard requirement for all levels of license is 15 hours of approved instruction made up of:

- three clock hours of local, state, and federal legislative and regulatory updates;
- one and a half clock hours dealing with fair housing;
- three clock hours of "Maryland Real Estate Commission's Code of Ethics, Flipping, and Predatory Lending";
- three clock hours of "Principles of Agency and Agency Disclosure" (all licensees) at alternate renewals on or after January 1, 2012;
- three clock hours of Requirements of "Broker Supervision" (brokers, branch managers, and team leaders) at alternate renewals on or after January 1, 2012; and
- additional electives needed to reach the required total hours.

FIGURE 1.3

Continuing Education Requirements

Category Designation on Certificate	Subject Matter and Those Required to Complete Specific Courses	Course Length and When Required
A	Legislative Update	3 hrs
C	Fair Housing (Licensees performing only commercial transactions may substitute Federal Americans with Disabilities Act)	1.5 hrs
D	Ethics, Flipping, and Predatory Lending	3 hrs
H	Principles of Agency and Agency Disclosure[†]	3 hrs*
I	Requirements of Broker Supervision[††]	3 hrs*
B, E, F, G	Other Approved Courses	1.5 hrs**
	Total Hours Required	15 hrs

[†]   All licensees

[††] Brokers, branch managers, and team leaders

*   At the first renewal after January 1, 2012; then, at alternate subsequent renewals

** In years when "Agency" and "Supervision" are NOT required

There are certain exceptions:

- Licensees who are qualified to practice law in the state and those who hold graduate degrees in real estate from accredited colleges or universities—and are not brokers, branch managers, or team leaders—need to complete only seven and a half hours (legislative update, fair housing, and ethics) of continuing education.
- Licensees who perform only nonresidential brokerage may substitute one and a half hours of instruction in the Americans with Disabilities Act for the fair housing requirement, but they still must complete a total of 15 hours.
- Holders of reciprocal licenses of any level are not required to complete any Maryland-approved hours of instruction when renewing their licenses, but they must comply with continuing education requirements in their home state.

In the Brokers Act, *nonresidential property* is defined in detail as

(1) real property improved by five or more single-family units; (2) improved and unimproved real property zoned for commercial, industrial, or non-residential use by the local zoning authority of the county or municipality in which the property is located; and (3) unimproved real property zoned for improvement as multifamily units by the local zoning authority of the county or municipality in which the property is located, [but not including]: (1) property zoned for agricultural use; or (2) single-family units, including a condominium or co-op unit, for sale or for lease, or otherwise conveyed or to be conveyed on a single basis.

All required continuing education must be completed before one's license can be renewed. Those renewing in a timely manner pay the Commission the required renewal fees and affirm that they have completed the required number of hours of continuing education. Licensees renewing electronically are notified at the end of their online session if they have been chosen for an audit of their course claims. If chosen, they will be required by the Commission to submit certificates for all of the courses they claimed in their renewal application.

A person whose license has expired for nonrenewal may normally apply for reinstatement of that license at any time within three years after its expiration date at a cost of $150. However, those who have made false claims of educational completion may be given one month to complete the missing education requirements, must pay a $1,500 penalty for the false application, as well as pay a $150 reinstatement fee. Their names, their violations, and their fines are then displayed on the Commission's website for several years.

There are several alphabetical categories for subject matter approved for continuing education courses:

A. Federal, state, or local legislative and regulatory changes

B. Antitrust law

C. Fair housing law

D. Real estate ethics or professional standards

E. Disclosure

F. Professional enhancement for practicing licensees

G. Technology relating to real estate brokerage services (not more than three hours allowed per renewal)

H. The principles of agency and agency disclosure

I. The requirements of supervision by brokers, branch office managers, and team leaders

To be approved by the Commission, all continuing education course subject matter must relate to real estate.

Approved courses may be presented by the Maryland Association of REALTORS® or its member boards, the Real Estate Brokers of Baltimore City, Inc., or any similar professional association or by an educational institution approved by the State Board of Higher Education. These courses must be taught by qualified instructors who are experienced in the real estate industry. The Commission's guidelines require that continuing education instructors have experience and expertise in the area or activity about which they are teaching.

When licensees complete each unit of study, the training institution that conducted the course issues certificates of completion to each student stating the

- number of clock hours,
- name and date of the course taken,
- code letter of the subject category, and
- names of the teacher and/or the organization presenting the training.

The education provider has 10 days to upload reports of credits earned to the Commission's database system.

The Commission may waive continuing education requirements for licensees who show good cause for being unable to meet the requirement.

Inactive Status [§17-316]

The Commission will place the licenses of associate real estate brokers and real estate salespersons into inactive status when they are no longer affiliated with licensed real estate brokers, and their license certificates and pocket cards are returned to the Commission.

A licensee whose license is on inactive status may not provide real estate brokerage services through that license. This prohibition forbids accepting fees for referrals. An inactive licensee is not affiliated with any broker and may not be compensated for any act of real estate brokerage. Individuals with inactive licenses may not be paid by a referral company.

The placement of a license on inactive status does not affect the power of the Commission to suspend or revoke the license or to take any other disciplinary action against the licensee.

Unless an inactive license is reactivated, it expires three years after the date it is placed on inactive status. Renewal of an inactive license requires complying with continuing education requirements. Please note that renewal is not reactivation.

The Commission will reactivate the license of real estate brokers on inactive status and reissue license certificates and pocket cards to them if they request reactivation and pay to the Commission the $50 reactivation fee. Salespersons and associate brokers returning from inactive status must do the same and also submit broker affiliation commitments, contingent on the reactivations. While on inactive status, a salesperson or an associate broker has no broker.

Location of Certificates; Loss or Destruction [§17-317]

Licensed real estate brokers are required to maintain their own license certificates in their offices at all times. The license certificates of licensees who are affiliated with a real estate broker must be retained at the office location out of which each of them usually work.

The Commission must immediately be notified of the loss or destruction of a license certificate or pocket card. Upon receipt of an affidavit of loss or destruction and payment of the required fee ($25) for a lost or destroyed pocket card or license certificate, the Commission will issue appropriate duplicates.

Change of Name [§17-318]

When a licensee or a firm takes a new name, upon receipt of the required application fee ($25), the old certificate, pocket card, and any required documentation, the Commission will issue the licensee a new license certificate and pocket card that reflect the change.

Licensure and the Deceased Broker [§17-319]

On the death of a licensed real estate broker, any adult member of the family may carry on the brokerage firm for up to six months to close and terminate the business. To do this, the certificate and pocket card of the deceased broker must be surrendered to the Commission. Any information required by the Commission must also be submitted.

Before the end of the six-month period for carrying on the business of a deceased real estate broker, an individual may qualify for and receive from the Commission the license of the deceased broker, if that individual

- is a member of the immediate family of the decedent,
- has been continuously licensed as a real estate salesperson for the immediately preceding three years,
- passes the real estate broker examination required by this subtitle, and
- either physically or electronically surrenders their real estate salesperson license certificate and pocket card to the Commission.

There must also have been compliance with the conditions for carrying on the business as stated in the first paragraph of this section.

A person receiving the reissued license of a deceased real estate broker may hold and use that license for as long as four years without meeting the 135-hour educational requirement. However, if the requirement has not been met within four years, the license expires.

Return of Licenses; Terminating Affiliation [COMAR 09.11.01.08]

The license certificates and pocket cards of an affiliate must be returned to the Commission by the affiliate's broker

- on the request of an affiliate (a real estate salesperson or associate real estate broker),
- on the death of an affiliate, or
- after a hearing before the Commission and on a finding that the license of an affiliate is to be suspended or revoked.

Real estate brokers are required to surrender to the Commission, promptly on demand, any such person's license that may be in their possession or control. Failure to do so is grounds for disciplinary action.

In the event of an affiliate's termination (discharge), a broker must:

- immediately mail to the licensee, at the last known address of that individual, notice of such termination;
- submit written notice to the Commission, including a copy of the notice mailed to the licensee; and
- return the license certificate of the licensee to the Commission.

Licensing Out-of-State Applicants [§17-514]

The Commission will issue licenses only to those nonresident applicants who file with the Commission a signed statement of irrevocable consent in addition to all other required documents and fees. By submitting this statement, applicants agree that suits and actions may be commenced against them without their actually being served papers notifying them of forthcoming legal actions. They are also consenting that official delivery of papers to the executive director of the Commission shall bind them in any action, suit, or proceeding brought against them in any county in which the cause of action arose or the complaining party resides.

When serving process on the executive director of the Commission, persons filing must immediately send a copy of the filing, by certified mail, to the principal office of the person against whom the action is directed.

Note that the signature block on license examination applications contains these words: "If the address of this registration is not within the State of Maryland, I do hereby irrevocably consent that suits and actions may be commenced against me in the proper courts of the State of Maryland as required by the Maryland Annotated Code."

Maryland law states that if any nonresident real estate broker, associate broker, or salesperson participates in any real estate transaction, divides a fee, and/or holds deposits from any such transaction in Maryland, that very act is construed (considered) to give irrevocable consent.

■ PROCESSING COMPLAINTS

The Commission's website provides a downloadable form on which complaints against licensees may be submitted. Upon receiving a properly completed complaint form, the Commission sends a copy of it to the broker of the company involved, together with a letter from the Commission's executive director, stating that the broker must respond in writing with a full explanation of the allegations and what action the broker recommends. A broker's failure to respond to this inquiry may be considered grounds for disciplinary action. A chart indicating the steps in handling a complaint against a licensee is found in Appendix C of this book.

A copy of the executive director's letter is also sent to the complainant. Later, when the broker's answer is received, the Commission sends its own reply, together with a copy of the broker's response, to the complainant.

The Commission may commence proceedings on a complaint made by a Commission member or by other persons (who must make such complaints under oath). Complaints must be in writing and state specifically the facts on which the complaint is based, and they may be accompanied by documentary or other evidence.

After reviewing the content of the complaint, the Commission may refer it for investigation if it appears an infraction has occurred. A complaint not referred for investigation is considered dismissed. Within 30 days of such dismissal, any member of the Commission may file an exception disagreeing with the dismissal. If such exception is taken, the full Commission will hold a hearing to consider proceeding with an investigation.

If an exception is not filed, the dismissal is considered a final decision of the Commission. "Final decision" means that any party aggrieved by the decision may then appeal to the appropriate court; decisions may not be appealed until they are final. Only final decisions may be appealed.

If the Commission or its designee, based on an investigative report, determines that grounds exist for disciplinary action, the matter is referred for a hearing. Complaints not referred for a hearing after investigation must be dismissed. This has the same effect as a final decision: any party aggrieved by that dismissal may make judicial appeal.

Hearings and Notices

Except as otherwise provided in the *State Government* Article (e.g., situations where summary action is needed), before the Commission takes any final action, it gives the individual against whom the action is contemplated an opportunity for a hearing before the Commission or a hearing board.

At least 10 days before the hearing, notice is served personally on the individuals against whom complaints have been made, or it is sent by certified mail to their last known addresses. If the individuals are licensees other than brokers, at least 10 days before the hearing, the Commission shall serve notice of the hearing to each real estate broker with whom the individuals are affiliated.

The individuals may have attorneys represent them at hearings. This does not mean they can fail to appear and merely send their attorneys. It means that they can bring attorneys to represent them in their hearings. If the individuals against whom action is contemplated fail or refuse to appear, the Commission may proceed to hear and determine the matter without their presence. Unlike the meetings of panels to hear complaints and examine reports of investigators, these final meetings of panels are open to the public.

Real Estate Hearing Board [§17-324]

The Commission establishes two or three real estate hearing boards—often called panels—each consisting of three Commission members. At least one member of each panel must be a professional member, and at least one must be a consumer member. From among each hearing board's members, the Commission designates a chairperson.

Referral of Cases

The Commission (or one of its hearing panels) may order a final public hearing on any complaint that has been filed with the Commission or on any other matter for which a hearing may be required.

Before deciding to hold hearings, a panel will meet privately to

- review complaints and consider whether they provide a reasonable basis for disciplinary hearings, and
- review claims against the Guaranty Fund to determine what further action to take.

Panels meet publicly to

- hear licensees' responses to and defenses against complaints; and
- then decide whether to authorize punitive actions against them.

Hearing boards exercise the same powers as, and conduct hearings for, the Commission. They report their decisions and actions to the Commission. Panels specifically advise the Commission of any action they take against licensees involved in monetary loss, misappropriation of funds, or fraud.

Hearing Regulations [COMAR 09.11.03]

COMAR—the Code of Maryland Regulations—provides for four types of hearings:

- Judicial hearings
- Applications for licensure
- Revocation or suspension of licenses
- Claims against the Guaranty Fund

Hearings are conducted under several levels of overlapping hearing regulations.

On dismissal of a complaint, the complainant and the licensee are notified in writing. The dismissal of a complaint after investigation is not reviewable further. Other complaints substantially based on the same facts are usually similarly dismissed.

Summary Actions [§17-328]

Summary actions are those taken before holding hearings to protect the public quickly against imminent loss. They are then followed *by* hearings for which formal, timely notice is given.

Revocation after Actions of Other Agencies [§17-327]

The Commission may summarily order the revocation of the license of any licensee after that licensee is convicted in a court of law of a violation of this title, the conviction is final, and the period for appeal has expired.

The license of any nonresident licensee may be revoked if the real estate regulatory agency of the state where the licensee is a resident revokes the license issued by that state and certifies its order of revocation to the Commission.

When the Commission orders summary revocations under this section, it gives licensees written notice of the revocations and the findings on which they were based. After the revocations are effective, the Commission grants the licensees whose licenses have been revoked an opportunity to be heard promptly, either before the Commission or before a hearing board.

Rather than summarily order revocations of licenses under this section, the Commission may elect not to revoke the licenses until after the licensees are given opportunity for hearings. If the Commission elects to give the licensees opportunity for hearings before revoking the license, the Commission gives notice and holds those hearings in the manner required for other hearings.

In any hearings held because of convictions or revocations by other agencies, the Commission considers only evidence of whether or not the alleged convictions or revocations, in fact, occurred. However, in such hearings, licensees may present matters in mitigation of the offenses charged.

Summary Suspension for Trust Fund and Other Violations [§17-328]

The Commission may summarily order the suspension of a licensee who:

- fails to account promptly for any funds held in trust;
- on demand, fails to display to the Commission all records and books, and fails to account for any funds held in trust;
- has been convicted of a crime as defined in §17–322(B)(24) (i.e., a felony, a misdemeanor that is directly related to the fitness and qualification of the applicant or licensee to provide real estate brokerage services, or a crime that constitutes a violation of any provision of the Brokers Act); or
- fails, within 10 days after the conviction or within 10 days following release from incarceration as a result of the conviction, whichever is later, to disclose to the Commission that the licensee has been convicted of a crime as previously defined.

The Commission gives the licensee notice and supporting reasons for its action and offers the opportunity to be heard later.

A summary suspension may start immediately or at any later date set by the order, and it shall continue until the licensee complies with the conditions set forth by the Commission in its order or until the Commission orders a different disposition after a hearing held under this section.

Judicial Review [§17-329]

A party who strongly disagrees with a final decision of the Commission may appeal to a circuit court. Upon appeal, that court may set a bond not to exceed $50,000 and stay (delay) the suspension or revocation. The bond money would be for the use and benefit of any member of the public who might suffer financial loss because of any further violations of the Brokers Act by the plaintiff licensee.

Notice of Revocation or Suspension [§17-330]

Whenever a licensee's license is revoked or suspended and a stay is not ordered by the Commission or a court, the Commission notifies

- the licensee,
- the real estate broker with whom the licensee is affiliated,
- the Maryland Association of REALTORS®, and
- the local Board or Association of REALTORS® and the Realtist organization in the area of the licensee's office.

If the Commission revokes or suspends the license of a nonresident licensee, the Commission also notifies the Real Estate Commission or other licensing authority in the state where the licensee is a resident, reporting the cause for the revocation or suspension of the license. Figure 1.4 clarifies some often-confused terms used in license activation.

FIGURE 1.4	Process	Occasion
License Activation Process	Renewal	Extends a license for another two-year term. Inactive licenses also require renewal. A license that is not renewed expires.
	Reissuance (Reactivation)	Licensee returns to active status and affiliates with a broker.
	Reinstatement	Revives license that expired for lack of renewal or restores license after suspension or revocation.

REAL ESTATE GUARANTY FUND (TITLE 17, SUBTITLE IV)

The Guaranty Fund exists to reimburse members of the public for actual financial losses at the hands of real estate licensees and their unlicensed employees. The maximum reimbursement for any claim is $50,000.

Use of Monies Collected

The Commission deposits all money collected for the Guaranty Fund with the State treasurer, who invests it, with the investment earnings credited to the fund.

Initial Assessment for Fund

Before granting initial licenses to applicants, the Commission requires that they pay $20 assessments that are credited to the Guaranty Fund. Regardless of how many times an individual applies to the Commission for licenses, the Commission makes only one such assessment. However, if the amount in the Guaranty Fund falls below $250,000, the Commission assesses all the individuals then holding licenses a fee—typically payable at renewal—sufficient to return the Guaranty Fund to that minimum level. At the end of 2013, the fund contained slightly more than $1.4 million.

Claims Against the Fund

A person may recover compensation from the Guaranty Fund only for actual financial losses. Claims must be based on acts or omissions that occurred in the provision of real estate brokerage services by licensees or unlicensed employees of a licensed real estate broker. Claims must involve transactions that relate to real estate located in Maryland and be based on acts or omissions in which money or property is obtained from a person by theft, embezzlement, false pretenses, forgery, or an act that constitutes fraud or misrepresentation. For example, when managing rental property, a licensee uses tenant security deposits for their own office expenses, leaving the landlord to refund the client at the landlord's own expense.

A claim against the Guaranty Fund must

- be in writing and under oath,
- state the amount of loss claimed,
- state the facts on which the claim is based, and
- be accompanied by documentation or other evidence that supports the claim.

At any claim hearing, the burden of proof shall be on the claimant to establish the validity of the claim.

A person may not recover from the Guaranty Fund any loss that relates to

- the purchase of any interest in a limited partnership that invests in real estate,
- a joint venture that is promoted by a real estate licensee for the purpose of investment in real estate, or
- the purchase of commercial paper secured by real estate.

A claim under the Guaranty Fund may not be filed by the spouse or by the personal representative of the spouse of the individual alleged to be responsible for the act or omission giving rise to the claim. Any claim must be filed with the Commission within three years of the loss or discovery of the loss.

Notice to Buyer

Real estate brokers must include in each sales contract a written notice that buyers are protected by the Guaranty Fund in an amount not exceeding $50,000. Although only buyers are mentioned in this notice, sellers may also submit claims.

Action by Commission on a Claim

Upon receiving claims, the Commission must act promptly by:

- forwarding copies to licensees and/or unlicensed employees alleged to be responsible and to their brokers;
- requiring a written response, within 10 days, from each of those individuals concerning the allegations set forth in the claim (this 10-day period is shorter than the 20 days required for response to other inquiries from the Commission);
- reviewing the claim and any responses to the claim; and
- conducting an investigation.

On the basis of its review of a claim and any investigation it conducts, the Commission either schedules a hearing or dismisses the claim.

Special Disposition of Smaller Claims

If the claim is $5,000 or less, the Commission, through a designated staff member, such as its executive director, may issue a proposed order either to pay or to deny the claim. Both the claimant and the licensee receive a copy of this proposed order.

Within 30 days, either the claimant or licensee may request a hearing or file written exceptions to the order. If either happens, the Commission must schedule a hearing on the claim. If no hearing is requested and no exceptions taken, the proposed order becomes a final order of the Commission.

Other Claims

The Commission gives notice of the hearing and opportunity to appear before the Commission to both the claimants and the licensees or unlicensed employees alleged to be responsible. The Commission must send the required notices to every party involved before conducting the hearing.

When the persons alleged to be responsible are licensees, the Commission may combine this hearing with disciplinary proceedings against licensees arising from the same facts alleged in a claim. A claimant may be party to that portion of the proceedings about the claim but may be a witness only in the disciplinary portion.

The misdemeanor penalty for knowingly making a false statement or material misstatement of fact about a Guaranty Fund matter is a fine and/or imprisonment. This procedure would have to be in a court of law; the Commission has no power to impose a sentence of imprisonment.

Payments by the Guaranty Fund

If a claim proves valid, the Commission orders its payment by the Guaranty Fund. The amount of compensation recoverable from the Guaranty Fund is limited to the actual monetary loss incurred by the claimant. The payout may never be more than $50,000 for any one claim. The amount paid may not include

- losses other than those from the original transaction,
- commissions owed to a licensee acting as either a principal or an agent in a real estate transaction, or
- any attorney's fees incurred in seeking money from the fund.

Payment is not made until either the time for seeking judicial review is over or any judicial stay has expired. The Commission orders payment of claims in the order in which they were awarded.

Reimbursement of Guaranty Fund

When payments are made from the Guaranty Fund, the Commission immediately and without further proceedings suspends the licenses of the offending licensees. Licensees suspended in this way are not reinstated until they repay to the fund the full amounts owed, plus interest, and make formal application for reinstatement. Reimbursement of the fund does not affect any sanction imposed by the Commission against the individual under the disciplinary provisions of Subtitle 3.

After payments of claims by the Guaranty Fund, responsible licensees are required to reimburse the fund in full for the amounts it paid, plus interest of at least 10%. (General Regulation .23 presently sets the rate at 12%.) The licensees responsible for an individual claim are jointly and severally liable. That is, each does not bear a proportionate share; rather, each remains individually responsible for the entire unpaid amount.

If licensees do not reimburse the Guaranty Fund as provided, the Commission may have the State Collections Unit sue them for the amount that has not been reimbursed and seek liens against their real property.

■ PROHIBITED ACTS [§17-322]

After giving proper notice, conducting any needed investigation, holding the required hearing, and reaching its conclusions, the Commission is empowered to deny a license to any applicant, and to fine, reprimand, suspend, or revoke the licenses of any licensees who, in residential or commercial dealings:

- fraudulently obtain or attempt to obtain licenses for themselves or others;
- fraudulently use licenses;
- willfully make misrepresentations or knowingly make false promises directly or through other persons;
- intentionally or negligently fail to disclose to any person with whom they deal material facts that they know or should know that relate to properties with which they deal;
- as affiliates, provide or attempt to provide real estate brokerage services on behalf of real estate brokers without informing in writing any other real estate broker under whom the affiliates are licensed;
- fail to follow the law concerning the conduct of dual agency;
- retain or attempt to retain the services of any unlicensed individuals (in such a way as to evade the law prohibiting payment of a commission to an unlicensed individual);
- guarantee, authorize, or permit other persons to guarantee future profits from the resale of real property;
- solicit, sell, or offer to sell real property so as to influence or attempt to influence a prospective party to the sale of real property by offering prizes or free lots, conducting a lottery or contest, or advertising "free appraisals" unless prepared to appraise real estate free of charge for any person and for any purpose;

- accept a listing contract to sell real property that fails to provide a definite termination date that is effective automatically, not requiring further notice from either the buyer or the seller;
- accept a listing contract to sell real property that provides for a net return to a seller and leaves the licensees free to sell the real property at any price higher than the net price;
- knowingly solicit a party to an exclusive listing contract with another licensee to terminate that contract and enter a new contract with the licensees making the solicitation;
- solicit a party to a sales contract, lease, or agreement that was negotiated by other licensees to breach that contract, lease, or agreement for the purpose of substituting a new contract, lease, or agreement, either for the benefit of the licensees making the solicitation or for their firm;
- for any transactions in which the licensees have served either as brokers or affiliates of brokers, fail to furnish promptly to each party to the transactions copies of the listing contracts to sell or rent real property, the contracts of sale, or the lease agreements;
- for any transactions in which the licensees have served as or on behalf of a real estate broker, fail to keep copies of all executed listing contracts to sell or rent real property, contracts of sale, or lease agreements;
- whether or not acting for monetary gain, knowingly induce or attempt to induce persons to transfer real estate or discourage or attempt to discourage persons from buying real estate by making representations about the existing or potential proximity of real property owned or used by individuals of a particular race, color, religion, sex, handicap, familial status, or national origin or by representing that the existing or potential proximity of real property owned or used by individuals of a particular race, color, religion, national origin, et cetera., will or may result in the lowering of property values; a change in the racial, religious, or ethnic character of a block, neighborhood, or area; an increase in criminal or antisocial behavior in the area; or a decline in the quality of the schools serving the area;
- use any of the following material if it includes the name of an organization or association of which the licensees are not members: contract forms for the listing of real property for sale, rent, or exchange; contract forms for the sale, rent, or exchange of real property; or any advertising matter;
- as real estate brokers or affiliates, advertise the sale or rent of or an offer to buy real property while failing to disclose in the advertisement the names of the licensee advertisers and the fact that the advertisers are indeed real estate licensees;
- advertise in any misleading or untruthful manner;
- as affiliates, advertise the sale or rent of or an offer to buy real property in their own names while failing to disclose in the advertisement the designated name of the real estate broker on whose behalf the affiliates are acting;
- for real estate brokerage services provided by associate real estate brokers or real estate salespersons, accept commissions or other valuable considerations from persons other than the real estate brokers with whom they are affiliated;
- fail to account for or to remit promptly any money that comes into their possession;
- pay or receive a rebate, profit, compensation, or commission in violation of any provision of this act;

- under the laws of the United States or of any state, are convicted in a court of law of felonies or misdemeanors that are directly related to their fitness and qualification to provide real estate brokerage services or of a crime that constitutes a violation of any provision of the Brokers Act;
- engage in conduct that demonstrates bad faith, incompetence, or untrustworthiness or that constitutes dishonest, fraudulent, or improper dealings;
- with actual knowledge of their violations, associate with licensees in transactions or practices that violate any provision of the Brokers Act;
- fail as real estate brokers to exercise reasonable and adequate supervision over the provision of real estate brokerage services by other individuals on their behalf;
- provide to any parties contracts that do not contain a notice of a buyer's right of selection, as required by the Brokers Act;
- require a buyer to employ a particular title insurance company, settlement company, escrow company, or title lawyer in violation of this act;
- fail to make the disclosure of representation as required by §17-528;
- violate any trust accounts provision of this act that relates to trust money;
- violate any other provision of this act;
- violate any regulation adopted under this act or any provision of the Code of Ethics; or
- violate §17-320(d) by failing as branch office managers to exercise reasonable and adequate supervision over the brokerage work of sales agents or associate brokers registered with their offices.

Instead of, or in addition to, suspension or revocation, for any violation of the Brokers Act (Title 17), the Commission may impose a penalty not exceeding $5,000 for a first violation, $15,000 for a second, and $25,000 for a third or subsequent violation. To determine the amount of the penalty imposed, the Commission considers

- the seriousness of the violation,
- the harm caused by the violation,
- the good faith of the licensee, and
- any history of previous violations by the licensee.

The Commission pays any penalty collected into the General Fund of the State.

The Commission considers several facts when granting, denying, renewing, suspending, or revoking licenses or reprimanding licensees when the individuals concerned have been convicted of certain crimes. In the case of felonies and misdemeanors, they consider

- the nature of the crime, and
- the relationship of the crime to the activities authorized by the license.

In the case of felonies, the Commission considers

- the relevance of the conviction to the fitness and qualification of the applicants or licensees to provide real estate brokerage services,
- the length of time since the conviction, and
- the behavior and activities of the applicants or licensees before and after their convictions.

The Drug Enforcement Act of 1990 authorizes the Commission to impose sanctions upon licensees for a controlled substance offense.

A Maryland statute, Child Support—Enforcement Procedures, subjects licensees to having their licenses suspended and renewals denied if they are overdue in the payment of child support awarded by Maryland or any other state.

■ ADDITIONAL PROHIBITED ACTS PUNISHABLE BY IMPRISONMENT

There are real estate–related criminal offenses for which imprisonment of an individual is a possible penalty. Note that the term *person* includes licensees, nonlicensees, individuals, and business entities such as corporations, partnerships, limited liability companies, and so forth. Although the Commission is empowered to pursue all violators of these provisions, including nonlicensees, and to impose monetary penalties of as much as $25,000, only a court of law can try, convict, and sentence an individual to prison.

In addition to being reprimanded, suspended, revoked, and fined by action of the Commission, the Brokers Act provides for imposition also, by a court of law, of fines not to exceed $5,000 and/or imprisonment not to exceed one year for a first offense, $15,000 and two years imprisonment for a second offense, and $25,000 and three years imprisonment for third or subsequent violations that involve the following sections of the Brokers Act:

§17–502   Proper handling of trust money

§17–525   Discriminatory real estate practices in Baltimore City

§17–526   Discriminatory real estate practices in Montgomery County

§17–527   Mass solicitation of listings that violates Baltimore City and Baltimore County laws

§17–530   Failure to disclose agency relationship to opposing parties or their agents

§17–532   Duties to client, including performance of dual agency and presentation of Property Condition Disclosure/Disclaimer Statement

§17–601   License generally required for performance of brokerage

§17–602   Forbidden misrepresentation by affiliates' holding themselves out to be brokers

§17–603   Broker's use of unauthorized individuals; lending license certificates

§17–604   Payment of prohibited compensation

§17–605   Payment to non-licensed lawyers simply for referrals; certain mass solicitation

§17–606   Requirements for advertisements placed upon property subject to ground rent

§17–607   Requiring use of any particular title insurance, settlement, escrow company, mortgage lender, financial institution,   or title lawyer

§17–608   Discriminatory representations to encourage sales or discourage purchases

§17–609   Solicitation intended to change racial composition of neighborhood

§17–610   Misstatement of facts in Guaranty Fund complaints

§17–611   Violation of suspension order in designated real estate conservation areas

Maryland courts are required to report to the Commission, for appropriate action, all convictions of licensees for violation of this act with respect to blockbusting and discriminatory real estate practices in Baltimore City or Montgomery County. The Commission enforces the provisions of the sections concerning Montgomery County. For this purpose, it receives complaints, conducts investigations, issues subpoenas, and holds hearings.

■ REAL ESTATE BROKERAGE PRACTICE IN BALTIMORE CITY

Although Baltimore City does not issue or require a separate real estate license to perform real estate activities there, local law does regulate the activities of licensees who practice in that city. Many of the prohibited acts are similar, if not identical, to State law. The Baltimore City real estate license law is found in §132 of Article 19 of the Baltimore City Code under the title "Real Estate Practices."

■ MARYLAND SECURITIES ACT

The Maryland Securities Act requires licensing of persons engaged in the offer and sale of real estate–related securities, including limited partnership interests in real property. The Maryland Securities Commission regulates all activities construed to be securities-related business. To inquire if certain activities could be construed as securities-related business, contact the Maryland Securities Commissioner.

■ REAL ESTATE APPRAISERS AND HOME INSPECTORS ACT

Title 16 of the *Business Occupations and Professions* Article of the Annotated Code of Maryland establishes licensing and certification procedures for real estate appraisers as well as for home inspectors. Title 16 creates a nine-member State Commission of Real Estate Appraisers and Home Inspectors within the Department of Labor, Licensing, and Regulation to administer that act.

■ COMPARATIVE MARKET ANALYSIS (CMA)

A comparative market analysis (CMA) is not an appraisal, and its preparation for a seller or purchaser does not require an individual to have an appraisal license or certificate. Individuals who are licensed to provide real estate brokerage services may prepare and present written CMAs without being licensed or certified as appraisers. (Note: a comparative market analysis may also be referred to as a competitive market analysis or a broker price opinion.)

Requirements for Preparing CMAs

Real estate licensees who have no appraisal license or certification may prepare comparative market analysis. However, The Real Estate Commission's Code of Ethics imposes specific requirements for licensees preparing a CMA for a prospect, customer, or client. For instance, the notice that follows must appear conspicuously on the first page of the CMA:

COMPETITIVE MARKET ANALYSIS DISCLOSURE

This analysis is not an appraisal. It is intended only for the purpose of assisting buyers or sellers or prospective buyers or sellers in deciding the listing, offering, or sale price of the real property.

In preparing CMAs, licensees must disclose to clients, prospective clients, or customers their use of any comparables in which they have any present or contemplated interest.

■ BUILDING INSPECTIONS

Business Occupations and Professions Article Title 16 requires individuals who provide home inspections to be licensed by the State Commission of Real Estate Appraisers and Home Inspectors. It is unlawful to provide such inspections for consideration without this license. For doing so, there are both civil and criminal penalties, including a fine of no more than $5,000 per violation. Exempt from this requirement are state and local government inspectors and building code enforcement officials acting within the scope of their employment, as well as licensed construction professionals acting within the scope of their licenses when their services may be required in the building or remodeling of real property as long as they are not claiming to be licensed home inspectors.

Real estate licensees are not required to be skilled in building inspection, but they are expected to be alert for red flags that exist in a property with which they are dealing. Red flags are physical indications that there may be a defect in the property not readily apparent to a layperson or an inexperienced home purchaser. Red flags often suggest the presence of latent defects, as defined in *Real Property* Article Section 10-702 (defined in Chapter 4, under "Seller Disclosure").

When known by any party, such defects must be brought to the attention of all parties entering into a transaction. Parties should be strongly advised to seek the expert advice of a licensed home inspector or a licensed structural engineer.

■ CHANGES IN THE MARYLAND REAL ESTATE BROKERS ACT AND RELATED REGULATIONS

From time to time, changes are made in the Brokers Act and the regulations of the Commission. The material included in this chapter is current as of the date of publication. However, readers are cautioned to ascertain whether changes have been made since publication of this book.

Before the Commission adopts, amends, or repeals regulations, it publishes notice of the proposed action in the *Maryland Register* together with an estimate of economic impact, a notice of opportunity for public comment on the proposal, and the text of the proposed changes. No less than 45 days after such publication, the Commission may take final action on the proposal. At that time, a report of its final action is published in the *Maryland Register*. The Commission's final action takes effect 10 days after that notice appears, unless the Commission specifies a later date.

While the Commission can make changes in its own regulations and code of ethics (both found in COMAR), only the General Assembly can make changes in the statute, the Brokers Act (Title 17).

CHAPER 1 QUIZ

1. Whom may licensed salespersons represent?
   1. Owners who employ them directly
   2. No more than one owner at one time
   3. Only brokers under whom they are licensed
   4. Any broker who is duly licensed

2. License certificates issued for salespersons must be
   1. carried by them when they are performing acts of brokerage.
   2. retained by their brokers in their company offices.
   3. retained by the Commission.
   4. retained by them in their homes.

3. Brokers need not notify the Commission when
   1. salespersons resign.
   2. changes occur in the location of any of their offices.
   3. changes occur in the names of their firms.
   4. changes occur in commission sharing.

4. As a licensed salesperson, you receive a lead from a friend who is not a real estate licensee. As previously agreed upon, you split the commission with your friend.
   1. This is a violation of the license law.
   2. This is not a violation of the license law.
   3. This is a violation of the license law only if the seller is not informed.
   4. This is not a violation of the license law if your broker has given you written permission.

5. Which of the following do licensees NOT need to do to be qualified real estate agents and eligible to use Schedule C–Self Employed when filing federal tax returns?
   1. Have a written employment contract with their brokers agreeing to this status
   2. Be free from their broker's control of how their work is done
   3. Substantially earn all of the income coming from their brokerage firms in the form of commissions
   4. Hold a real estate license

6. Which of the following is paid biennially?
   1. Initial Guaranty Fund fee
   2. Brokers' and salespersons' original license fee
   3. Brokers' and salespersons' license renewal fee
   4. Guaranty Fund reassessment

7. How is the act of blockbusting regarded by Maryland law?
   1. Unethical but not prohibited by law
   2. A felony
   3. A misdemeanor
   4. A legitimate listing technique

8. Who may fine individuals found guilty of operating in the real estate business without a license?
   1. The district attorney
   2. The Commission
   3. The state or local Association of REALTORS®
   4. The attorney general

9. What is an unlicensed person improperly collecting a real estate commission guilty of?
   1. Duress
   2. A felony
   3. A misdemeanor
   4. Fraud

10. Which of the following could result in discipline by the Commission?
    1. Slandering competitors
    2. Intemperance
    3. Bad faith
    4. Puffing

11. What is the maximum penalty possible for filing false statements with the Commission in reference to a Guaranty Fund claim?
    1. $5,000
    2. $10,000
    3. $15,000 and imprisonment for two years
    4. $25,000 and imprisonment for three years

12. Who may hold standard licenses to provide Maryland residential real estate brokerage services?
    1. Corporations
    2. Limited liability companies (LLCs)
    3. Partnerships
    4. Individuals

13. Who appoints members to the Maryland Real Estate Commission?
    1. The State Senate
    2. The Governor of Maryland
    3. The House of Delegates
    4. The Executive Director of the Commission

14. When will a salesperson license issued by the Commission on November 1 expire?
    1. One year from the date of issue
    2. Two years from the date of issue
    3. April 30 of the next even-numbered year
    4. March 1 of the next even-numbered year

15. What is the primary purpose of the Brokers Act?
    1. To raise revenue
    2. To protect the public interest
    3. To control salespersons
    4. To restrict competition

16. How is the executive director of the Commission chosen?
    1. Appointed by the Governor
    2. Confirmed by the State Senate
    3. Appointed by the Secretary of Labor, Licensing, and Regulation
    4. Selected from the Maryland State Employees Classified System

17. What must ads placed by licensees for a property listed in their firm show?
    1. Name and address of the property owner
    2. Name of the listing salesperson
    3. Designated name of the broker
    4. General location of the property

18. What is the minimum level the Guaranty Fund must be maintained?
    1. $250,000
    2. $25,000
    3. $2,000
    4. $200,000

19. Which of the following relations are NOT addressed in the Commission's Code of Ethics?
    1. Members of the public
    2. The Real Estate Commission
    3. Clients
    4. Fellow licensees

20. What is the membership of the Maryland Real Estate Commission comprised of?
    1. Five members
    2. Four members that are not real estate licensees and five that are not licensees
    3. Four professional and five consumer members
    4. Representative brokers from real estate boards or associations throughout Maryland

21. The Commission may refuse to issue a broker license to a Maryland resident who has filed a proper application and met the legal requirements
    1. if it then offers the applicant a hearing on the matter.
    2. if the applicant has been convicted of a traffic violation within the past year.
    3. without offering to hold a hearing on the matter.
    4. if the applicant has not reached the age of 21 years.

22. Which of the following has authority to set license fees?
    1. The Commission
    2. Associations and boards of licensees
    3. The Secretary of the Department of Labor, Licensing, and Regulation
    4. The General Assembly

23. In which of the following situations does an act of real estate brokerage require a real estate brokerage license?
    1. A mortgage lender sells real estate acquired through foreclosure.
    2. A person charges a modest consulting fee to guide their friend in the sale of a home.
    3. An attorney-at-law handling a divorce action charges 3% to help sell a house the couple owns.
    4. A property owner subdivides his land and sells five lots in one calendar year.

24. Where do fees paid for Maryland real estate licenses finally go?
    1. The Maryland General Fund
    2. The Guaranty Fund
    3. The Real Estate Board or Association active in the area
    4. The State Real Estate Commission Fund

25. Which is *TRUE* of the Commission employees?
    1. They include an executive director and field inspectors.
    2. They must be licensed as brokers or salespeople while employed by the Commission.
    3. They must have been licensed to get their position.
    4. They are permitted to perform acts of brokerage for which a license is required.

26. Licenses of salespersons who are released by their brokers are to be
    1. returned to the Commission by the brokers.
    2. returned to the Commission by the salespersons.
    3. removed from display but retained by the brokers.
    4. returned to the salespersons.

27. What is the upper limit, if any, of a financial loss protected by the Guaranty Fund?
    1. $50,000
    2. $25,000
    3. $5,000
    4. $2,500

28. Which statement about licenses held by Maryland real estate brokerage licensees is *NOT* correct?
    1. Their holders are regulated by authority of the *Business Occupations and Professions* Article of the Maryland Annotated Code.
    2. They are issued and administered by the Maryland Real Estate Commission.
    3. They are not issued to corporations or associations.
    4. They are required for every person who sells real estate for consideration.

29. What is a requirement for licensed real estate salespersons to deliver real estate brokerage services?
    1. Affiliation with properly licensed real estate associate brokers
    2. Performance of real estate acts only on behalf of brokers under whom they are licensed
    3. Membership in the local Board or Association of REALTORS®
    4. Operation of a real estate business under their own name or designated name

30. Which of these must hold a valid real estate license to perform the acts mentioned in return for consideration?
    1. An attorney-at-law who advertises real estate services and agrees to serve as a prospect's buyer broker
    2. A person who serves as a real estate salesperson for a homebuilder
    3. Attorneys-in-fact who use powers of attorney to earn commissions for the sale of real estate
    4. Trustees who sell properties upon which their lender has foreclosed

CHAPTER 2

Real Estate Agency

■ KEY TERMS

adverse

affirmative

assist

agency in commercial
  brokerage

agency in residential
  brokerage

brokerage

buyer's agent by written
  agreement

clients' confidential
  information

cooperating agents

customers

disclosure

dual agents

exclusive-buyer-agency
  company

exclusive-seller-agency
  company

fiduciary duties

full client treatment

implied agency

intra-company agents
  (ICAs)

presumed buyer agent

represent

seller's agents

single-agency company

■ OVERVIEW

While most of this chapter emphasizes Maryland real estate law and practice, some general terms are also clarified here. On occasion, a brief restatement (in parentheses) may follow a technical term. In this book, *Purchaser* will be used for *purchaser* or *tenant* and *Seller* will be used for *seller* or *landlord*.

Topics addressed include the application of agency law to real estate brokerage; consumer confusion about various kinds of possible agency relationships; presumed buyer representation; various consent, disclosure, and notification forms; and the organization and management of brokerage firms, including advertising and handling of trust funds.

■ BROKERAGE AND AGENCY: NOT ALWAYS THE SAME

In general, brokerage involves bringing parties together and helping them negotiate agreements in return for a fee. Many kinds of brokers—commodity brokers, for instance—often do not represent either buyers or sellers. Instead, they merely facilitate transactions. The student should understand that performing certain kinds of brokerage does not always require a broker to represent—be an agent of—either party. This book, however, deals with brokerage based upon agency because Maryland law does not recognize or permit transactional brokerage in which the licensee is allowed to act as a middle man. Salespersons are general agents of their brokers who are, in turn, special agents of client buyers and sellers, lessors and lessees. Maryland real estate salespersons and associate real estate brokers engage in brokerage activity on behalf of their brokers, who always represent principals in a transaction.

■ AGENCY

Agency Duties of Licensees [§17-528–§17-535]

From §17-528 to §-17-535, the Brokers Act, *Business and Occupations* Article Title 17 of the Maryland Code, sets forth in detail the agency duties of residential real estate licensees. Specific additional duties are imposed by regulation in the Code of Maryland Regulations (COMAR), Sections 1 to 9 of Title 9, Subsection 11.

Licensees delivering brokerage services for commercial real estate are not governed by §17-528 to §17-535, (Part III. Duties of Licensees) but by other sections of Title 17 and other requirements of the Maryland Code. They are also subject to the unwritten law, which is common law that is made up of firmly established custom and judicial opinions uttered by courts of appeal—statewide and nationally.

For this reason, licensees who will perform commercial real estate brokerage should consider taking the Commission-mandated continuing education course, agency-commercial, as soon as it is available to them. All brokerage licensees must take three clock hours of agency continuing education at every other license renewal (once every four years). It is up to the licensee whether they take the agency-residential or the agency-commercial course. If a licensee takes both, one can satisfy the mandated core agency course requirement; the second can be applied to optional hours required to satisfy the 15-hour requirement.

Maryland residential agency law applies only to the sale or lease of real property that is improved by one to four single-family units. This includes a condominium, town house, or single-family home. It also applies to residential properties that have been divided into up to four apartments. However, the law does not apply to all residential property. For example, a 50-unit residential apartment building would be considered a commercial transaction, and the residential agency law would not apply.

The residential agency law does not apply to leases of 125 days or less either. Moreover, there are other certain residential property transactions that are not governed by the Maryland residential agency law. For example, the sale of a 40-unit residential apartment building would be considered a commercial transaction, and the residential agency law would not apply.

Commercial real estate is defined §17-536 as:

- real property improved by five or more single-family units;
- improved and unimproved real property zoned for commercial, industrial, or nonresidential use by the local zoning authority of the county or municipality in which the property is located; and
- unimproved real property zoned for improvement as multifamily units by the local zoning authority of the county or municipality in which the property is located.

Commercial real estate does not include:

- property zoned for agricultural use; or
- single-family units, including a condominium or co-op unit, for sale or for lease, or otherwise conveyed or to be conveyed on a single basis.

Both Title 17 and the regulations are available for study and downloading through the Maryland Real Estate Commission website (www.dllr.state.md.us/license/mrec/) by clicking the tab "Laws." At "Regulations Online – 09.11,"students preparing for the salesperson or broker license exam may wish to download each part of Chapters 1 and 2, entitled "General Regulations" (09.11.01.01 to 09.11.01.27) and "Code of Ethics" (09.11.02.01 to 09.11.02.03), paragraph by paragraph and consolidate them into a single document for study.

Agency Relationships

Maryland real estate licensees, when acting as agents, owe their clients—the persons they represent—fiduciary duties. As described in the principles text, these duties are

- **c**are,
- **o**bedience,
- **l**oyalty,
- **d**isclosure,
- **a**ccounting, and
- **c**onfidentiality

(Acronym: COLDAC).

These fiduciary duties agents owe to their clients are of fundamental importance.

Note that when acting as agents with fiduciary duties, licensees themselves are called fiduciaries.

Licensees owe non-clients, customers, other third parties, and clients

- honesty and fair dealing,
- reasonable care,
- prompt presentation of all offers and counteroffers,
- honest answers to all questions—except those that are properly declared to be confidential by a client or are otherwise protected by the law, and
- affirmative (voluntary) disclosure of material facts. (See Figure 2.1.)

FIGURE 2.1

Licensee Duties and Services to Clients and Customers

Duty or Service	Provided to Principals (Clients)	Provided to Third Parties (Customers)
Care ("Utmost" care) *Trust / Confidenel*	X	
Obedience *advise*	X	
Loyalty *Negohotion*	X	
Disclosure of all facts relevant to a transaction	X	
Accounting	X	
Confidentiality	X	
Magisterial acts: Offering expert guidance and judgment	X	
Ministerial acts (When authorized in the agency agreement): Actions of service, not requiring exercise of judgment or giving expert guidance	X	X
Affirmative disclosure of material facts	X	X
Honesty and fair dealing	X	X
Reasonable care and skill in performance	X	X
Prompt presentation of all written offers and counteroffers	X	X

Fair ~~Honesty~~ Fairness Honesty X   X

Assist and Represent: Terms with Different Meanings

Maryland real estate brokerage licensees may work with a prospective buyer either as a client or a customer. Clients are represented, but customers are assisted. Title 17 states that a prospective buyer is initially entitled to full fiduciary duties under the concept of presumed representation. If the prospect refuses this presumed status (or the licensee working with the prospect refuses to provide it), the prospect could continue to work with the licensee, simply receiving assistance as a customer; enter into a written contract for client representation, a buyer-representation agreement; or the prospect could reject both alternatives and simply walk away.

Understanding the difference between client-level service and customer-level service is fundamental to the effective and lawful provision of real estate brokerage services. Licensees always represent someone. They need to clearly understand who that "someone" is and what duties are owed to that person. Again, licensees represent clients, but they assist customers. Further, under Maryland law, real estate licensees represent one side or the other in any act of brokerage; the law does not recognize or permit transactional brokerage in which the licensee is allowed to act as a middle man.

A broker relates to prospective buyers either by

- representing them as clients under a written buyer-representation agreement,
- representing them as presumed agents, or
- treating them as customers when they are seeking to buy property listed with the broker's firm.

They relate to sellers either by

- representing them under a written agency contract (listing), or
- treating them as third parties when representing buyer clients.

An owner who lists property with a broker becomes the broker's client. Note that the legal term for *client* is *principal*. Brokerage requires a supporting valid agreement.

Representation agreements

- need to be in writing and signed by all necessary parties;
- need to state consideration stated as a dollar amount or as a percentage of the sales price;
- need to state when consideration is earned;
- need to state when consideration may be paid;
- need to state a definite termination date;
- cannot include automatic extensions;
- need to define the duties and the authority of agent;
- need to include responsibilities of principal;
- require copies to be distributed to all signers; and
- need to include permission for the agent to perform ministerial acts.

Ministerial acts

- are servant actions performed to help the purchaser meet purchaser's obligations to principal (e.g., meeting various well/septic inspectors, appraisers, etc. with keys when the purchaser and purchaser's agent are not available); and
- help the purchaser that requires no expertise.

■ THE CHALLENGE OF DUAL AGENCY

Demand for Buyer Representation

Knowledgeable, prospective purchasers frequently demand that the licensee working with them actually serves as their agent (i.e., be "on their side" and give them client-level service). They want to be served by skillful professionals who will be loyal to them and not only help them locate property to purchase, but also protect their interests, keep their confidence, and skillfully coach them in negotiating price and many other matters throughout the transaction.

Most firms throughout Maryland, in response to this consumer demand, offer representation to buyers by offering them client-level service. Brokerage firms were already providing—and continue to provide—client-level representation for sellers who list their properties with them.

The first example below illustrates a simple case of buyer representation; the second, a more complex one.

■ **EXAMPLE 1**   Broker Norman, formally representing buyer Elizabeth under a written buyer representation agreement, shows her a property listed by broker Eugene. Arturo is the owner/seller of that property and is, therefore, Eugene's client and receives client-level service from Eugene's company. Elizabeth is receiving client-level service from Norman's. Both brokerage firms in this case are providing single-agency service; each broker is the agent of one party to this transaction.

■ **EXAMPLE 2**   Client-buyer Rebecca asks her salesperson, Brian, to help her prepare a contract to purchase a property listed with Brian's broker, Yvonne—a property owned by the seller, John. As John listed with Yvonne's company, he is obviously already a client of Yvonne's company. So at this moment, Yvonne's company is being asked to represent client-buyer Rebecca and client-seller John—parties on opposite sides of the same transaction.

No individual (natural person) can possibly give total loyalty to opposing parties. That is the situation Broker Yvonne is facing. She wants to earn a commission for selling her company's listing and also a fee for representing the buyer-client in that same transaction. How can Yvonne's company properly represent both seller John and buyer Rebecca?

The Maryland Solution: Intra-Company Agents (ICAs) [§17-530]

The situation described in Example 2 (dual agency) has such potential for conflict of interest that, in the late 1990s, the Maryland legislature added to the Brokers Act certain actions that Brian's broker, Yvonne, is required to take if she wishes to earn commissions by representing both Rebecca and John as clients. In order to do this, the law requires the firm to have the written consent of all parties to this *dual agency*. The firm must then appoint two of its licensed affiliates to serve as intra-company agents (ICAs). (The term *intra* means *within*, as in intramural games—those played within the walls of an institution.) So, Broker Yvonne appoints two affiliates, Viola and Brian, as ICAs of John and of Rebecca, respectively. As the firm's broker, Yvonne is prevented by law from appointing herself as one of the ICAs. The firm—upon receiving informed, written consent to this arrangement from both buyer and seller—may now serve as agent of both parties in the contemplated transaction.

To maintain each side's confidentiality, the broker personally backs away from direct involvement in the transaction and lets the ICAs represent their respective clients. The ICAs will give their respective parties full client treatment: care, obedience, loyalty, disclosure, accounting, and confidentiality.

If Yvonne's company were very small and had only its broker and one other licensee, it could not perform the dual agency otherwise allowed by Maryland law because the law requires that the broker appoint two persons other than the broker to be ICAs. In a multioffice company, an office manager, designated to do so by the firm's broker, may appoint ICAs but may not serve as one of them.

Consent to Dual Agency by the Parties

At the time of entering into a written buyer-representation agreement, buyers may (or may not) choose to also sign a Consent for Dual Agency form, agreeing to the dual agency that could arise if they were shown a property listed with their buyer-broker's firm. They can revoke this consent at any time before actually entering into a dual agency sales agreement. If they did not sign such a form earlier, they can still sign one if, and when, they later decide to engage in dual agency.

A firm can show client-buyers only those properties listed with that firm whose owners have already consented to dual agency. Before sellers can accept a dual-agency offer, though, the sellers' Consent for Dual Agency form—even though already given—must be reaffirmed with their signatures in the space provided on their consent form. The names of the specific purchasers must also be entered. Similarly, the client-purchasers must reaffirm their consent in the space provided on their Consent for Dual Agency form before their offer can be presented. The form must show the specific property involved and the name(s) of its owner-sellers. This consent is only good for this deal, these parties, and the stated property.

F I G U R E   2.2

Consent for Dual Agency

STATE OF MARYLAND
REAL ESTATE COMMISSION

Consent for Dual Agency (agreement)

(In this form, the word "seller" includes "landlord"; "buyer" includes "tenant"; and "purchase" or "sale" includes "lease")

When Dual Agency May Occur

The possibility of Dual Agency arises when:

1) The buyer is interested in a property listed by a real estate broker; and

2) The seller's agent and the buyer's agent are affiliated with the same real estate broker.

Important Considerations Before Making a Decision About Dual Agency

A broker acting as a dual agent does not exclusively represent either the seller or buyer; there may be a conflict of interest because the interests of the seller and buyer may be different or adverse. As a dual agent, the real estate broker does not owe undivided loyalty to either the seller or buyer.

Before the buyer and seller can proceed to be represented by a broker acting as a dual agent, they must both sign Consent for Dual Agency. If the <u>buyer</u> has previously signed Consent for Dual Agency, the buyer must **affirm** the buyer's consent for the purchase of a particular property before an offer to purchase is presented to the seller. If the <u>seller</u> has previously signed Consent for Dual Agency, the seller must **affirm** the seller's consent for the sale of the property to a particular buyer before accepting an offer to purchase the property. The **affirmation** is contained on Page 2 of this form.

Your Choices Concerning Dual Agency

In a possible dual agency situation, the buyer and seller have the following options:

1. **Consent in writing to dual agency.** If all parties consent in writing, the real estate broker or the broker's designee (the "dual agent") will assign one real estate agent affiliated with the broker to represent the seller (the seller's "intra-company agent") and another agent affiliated with the broker to represent the buyer (the buyer's "intra-company agent"). Intra-company agents may provide the same services to their clients as an exclusive seller's or buyer's agent, including advising their clients as to price and negotiation strategy.

2. **Refuse to consent to dual agency. If either party refuses to consent in writing to dual agency**, the real estate broker must terminate the brokerage relationship for that particular property with the buyer, the seller, or both. If the seller's agreement is terminated, the seller must then either represent him or herself or arrange to be represented by another real estate company. If the buyer's agreement is terminated, the buyer may choose not to be represented by an agent of his or her own but simply to receive assistance from the seller's agent, from another agent in that company, or from a cooperating agent from another company. Alternatively, the buyer may choose to enter into a written buyer agency agreement with a different company.

1 of 2

FIGURE 2.2

Consent for Dual Agency (continued)

Duties of a Dual Agent and Intra-Company Agent

Like other agents, unless the client gives consent to disclose the information, dual agents and intra-company agents must keep confidential information about a client's bargaining position or motivations. For example, without written consent of the client, a dual agent or intra-company agent may not disclose to the other party, or the other party's agent:

1)   Anything the client asks to be kept confidential; *
2)   That the seller would accept a lower price or other terms;
3)   That the buyer would accept a higher price or other terms;
4)   The reasons why a party wants to sell or buy, or that a party needs to sell or buy quickly; or
5)   Anything that relates to the negotiating strategy of a party.

*   Dual agents and intra-company agents must disclose material facts about a property to all parties.

How Dual Agents Are Paid

Only the broker receives compensation on the sale of a property listed by that broker.

If a financial bonus is offered to an agent who sells property that is listed with his/her broker, this fact must be disclosed in writing to both the buyer and seller.

Consent for Dual Agency

I have read the above information, and I understand the terms of the dual agency. I understand that I do not have to consent to a dual agency and that if I **refuse** to consent, there will not be a dual agency; and that I may withdraw the consent at any time upon notice to the dual agent. I hereby **consent** to have

_____ act as a Dual Agent for me as the
(Firm Name)

_____**Seller** in the sale of the property at: _____.

_____**Buyer** in the purchase of a property listed for sale with the above-referenced broker.

_____   _____   _____   _____
Signature   Date   Signature   Date

AFFIRMATION OF PRIOR CONSENT TO DUAL AGENCY

• The undersigned **Buyer(s)** hereby affirm(s) consent to dual agency for the following property:

_____
Property Address

_____   _____   _____   _____
Signature   Date   Signature   Date

• The undersigned **Seller(s)** hereby affirm(s) consent to dual agency for the Buyer(s) identified below:

_____
Name(s) of Buyer(s)

_____   _____   _____   _____
Signature   Date   Signature   Date

■ A FIRM'S AGENCY OPTIONS IN REPRESENTATION

Licensed real estate brokers in Maryland, as in other states, may choose to operate as either single-agency, dual-agency, or hybrid companies. Those operating as single-agency companies typically choose to act as one of the following:

■ A single-agency company that offers to represent either buyers or sellers, but not both, in any given transaction

■ An exclusive-seller-agency company that offers to represent only sellers in all transactions

■ An exclusive-buyer-agency company that offers to represent only buyers in all transactions

A company willing to perform both single- and dual-agency transactions is acting as a hybrid company that offers to conduct dual-agency transactions when all parties agree and the details of governing law are satisfied, and to provide single-agency services in other transactions. Most Maryland residential brokerage firms are hybrid companies.

Single-agency companies offer to represent sellers while treating prospective buyers as customers (not clients) of that brokerage. They also represent sellers when customers are brought to them by cooperating agents, as described in the next section: "Categories of Representation." These single-agency companies also offer to represent buyers in dealing with properties listed with other companies. Even though permitted to do so by Maryland law, single-agency companies—by definition—do not perform dual agency.

It is essential that each company decide which agency service or services it will offer and present that policy and its associated procedures to everyone in the organization. All persons affiliated with the company should be trained in the proper performance of these services. It is the joint responsibility of brokers, branch office managers, and team leaders to ensure these services are being performed according to the detailed requirements of the Brokers Act.

■ CATEGORIES OF REPRESENTATION [§17-530]

The Brokers Act and the Understanding Whom Real Estate Agents Represent form, the Maryland Real Estate Commission's relationship information form (Figure 2.3), present six roles played by licensees in Maryland real estate brokerage: seller's agent, cooperating agent, presumed buyer's agent, buyer's agent (by written agreement), dual agent, and intra-company agent.

■ A **seller's agent** is a licensee who is affiliated with or acting as the listing broker for a property. A seller's agent represents the sellers (the agent's client) but may also assist a prospective buyer (the agent's customer) in buying that property. The licensee is the seller's agent but merely the buyer's salesperson.

■ A **cooperating agent** in a property transaction works for a real estate firm other than the one that listed the property. Although not part of the listing company, the cooperating agent still represents the seller (as a subagent) through and under the listing broker. The cooperating agent assists the prospective buyer (their customer) in acquiring the property. In the past, this was the typical arrangement in transactions involving both a listing firm and a selling firm. This practice, which creates subagency, is no longer favored and is becoming increasingly rare.

Although firms work together on a transaction (as co-brokers), it does not necessarily make either of them a cooperating agent. Co-brokering can occur between a listing firm and one of the following two types of "outside" firms:

— A cooperating firm
— A buyer-broker firm

In the first instance, the buyer is assisted by the cooperating firm, and the seller is represented by the listing firm. In this situation, *cooperating agent* is the term used in the statute. When a buyer-broker firm is involved, though, the co-brokering involves no cooperating agent.

■ A **presumed buyer's agent** has no written agreement to represent the prospect. This agent owes the prospect fiduciary duties but has no right to claim any payment for this representation and is not assured buyer loyalty. A licensee becomes a presumed buyer's agent whenever a prospective buyer goes to a licensee for help in finding a home to purchase. It is the default relationship that all such buyers' approaches create. Either the prospect or the licensee can end this situation at any time by orally refusing to continue it. This refusal makes the prospect a customer unless the prospect enters into a written buyer representation agreement with the licensee. Even if the representation is terminated, the licensee continues to owe the prospect full confidentiality for matters revealed during conversations before the termination. The sooner a presumed relationship is either terminated or replaced by a written agency agreement, the better for all those involved.

■ A **buyer's agent** is a licensee who has a written agreement to represent prospective buyers (their clients) in the acquisition of real estate. When representing buyers in acquiring a property listed with another company, buyer's agents are not subagents of the owner-seller. Although they are co-brokers, they are not cooperating agents. As emphasized in the previous paragraphs, buyer's agents represent the buyer. Such a buyer's agent owes the buyer client fiduciary duties and performance of any other responsibilities set forth in the written buyer representation agreement. A buyer's agent is entitled to fees established in the representation agreement.

■ **Dual agents** represent not only sellers but also prospective purchasers in the same property transaction. All parties must sign a completed Consent for Dual Agency form (see Figure 2.2) for dual agency to be conducted lawfully. Additional steps to protect the parties are also mandated.

■ **Intra-company agents** must be used when a firm performs residential dual agency. They are pairs of licensees affiliated with the broker (or branch manager, if authorized by the broker), who assigns them—one to the seller and one to the buyer—to deliver client-level services to each in the sale of a specific parcel of real estate listed with their company. They are acting on behalf of their firm, which is the dual agent. Both buyer and seller must agree to this arrangement for it to go forward. The assigned licensees are designated as intra-company agent for the seller and intra-company agent for the buyer. They were formerly called dual agent for the buyer and dual agent for the seller. The more recent designation is more accurate because only their broker—acting for the firm—is a true dual agent.

F I G U R E   2.3

Understanding Whom Real Estate Agents Represent Form

STATE OF MARYLAND

REAL ESTATE COMMISSION

Understanding Whom Real Estate Agents Represent

At the Time of the First Scheduled Face to Face Contact with You, the Real Estate Licensee Who is Assisting You is Required by Law to Provide this Notice to You. This Notice is Not a Contract or Agreement and Creates No Obligation on Your Part.

Disclosure

Before you decide to sell or buy or rent a home you need to consider the following information

In this form "seller" includes "landlord"; "buyer" includes "tenant"; and "purchase" or "sale" includes "lease"

Agents Who Represent the Seller

Seller's Agent: A seller's agent works for the real estate company that lists and markets the property for the sellers and exclusively represents the sellers. That means that the Seller's agent may assist the buyer in purchasing the property, but his or her duty of loyalty is only to the sellers.   *customer*

Cooperating Agent: A cooperating agent works for a real estate company different from the company for which the seller's agent works. The cooperating agent can assist a buyer in purchasing a property, but his or her duty of loyalty is only to the sellers.   *customer*

If you are viewing a property listed by the company with whom the agent accompanying you is affiliated, and you have not signed a "Consent for Dual Agency" form, that agent is representing the seller

Agents Who Represent the Buyer

Presumed Buyer's Agent (no written agreement): When a person goes to a real estate agent for assistance in finding a home to purchase, the agent is presumed to be representing the buyer and can show the buyer properties that are *NOT* listed by the agent's real estate company. A presumed buyer's agent may *not* make or prepare an offer or negotiate a sale for the buyer. The buyer does *not* have an obligation to pay anything to the presumed agent.

If for any reason the buyer does not want the agent to represent him or her as a presumed agent, either *initially* or *at any time,* the buyer can decline or terminate a presumed agency relationship simply by saying so.   *oral*

Buyer's Agent (by written agreement): A buyer may enter into a written contract with a real estate agent which provides that the agent will represent the buyer in locating a property to buy. The agent is then known as the buyer's agent. That agent assists the buyer in evaluating properties and preparing offers, and negotiates in the best interests of the buyer. The agent's fee is paid according to the written agreement between the agent and the buyer. If you as a buyer wish to have an agent represent you, you must enter into a written buyer agency agreement before a contract offer can be prepared.

Dual Agents

The possibility of **dual agency** arises when the buyer's agent and the seller's agent both work for the same real estate company, and the buyer is interested in property listed by that company. The real estate broker or the broker's designee, is called the "dual agent." Dual agents do not act exclusively in the interests of either the seller or buyer, and therefore cannot give undivided loyalty to either party. There may be a conflict of interest because the interests of the seller and buyer may be different or adverse.

If both seller and buyer agree to dual agency by signing a Consent For Dual Agency form, then the "dual agent" (the broker or the broker's designee) will assign one agent to represent the seller (the seller's "intra-company agent") and another agent to represent the buyer (the buyer's "intra-company agent"). Intra-company agents may provide the same services to their clients as exclusive seller's or buyer's agents, including advising their clients as to price and negotiation strategy, provided the clients have both consented to be represented by dual agency.

designee

Source: Maryland Real Estate Commission

F I G U R E   2.3

Understanding Whom Real Estate Agents Represent Form (continued)

If either party does not agree to dual agency, the real estate company must withdraw the agency agreement for that particular property with either the buyer or seller, or both. If the seller's agreement is terminated, the seller must then either represent him or herself or arrange to be represented by an agent from another real estate company. If the buyer's agreement is terminated, the buyer may choose to enter into a written buyer agency agreement with an agent from a different company. Alternatively, the buyer may choose not to be represented by an agent of his or her own but simply to receive assistance from the seller's agent, from another agent in that company, or from a cooperating agent from another company.

No matter what type of agent you choose to work with, you have the following rights and responsibilities in selling or buying property:

>Real estate agents are obligated by law to treat all parties to a real estate transaction honestly and fairly. They must exercise reasonable care and diligence and maintain the confidentiality of clients. They must not discriminate in the offering of properties; they must promptly present each written offer or counteroffer to the other party; and they must answer questions truthfully.

>Real estate agents must disclose all material facts that they know or should know relating to a property.   An agent's duty to maintain confidentiality does not apply to the disclosure of material facts about a property.

>All agreements with real estate brokers and agents should be in writing and should explain the duties and obligations of both the broker and the agent. The agreement should explain how the broker and agent will be paid and any fee-sharing agreements with other brokers and agents.

>You have the responsibility to protect your own interests. You should carefully read all agreements to make sure they accurately reflect your understanding. A real estate agent is qualified to advise you on real estate matters only. If you need legal or tax advice, it is your responsibility to consult a licensed attorney or accountant.

Any complaints about a real estate agent may be filed with the Real Estate Commission at 500 North Calvert Street, Baltimore, MD 21202. (410) 230-6206.

We, the ☐ Sellers/Landlord   ☐ Buyers/Tenants acknowledge receipt of a copy of this disclosure and

that _____(firm name)

and _____(salesperson) are working as:

(You may check more than one box but not more than two)
- ☐ seller/landlord's agent
- ☐ co-operating agent (representing seller/landlord)
- ☐ buyer's /tenant's agent
- ☐ intra-company agent/dual agent **(CHECK BOX ONLY IF CONSENT FOR DUAL AGENCY FORM HAS BEEN SIGNED)**

_____   _____
Signature   (Date)   Signature   (Date)

* *

I certify that on this date I made the required agency disclosure to the individuals identified below and they were **unable or unwilling** to acknowledge receipt of a copy of this disclosure statement

_____   _____
Name of Individual to whom disclosure made   Name of Individual to whom disclosure made

_____
Agent's Signature   (Date)

p.2 of 2   **Rev 1/2011**

■ PRESUMED BUYER'S AGENCY RELATIONSHIP [§17-533]

The Brokers Act states that a licensee who assists a prospective buyer or lessee in locating residential real estate for purchase or lease, and is neither affiliated with nor acting as the listing real estate broker for any real estate shown or located, is presumed to be acting as the buyer's or lessee's agent representing the buyer or lessee. The licensee represents the prospects in this way unless or until either the licensee or the prospects decline the presumed representation. At the earliest opportunity, the licensee should present the Commission's form describing the various kinds of agents to the prospects. The Brokers Act requires that the form, Understanding Whom Real Estate Agents Represent, be presented no later than "the first scheduled face-to-face meeting" with prospects. In the industry, this form is often referred to as the "Understanding Whom" form. The REALTOR® Code of Ethics, in contrast, requires that disclosure of agency representation be made "at first contact." Prudence dictates that it be presented by licensees as early as possible, not waiting for a scheduled meeting. It is extremely important to remember that presenting the agency disclosure form does not create a buyer-broker relationship for which compensation may be claimed, and it does not bring to an end any presumed representation. Until presumed buyer representation is ended, the licensee still owes much to the prospect (the presumed client), but the prospect owes nothing to the licensee.

Affiliates acting under presumed buyer representation (PBR) may lawfully show prospects properties listed with other firms. However, because the prospects have not agreed to written, contractual buyer representation, they are free to walk away and later buy, through another firm, any or all property they have been shown by the first firm. These presumed clients may walk away as long as the licensee continues in the role of presumed buyer representative. They have all the freedom of customer-prospects combined with the right to expect client-level service, all without any financial responsibility to the firm that is serving them. Of course, prospects being assisted as customers also are free to walk away from the company that has been assisting them, but they have had no claim to fiduciary duties—client-level service.

A licensee can end this undesirable situation with prospects simply by telling them "I do not perform presumed buyer representation," or "Our firm does not perform presumed buyer representation." A good time to say this is while presenting and explaining the Commission's Agency Disclosure at the paragraphs entitled "Presumed Buyer's Agent." Firms should establish a policy as to when and how to do this.

Events that End Presumed Buyer Representation

Buyer representation may be terminated when:

■ the licensee or the prospects reject the presumed relationship, which can be done orally;
■ the buyers either want to begin negotiations on—or wish to draw up an offer for—the purchase of a specific property listed with another firm;
■ prospective buyers want to be shown a property listed with their presumed agent's firm; or
■ the buyers enter into a written representation agreement with the licensee, thus preserving and extending the benefits of their formerly presumed status.

The termination of presumed representation, even when it is required by law, should be brought to the attention of the presumed clients to make them aware that some of the protections and advantages of presumed representation will now be lost unless they move to contractual representation. Some licensees present a new Understanding Whom Real Estate Agents Represent form because their relationship with the prospect has changed, and the updated form reveals that to the prospect. The form doesn't make it happen; it reports what happened and what the new relationship is.

Confidentiality—A Potentially Troublesome, Long-Lasting Feature of Presumed Buyer Representation

Fiduciary duties owed to a presumed client include confidentiality. That confidentiality continues even when:

- the presumed agency ends;
- the presumed clients (buyer/tenant prospects) walk away and never come back;
- the presumed clients later refuse both presumed representation and contractual, formal representation;
- the prospects turn into customers; or
- the presumed clients die.

Matters that must be kept confidential by the licensee and not used to the clients' disadvantage in any later negotiations include

- reasons for buying or selling,
- urgency to buy or sell,
- highest/lowest prices acceptable, and
- bargaining strategies learned from prospects during the period of presumed buyer representation.

To reduce conflict-of-interest problems, some firms make it their policy for affiliates to decline presumed buyer representation very early in their contacts with prospects. This refusal to engage in presumed buyer representation can be made orally or in writing. Other firms allow each affiliate to decide whether to engage in presumed representation.

■ AGENCY DISCLOSURE: UNDERSTANDING WHOM REAL ESTATE AGENTS REPRESENT

Timing of Presentation [§17-530 (b)(2); §17-533 (i)(2)]

The Brokers Act requires that

- a licensee who participates in a residential real estate transaction as a seller's agent, buyer's agent, or as a cooperating agent shall disclose that fact in writing to adverse parties;
- the disclosure shall occur no later than the first scheduled face-to-face contact with the adverse party;
- in any residential real estate transaction involving a cooperating agent, it shall be the obligation of the cooperating agent to make the written disclosure to the buyer;
- in any residential real estate transaction that does not involve a cooperating agent, it shall be the obligation of the seller's agent to make the required, written disclosure to the buyer;

- all licensees who are representing sellers disclose, in writing, to buyers the fact that they (the licensees) are representing sellers;
- when licensees represent buyers (under a written representation agreement), they are required to disclose that fact to sellers or sellers' agents; and
- when licensees are acting as presumed buyer's agents, the mandatory disclosure of this fact to the seller may be made orally, and they do not need to get the signature of the seller on the Understanding Whom Real Estate Agents Represent form.

The form that the Commission requires all licensees to use in written disclosure of representation to buyers is shown in Figure 2.3.

The Understanding Whom Real Estate Agents Represent form is not a contract; it is an information piece on which signatures of prospects and licensee are requested. However, the prospects' signatures are not required for the presentation of the form to be sufficient. If the prospects will not sign it, the law allows the licensee himself to sign it, stating that the prospects could not or would not sign. Dates recorded on the signatures can show that the disclosure was made in a timely way so as to satisfy the law. Prospects are to be given a copy of the otherwise completed form, even if they have refused to sign it.

What This Form Does Not Do

Whether it is signed or not, there are at least two things that presenting this form does not do. It does not end presumed buyer representation, and it does not create a formal buyer-representation contract. Though many licensees think that the form does one or both of those two things, note that it does neither.

Contents of Form

On this form, the licensee reveals, to those receiving it, which of the four types of agent their salesperson is acting as in dealing with them. A completed form tells both how real estate agents in general may work and how the licensee who presents it is working at that particular moment.

Decisions at Presentation

Buyers who receive this form may simply read it and, possibly, sign it. If they do not expressly reject presumed buyer representation at this point, the presumed representation continues. Buyers are free to refuse both presumed and formal written representation. If they do so, they continue as customers to be assisted in seeking a property to buy. They will then, of course, receive customer-level service.

If the buyers want formal buyer representation, with client-level service, they must enter into a written agreement with the licensee's firm to represent them as purchasers. Buyer representation agreements are discussed in Chapter 4.

■ THE CLIENT'S RIGHT OF CONFIDENTIALITY [§17-532]

Whatever confidential information a licensee learns from individuals while representing them—either under a formal representation agreement or as a presumed buyer representative—such as information about their personal finances, bargaining strategy, and motivations to buy or to sell, must be kept confidential throughout the transaction. Licensees should keep in mind that the client's right of confidentiality continues after the agency ends, after the transaction is completed, and even after a written agency agreement expires. Confidential information may be disclosed later, only with the written permission of the former client or when the information has become public knowledge by the former client's publication of it.

Agents are forbidden, for example, to reveal confidential information to other clients whom they may later represent—or to other agents in their own company who may represent parties negotiating with the previous clients—or to use such inside information to the disadvantage of the previous clients. When licensees later represent new clients in a transaction involving the former client, they must disclose to the new clients that they cannot reveal to them confidential matters about the old client.

The subject of confidentiality is so important that it deserves repeated explanation and clarification at a company's regular training sessions for sales personnel. Awareness of the need for greater confidentiality should extinguish casual office conversation about cases, clients, and customers.

Brokerage offices that practice dual agency should provide locked files or other security arrangements so that confidential information about buyers or sellers in the same transaction is kept securely segregated and does not fall into the hands of an intra-company agent representing an adverse (opposite) party. The broker—who is actually the dual agent—has full access to all this information but is forbidden by law to share it with adverse parties in any transaction unless mandated by court order or by the requirement to disclose newly discovered material facts. Of course, material facts should never be treated as confidential because they must be voluntarily revealed to all parties in every case. This is affirmative disclosure.

■ AGENCY RELATIONSHIP NOT DETERMINED BY WHICH PARTY PAYS [§17-534]

Maryland law now clearly states that agency relationships and responsibilities are not determined by which party pays for brokerage services. Before 1998 when this principle was spelled out in the Brokers Act, it was already part of the common law but unknown to many licensees.

Application of This Principle

For example, when sellers pay—or agree to pay—a brokerage fee charged by a buyer's broker, this payment does not make that broker the sellers' agent. In this example, this fact blocks any claim by the seller that the licensee representing the buyer should have worked in the seller's best interest. It also prevents buyers from claiming that the licensee engaged to represent them was really under the control of the seller. Before the statute clarified this issue, such claims had been used (however improperly) to attack and seek rescission of sales agreements on the basis of undisclosed dual agency.

This matter is counterintuitive—that is, it goes against conventional wisdom and also against what many students may have heard in previous classes. Pay particular attention to the language in Title 17:

> The payment or promise of payment of compensation to a licensed real estate broker by a seller, lessor, buyer, or lessee, or by a licensee acting for a seller, lessor, buyer, or lessee: (1) is not determinative of whether a brokerage relationship has been created or exists; and (2) does not create or

determine the existence of a brokerage relationship between a broker and a seller, lessor, buyer, lessee, or licensee. [§17-534(d)]

Even more counterintuitive is the fact that it is not necessary for a brokerage fee to be promised or paid to create an agency relationship with a licensee. Certain behaviors and statements of a licensee may properly be construed (interpreted) by a member of the public—and later by a court—to indicate that the licensee is indeed that person's agent, even without a formal agreement.

Consider this example: A licensee who says to a customer, "Trust me; I'll get you a great deal," is asking the customer to regard her as trustworthy and loyal—that is, as the customer's agent. If this occurs while the licensee is already serving as an agent or subagent for the sellers, an undisclosed (probably unintended but certainly unlawful) dual agency is created, which may later prove to be the basis for rescission of sales contract, loss of commission, suit for damages, and disciplinary action by the Commission.

Last, but unfortunately not least, the person to whom the licensee comes to owe loyalty (because of a careless remark) owes the licensee nothing for his trouble. This implied agency, like presumed representation, can amount to all work and no pay.

Remember: No individual licensee can directly and personally represent adverse (opposing) parties in a Maryland residential transaction. When a brokerage firm is properly involved in a dual agency situation, its broker is the dual agent but does not directly and personally deal with the parties. Instead, the broker appoints two intra-company agents to represent the opposing parties.

■ DISCLOSURE AND FAIRNESS [COMAR 09.11.02.02A]

According to the Code of Ethics of the Commission, the obligation of absolute fidelity to the client's interest is primary, but it does not relieve licensees from the statutory obligation to deal fairly with all parties to a transaction and to reveal material facts affirmatively (without being asked).

Statutory attempts to guarantee fairness by requiring disclosures often miss their mark. This is because members of the public often receive so many lengthy, technical disclosures that they end up with little or no understanding of what is being disclosed. Hurrying prospects through the signing of disclosure forms and perhaps saying, "These are merely formalities required by law," makes it even more likely that the disclosures will not disclose anything. Such behavior is unethical and must be avoided.

CHAPTER 2 QUIZ

1. Brokers' principals are called
    1. managers.
    2. clients.
    3. prospects.
    4. customers.

2. Which is *TRUE* when brokers handle the purchase and sale of residential real property?
    1. They are agents of the owner of the property being bought or sold.
    2. They may not act as the agent of the buyer.
    3. They may not represent both buyer and seller in the same transaction without the designation of two intra-company agents.
    4. They may personally represent both buyer and seller if both parties agree.

3. Arthur has been assigned by his broker, Bettina, to work with Carlos to provide buyer representation for the purchase of a property listed by Dorene, a salesperson with Bettina's company. Bettina has named Dorene to represent the seller. In this situation, which of the following is *TRUE?*
    1. Carlos is a prospect; Arthur is his intra-company agent; Bettina is a single-agency broker; and Dorene is the intra-company agent for the seller.
    2. Carlos is a client; Arthur is his intra-company agent; Bettina is a disclosed dual agent; and Dorene is the intra-company agent of the purchaser.
    3. Carlos is a customer; Arthur is his salesperson; Bettina is an intra-company agent; and Dorene represents the seller.
    4. Carlos is a client; Arthur is his intra-company agent; Bettina is not a single-agency broker; and Dorene is the intra-company agent for the seller.

4. Which of the following is *TRUE* of brokers when they represent buyers of real estate?
    1. They are regarded by the law as dual agents in such transactions.
    2. They must disclose this agency relationship to sellers.
    3. They are in violation of the Brokers Act.
    4. They will not be compensated.

5. Which of the following is *TRUE* concerning presumed buyer representation?
    1. Presumed buyer representation begins when a licensee shows a prospective purchaser property listed by another brokerage firm.
    2. Presumed buyer representation ends when a licensee shows a prospective purchaser property listed with another brokerage firm.
    3. A prospective purchaser who declines to enter into a buyer representation agreement is no longer owed confidentiality about matters previously discussed.
    4. The licensee can no longer be the presumed buyer representative of a purchaser who makes an offer on a property.

6. Which statement concerning agency is *TRUE?*
    1. A broker may be considered the agent of the party from whom the broker receives payment.
    2. A broker is allowed to be a dual agent in a transaction if no harm is done.
    3. A salesperson may personally perform dual agency if both buyer and seller agree in writing.
    4. A broker who represents both buyer and seller in the same transaction must appoint two intra-company agents.

7. Which of the following is *NOT* a duty agents owe to their principals?
    1. Disclosure of all facts
    2. Loyalty
    3. Timely presentation of all written offers and counteroffers
    4. Reporting to a client-buyer that one of the seller's family members had AIDS

8. When must a licensee who is representing a seller disclose this fact to the buyer?
    1. At first contact
    2. When an offer is made
    3. No later than the first scheduled face-to-face meeting
    4. When the buyer or agent of the buyer asks

9. Which of the following does a licensee *NOT* owe to a customer?

1. Due care
2. Disclosure of material facts
3. Obedience
4. Honesty

10. Which of the following statements about agency is *TRUE* in Maryland?

1. Maryland does not allow a brokerage firm to represent both buyer and seller in the same transaction.
2. Dual agency is permitted only in brokerage firms consisting of three or more licensees.
3. A licensee's performance of ministerial duties for a customer justifies the claim by that customer that the licensee ". . . acted in a way that indicated she was my agent."
4. The broker of a firm may act as one of the two intra-company agents required for dual agency.

11. Which of the following does *NOT* end presumed buyer representation?

1. Prospects orally decline presumed representation.
2. Prospects decide to make an offer for property listed by a company other than the company representing them.
3. Licensee working with prospects fails to present a disclosure of representation form.
4. Licensee shows prospects a property listed with a firm other than the licensee's.

12. When may a brokerage lawfully perform dual agency?

1. When the firm has been certified by the Commission for dual agency brokerage
2. When the firm has only two individual licensees in it
3. When the firm's broker (or the branch manager) designates two company licensees—one to represent (be the intra-company agent for) the seller and another for the buyer
4. When both sellers and buyers have agreed to dual agency on a particular property

13. How and when should it first be revealed to prospects that they have presumed buyer representation?

1. Orally, at the initial interview between the licensee and prospect
2. In writing, when the prospect signs a written agreement to be a client
3. In writing, before the end of the first scheduled face-to-face meeting
4. In writing, when the possibility of dual agency arises

14. Which statement about cooperating agents (as defined on the Understanding Whom Real Estate Agents Represent form) is *FALSE*?

1. Cooperating agents can represent the buyer.
2. Cooperating agents are subagents of the listing broker.
3. Cooperating agents bring in customers/buyers and are from a company other than the listing company.
4. A cooperating agent who brings in a buyer has fiduciary duties to the seller-owner.

15. Which of the following is *TRUE* about the Understanding Whom Real Estate Agents Represent disclosure of agency representation form?

1. It constitutes a contract for buyer representation when the fourth box is checked and the prospect signs the form.
2. It ends presumed buyer representation no matter what box is checked, whether or not the prospect signs it.
3. Failure to properly present the form constitutes a violation of the Brokers Act by the licensee.
4. The prospect is required by law to acknowledge receipt of the form by signing it.

CHAPTER 3

Real Estate Brokerage

■ KEY TERMS

beneficial owner	designated name	supervision
branch office manager	independent contractor	trust money
team leader	real estate brokerage	unlicensed person

■ OVERVIEW

In this chapter, you will be introduced to many aspects of the provision of real estate brokerage services. These matters include forms of business organization through which services may be delivered; supervisory responsibilities of brokers, branch managers, and team leaders; examples of reasonable and adequate supervision; the role of teams in a real estate brokerage firm; activities in which personal assistants may and may not engage; conducting an open house; ways in which affiliates relate to the brokerage firm; and requirements for disclosing licensee identities in advertising. This information is not only basic to passing the state licensing examination but also is essential to proper conduct of real estate brokerage.

■ BROKERAGE [§17-101]

The Brokers Act defines real estate brokerage as performing certain services for another person in return for consideration. These services are:

■ selling, buying, exchanging, or leasing real estate;

■ collecting rent for the use of any real estate;

■ giving assistance in locating or obtaining any residential real estate for purchase;

■ regularly dealing in real estate or in leases or options on real estate;

■ promoting the sale of real estate by listing it in a publication issued primarily for promoting real estate sales;

■ subdividing land and selling the divided lots; and

■ acting as a consultant in any of these activities.

Title 09 of the Code of Maryland Regulations (COMAR) recites numerous specific ways in which the Brokers Act governs every aspect of providing brokerage services. Relevant sections of COMAR, as well as Title 17 of the Brokers Act, are available online as described in Chapter 1.

COMAR includes the General Regulations issued by the Real Estate Commission with the guidance of the Department of Labor, Licensing, and Regulation and under the authority of the Brokers Act. Unless proven unconstitutional, without statutory support, or against public policy, these regulations have the force of law.

■ ORGANIZATION OF BROKERAGE FIRMS [§17-321]

The Role of the Broker

In every Maryland real estate firm, no matter how many branch offices and agents it has, only one individual is the broker. A real estate brokerage firm may be in any one of several forms of legal entity: corporation, LLC, partnership, sole proprietorship, and so forth. A licensed broker may provide real estate brokerage services through any of these forms of business organization if they have been employed by that organization and have been designated as the broker—the individual personally responsible for provision of its real estate brokerage services.

Owners may hire a broker under whose license the firm is to be operated. The broker of a firm is not required to be its sole proprietor, partner, stockholder, board member, officer, or owner. On the other hand, a broker is permitted to be the sole proprietor-owner, stockholder, partner, and so forth. Any individual who participates in providing brokerage services for a firm while associated with the firm as a partner, officer, shareholder, or in any other capacity must hold either a salesperson's or an associate broker's license. However, company officers, shareholders, corporate board members, and so forth, who are not personally involved in providing brokerage services, do not need to be licensed.

Prior to delivering brokerage services through any one of the organizational forms, brokers must submit to the Real Estate Commission notice of their intention to do so. The notice must include

■ the name of the real estate broker submitting the notice,

■ a statement that the named individual has been designated as the broker of the firm,

- the address of the firm's principal place of business and of each proposed branch office,
- any designated name that the firm intends to use in conducting its business [doing business as . . .(DBA)],
- a list of all the licensed associate real estate brokers and licensed real estate salespersons who will be affiliated with the broker of the firm, and
- any other information the Commission may require by regulation.

The Commission maintains current information regarding every corporation, partnership, LLC, and sole proprietorship through which Maryland real estate brokerage services are provided. A brokerage firm—whether corporation, partnership, or LLC—that provides real estate brokerage services is not relieved from responsibility for the acts or omissions of its officers, partners, employees, or agents. The form of the organization does not shield it or them from accountability.

Similarly, individuals who provide real estate brokerage services through—or on behalf of—corporations, partnerships, and so forth, are not relieved of individual responsibility for their actions in providing those services because of the way they are affiliated with the firm, either as employees or nonemployees.

Limitation on Affiliates' Interests [§17-511]

No more than 50% of the ownership control in any form of business organization providing real estate brokerage services may be held directly or indirectly by salespersons or associate brokers or any combination thereof. Otherwise, affiliates might become able to control their principal, the broker, rather than the other way around. Whenever affiliates apply for new licenses or renewals, they must disclose to the Commission the percentage of control they hold in the firm. This percentage must include other percentages held by the applicant's immediate family members who are not themselves licensees in that firm. Immediate family members who are licensees will report their own percentages of ownership on their license applications.

How Salespersons and Associate Brokers Affiliate with a Brokerage Firm [§17-321]

Brokers may provide brokerage services personally and/or through affiliates—real estate salespersons and associate brokers licensed under them. Such affiliates typically are statutory nonemployees (IRS-qualified real estate agents, as explained in Chapter 1), but employee status is also a possibility. Such "qualified" real estate agents (nonemployee affiliates) are often referred to as independent contractors, although independent contractor status, as defined by common law, is a very elusive situation to describe or to demonstrate. Qualified agent status, on the other hand, is easy both to define and prove, as shown in Chapter 1. Any individual, including a licensed associate real estate broker, who provides real estate services on behalf of a real estate broker, is considered a real estate salesperson with respect to the provision of those services. Except when serving as branch managers or team leaders, licensed associate brokers have no more authority than salespersons and only perform the duties of salespersons.

■ SUPERVISION [§17-320 AND COMAR 09.11.05]

Supervision requires direction and review of professional real estate activities. Commission General Regulation .05 requires that brokers supervise all licensees affiliated with them, whether those affiliates are employees, qualified real estate agents, or independent contractors. Affiliates may not operate unsupervised no matter how they are related to the firm.

There is a misunderstanding of this matter among many affiliates and some brokers, who dwell on the word *independent* in "independent contractor." Affiliates are never independent from their broker or from the broker's supervision and control. Brokers can tell their affiliates not only what to do but how to do it. After all, the broker is responsible both to the Commission and to the courts for the conduct of their agents (affiliates). Salespersons and associate brokers are general agents of their broker; their broker is their principal. They are subject to the broker's authority and control.

A general legal rule is that principals are responsible for the actions of their agents in the agents' performance of their duties. It follows that because brokers are responsible for the actions of their agents, they must have authority to control them. Moreover, a broker cannot escape the duty to supervise by claiming "My salespersons are independent contractors, so I can't tell them how to conduct their brokerage activities," or "I can't be watching my agents all the time." There is no acceptable excuse for failure to supervise.

Brokers are also to direct and review the supervisory activities of each branch office manager and any team leaders in the firm. These branch office managers and team leaders (who must be licensees, generally with at least a three-year active license history) are charged with responsibility to supervise the professional real estate activities of associate brokers and salespersons registered to their offices or in their teams. Brokers do not supervise affiliates in branch offices personally but do so through their branch office managers and team leaders. Supervision by branch managers and team leaders is in addition to rather than in place of supervision by the firm's broker. For example, a salesperson-member of a team is subject to supervision by the team's leader, the branch office manager, and the firm's broker.

Factors that define reasonable and adequate supervision include, but are not limited to, supervisors providing:

- regular training or education sessions held at least once every two months;
- experienced supervisory personnel to review and discuss contract provisions, brokerage agreement provisions, and advertising;
- written procedures that give clear guidance for handling deposit monies and other funds;
- mechanisms to ensure compliance with all fair housing laws and regulations;
- clear advertising requirements for real estate transactions;
- review of all contracts that have been signed by all parties;
- procedures for, and limitations on, the use of unlicensed personal assistants;
- emphasis on disclosure of agency relationships by licensees in real estate transactions;
- emphasis on the obligation of all licensees to comply with the Brokers Act, the Commission's Regulations and Code of Ethics, as well as all applicable local, state, and federal laws and regulations;

- restrictions on the sale or lease of a licensee's real property and the purchase or leasing of real property by licensees for their personal use; and
- prohibitions on unauthorized practice of law by a licensee.

In addition, supervisors—brokers, office managers, and team leaders—needing to prove reasonable and adequate supervision need to have evidence of

- affiliates' attendance at sales and training meetings,
- review of all executed contracts,
- review of all advertisements placed by any affiliate,
- compliance with the firm's written procedures and policies distributed to its affiliates, and
- procedures for informing affiliates of new or changed real estate laws and regulations.

These examples of "reasonable and adequate" supervision impose a substantial burden on brokers, office managers, and team leaders to maintain a paper trail of many events and actions. When those charged with responsibility for supervision cannot show sufficient evidence of meeting most of these requirements, they are presumed to have failed to supervise and the burden of proving otherwise falls on them.

■ PERSONAL ASSISTANTS

Some salespersons and associate brokers use personal assistants to help them in the conduct of their work. Some of these assistants hold real estate licenses, while others do not. The Brokers Act makes no specific mention of personal assistants. COMAR mentions them but does not define the term or list privileges or prohibitions. However, *Guidelines for the Use of Unlicensed Employees* from the Office of the Maryland Attorney General, posted on the Real Estate Commission's website, lists what unlicensed employees in a brokerage firm may and may not lawfully do. Notice that an individual working in a brokerage firm who holds a license, but not under that firm's broker, is considered to be unlicensed for the purposes of those guidelines.

Actions of Unlicensed Persons

Persons in a firm who are regarded as unlicensed are:

- those not holding an active salesperson, associate broker, or broker license under the firm's broker;
- those licensed under the license of another company (or perhaps another brokerage firm not active in the area); or
- office administrators employed by the firm, whose licenses are on inactive status, even if they have an active license in the firm's referral company.

What Such Persons May and May Not Do[1]

Unlicensed persons *may* do the following:

- Answer the telephone and forward calls to a licensee
- Submit listings and changes to a multiple listing service

---

[1]   Office of the Attorney General, "Guidelines on the Use of Unlicensed Employees," Department of Labor, Licensing and Regulation, http://www.dllr.state.md.us/license/mrec/mrecdodonts.shtml (accessed April 29, 2014).

- Follow up on loan commitments after a contract has been negotiated
- Assemble documents for closing
- Secure documents (public information) from courthouses, public utilities, and so forth
- Have keys made for company listings
- Write and place ads subject to the review and approval of an (employing) licensee and supervising broker
- Type contract forms at the direction of and for approval by licensee and supervising broker
- Compute commission checks
- Place signs on property
- Arrange the date and time of home, termite, and well/septic inspection; mortgage application; presettlement walk-through; and settlement
- Prepare flyers and promotional information for approval by licensee and supervising broker
- Act as courier service to deliver documents, pick up keys, etc.
- Schedule an open house
- Schedule appointments for licensee to show listed property
- Accompany a licensee to an open house or showing for security purposes or to hand out preprinted materials

Unlicensed persons *may not* do the following:

- Prepare promotional materials or ads without the review and approval of the licensee and supervising broker
- Show property
- Answer any questions about listings, title, financing, closing, and so forth
- Discuss or explain a contract, listing, lease, agreement, or other real estate document with anyone outside the brokerage
- Be paid on the basis of real estate activity, such as a percentage of commissions, or any amount based on listings, sales, and so forth
- Negotiate or agree to any commission, commission split, management fee, or referral fee on behalf of a licensee
- Discuss the attributes or amenities of a property, under any circumstances, with a prospective purchaser or lessee
- Discuss the terms and conditions of the real property offered for sale or lease with the owner of real property
- Collect, receive, or hold deposit monies, rent, other monies, or anything else of value received from an owner or lessor of the real property or from a prospective purchaser or lessee
- Provide owners of real property or prospective purchasers or lessees with any advice, recommendations, or suggestions as to the sale, purchase, exchange, or leasing of real property to be listed or real property presently available for sale or for lease
- Hold themselves out in any manner, orally or in writing, as being licensed or affiliated with a particular company or real estate broker as a licensee
- Contact the public concerning the availability of real estate brokerage services, unless an inquiry about a specific property is immediately referred to a licensee

Under the Internal Revenue Code, the IRS will likely consider unlicensed persons whom affiliates hire as personal assistants to be the affiliates' employees. As employers, licensees must comply with all IRS requirements on recordkeeping and payroll deductions, as well as meet the responsibility for workers' compensation insurance, retain employee withholdings for Social Security and Medicare, and pay employers' portions of each. Income earned by providing personal assistance does not meet the definition of income to an IRS-qualified agent. Personal assistants are employees whether they are engaged and paid by an affiliate or by the brokerage firm.

■ REAL ESTATE "TEAMS" [§ 17-543 THRU § 17-548]

Before 2010, groupings of salespersons and associate brokers have appeared in many real estate firms throughout the State, bringing together persons with varied talents into cohesive units in order to facilitate service to the public and maximize income to their members. Since there was no legislation specifically governing teams as to membership, supervision, naming, advertising, and so forth, real estate teams took various forms and operated in various ways; they typically had a team leader.

By legislation passed in 2010, the Brokers Act recognized and addressed, in detail, the behavior and supervision of teams, groups, and similar entities within a brokerage firm. The statute defines *team*, sets forth the requirements for being a team leader, states how a team's leader is to be selected, and explains the leader's responsibilities and the requirement for each team leader to complete additional, specific continuing education in supervision. This requirement is detailed in Chapter 1 under "License Renewal." The statute also limits membership on a team to salespersons and associate brokers licensed under the firm's broker in the same office and to any of their personal assistants or employees. In other words, it means that a broker is never to be on a team.

Moreover, the updated statute addresses in detail how the team may advertise, requiring it to clearly reveal that it is part of a brokerage firm and is not itself such a firm. The law requires every team to work only from the office of the firm where its members' licenses are retained. A team is not to provide brokerage services from any other location.

When a licensee who is part of a group or team signs real estate documents in the course of performing brokerage activities, that signature must be the licensee's own name and not the name of a brokerage group or team.

The Brokers Act does not authorize teams or groups to maintain any account for the funds of others. Trust money, such as earnest deposits or rental security deposits, is to be submitted immediately to the party authorized in the firm's policy and procedures manual to receive such funds. If allowed to do so by the firm, a team may properly have an account for its own operating funds but must never place funds of others—trust funds—into such an account.

Responsibility for Team Supervision

Licensees on a team are supervised by their team leader, their branch office manager (when they work from a branch office), and their broker. In a large firm the broker provides for branch manager supervision, each branch manager supervises the team leaders in the branch, and team leaders supervise the members of their teams. Supervision at all levels is simultaneous; no level is excused from its supervisory responsibility by the existence of another level with overlapping responsibility.

Teams: Definition and Naming

A team is made up of two or more licensees—salespersons and/or associate brokers—and their assistants and employees who work together on a regular basis to provide real estate services. All of a team's licensee members must be licensed under the same broker and have their licenses retained in the same office. A broker may not be a team member. Team members present themselves to the public as being part of one entity. They designate themselves by a collective name such as *team*, *group*, or some similar term. The name must not lead the public to see the group as a separate brokerage company. Therefore the words *real estate*, *realty*, *brokerage*, and the like, may not be used in the name.

Requirements for Team Advertising

All advertising by a team must clearly and conspicuously show the team's connection to the brokerage firm that it is a part of. In public discussion of this matter, the Commission has indicated that it would welcome the use of a preposition like *of* or *with* between the name of the team and the name of the firm.

■ **FOR EXAMPLE**   The ABC Service Team *of* XYZ Realty Co.

Whenever the team name is mentioned in advertising, the company name is to be immediately associated with it (on that very page, website screen, pencil, handout, business card, poster, truck, van, or sign and in any audible announcement).

Every advertisement of a team must contain the name of at least one of its license members as well as the phone number of the brokerage office of the firm that it is a part of.

Team Leader: Qualifications, Selection, and Duties

To be a team leader, a licensee must either be an associate broker or have held an active salesperson license for three years. Team leaders are chosen by the members of the team (and, presumably, therefore, they serve at the pleasure of the team). They must keep an accurate list of the members of their teams and provide it to their branch manager (or broker, if the broker manages the office). This list must be constantly updated whenever there is a change in team membership and the update provided to the leader's supervisor. The updated list is to be provided by the branch manager or by the broker at the request of the Commission. The team leader must—as must the firm's broker and the branch's manager—exercise reasonable and adequate supervision of the members of the team so that team members conform to all relevant governmental rules and regulations, as well as to the firm's policies and procedures.

Team Involvement in Disclosed Dual Agency

In instances of dual agency, only the real estate broker or the broker's designee may designate two members of a team as intra-company agents (ICAs) for the seller and the buyer in the same transaction and only after the parties have been advised, in writing, that the licensees are part of the same team and that the team could have a financial interest in the outcome of the transaction. For this purpose, the Commission provides the Notification of Dual Agency Within a Team form shown in Figure 3.1. The broker, or a designee of the broker, may designate two members of a team to serve as ICAs for buyer and seller. The person making such a designation shall not be a member of the team. Note that the team leader is not authorized to select intra-company agents.

When a broker appoints two members of the same team to be intra-company agents for the parties, those individuals must exercise great care in ensuring that disclosure of confidential information does not take place among or between team members. The existence of financial incentives (bonuses) offered within a team must also be disclosed to all parties.

FIGURE 3.1

Notification of Dual Agency Within a Team (Provided by the Maryland Real Estate Commission)

NOTIFICATION OF DUAL AGENCY WITHIN A TEAM

Under Maryland law, a team that provides real estate brokerage services must consist of two or more associate brokers or salespersons, or a combination of the two, who:

- work together on a regular basis;
- represent themselves to the public as being part of one entity; and
- designate themselves by a collective name such as "team" or "group."

The team operates within a brokerage, and team members are supervised by a team leader as well as by the broker, and, if they work in a brokerage branch office, by the branch office manager.

The law permits one member of a team to represent the buyer and one member to represent the seller in the same transaction only if certain conditions are met. If both parties agree, the **broker** of the real estate brokerage with which the salespersons or associate brokers are affiliated may designate one team member as the intracompany agent for the buyer and another team member as the intracompany agent for the seller. No one else may make that designation.

The law also requires that the buyer and seller each be notified in writing that the two agents are members of the same team, and that the team could have a financial interest in the outcome of the transaction in addition to any financial benefit obtained by selling one of the broker's own listings. THIS FORM CONSTITUTES YOUR NOTICE OF THOSE FACTS.

Dual agency may occur only if both parties consent to it, and sign the Consent for Dual Agency form prescribed by the Real Estate Commission. If you have concerns or questions about being represented by a team member when another team member represents the other party, you should address these to the broker or branch office manager before signing the Consent form.

This form must be presented to the buyer and seller at the time that the real estate licensee presents the disclosure of agency relationships. For the seller, that should occur no later than when the seller signs the listing agreement. For the buyer, that should occur no later than the initial scheduled showing of property.

ACKNOWLEDGMENT OF RECEIPT OF NOTICE

I/we acknowledge receipt of the Notification of Dual Agency within a Team.

_____   _____
                                          Date

_____

Forms of Organization

As permitted by §17-512 of the Brokers Act, with their brokers' permission, salespersons and associate brokers may organize themselves into limited liability companies (LLCs) or into professional service companies (PSCs). If they are so organized, the statute authorizes individual licensees within a group to direct the broker to pay commissions they earn to the LLC or PSC. Brokers are not authorized to be part of either such LLCs or PSCs. There is no permission in the Brokers Act for such organizations to be incorporated.

The Brokers Act clearly requires every shareholder in an LLC and every member of a PSC to be licensed either as a real estate salesperson or an associate real estate broker under the broker of that firm. The Commission regards a licensee working in Firm A but licensed only in another firm as an unlicensed person with respect to Firm A.

Disclosed Dual Agency

Conduct of Disclosed Dual Agency The Brokers Act requires that dual agency must only occur under clearly defined conditions. The broker or a designee of the broker must obtain the written informed consent of all parties for the broker to act as the dual agent. The broker or the broker's designee then assigns one licensee to act as the intra-company agent for one party and a second licensee to act as the intra-company agent for the other party. An intra-company agent must be either an associate broker or a salesperson of the firm. Brokers may not act as intra-company agents; they are already the dual agents.

Disclosure of Bonuses in Dual Agency §17-514(d)(1)(30) of the Brokers Act states: "If a real estate broker offers any financial bonuses to licensees affiliated with the broker for the sale or lease of real property listed with the real estate broker, the real estate broker shall provide to each party to a real estate transaction a statement that discloses that financial bonuses are offered."

Trust Money [17-502 (b) (1)]

A real estate broker promptly, but not more than seven business days after the acceptance of a contract of sale by both parties, shall deposit trust money in an account that is maintained by the real estate broker:
  (i)   separately from the real estate broker's own accounts; and
  (ii) solely for trust money.

All trust money must be promptly submitted to the broker for deposit in the broker's escrow account unless a written contract provision calls for a different destination (perhaps a title company) but not a different time period. The Brokers Act makes no provision for any accounts, other than the broker's, for trust monies. However, in practice, a growing number of brokers are suggesting that earnest money deposits be held by the title company that is to perform title and settlement work. Title companies are not subject to the procedures required by Title §17-505 for the return of trust monies.

Licensee Sales Commission Disputes

The licensing law does not authorize the Real Estate Commission to arbitrate any disputes between brokers or between brokers and salespersons over distribution of commissions. Such disputes may be submitted for arbitration to the respective Board or Association of REALTORS®, if the parties to the dispute are members of the same board, or to the Maryland Association of REALTORS®, if the parties to the dispute are members of different boards or associations. Arbitration may also be pursued through other agencies. To prevent commission disputes, the percentage and distribution of commissions should be agreed to in writing, especially those setting forth the agreement between brokers and their salespersons.

Division of compensation between brokerage firms, however, is usually based on information in the published multiple listing and, typically, confirmed orally.

■ PLACES OF BUSINESS: OFFICES [§17-517]

Each licensed nonresident real estate broker shall also maintain an office in Maryland, if the state in which the nonresident broker resides requires a resident of Maryland who is licensed in that other state, to maintain an office in that state.

The place of business in Maryland required by the Brokers Act for all broker licensees must be an office or headquarters where they and their employees and/or affiliates regularly transact real estate business. The Commission does not recognize mobile (rolling) offices. The broker's office is to have a specific street address where investigators can readily find financial and other records. Records of the firm's transactions, including the records of the broker's escrow account, must be kept in a secured location at this stationary office. Commercial answering services, mechanical recording devices, or mail drops, singly or in combination, do not satisfy the requirement for an office. Brokers must retain, in their main offices, their own licenses and the licenses of all their affiliates registered with the Commission as working at that location.

The federal Americans with Disabilities Act requires that places of public accommodation make reasonable modifications to meet the needs of persons with disabilities. Real estate offices are such places. Access for the public should be barrier-free, and employees should be alerted to assist any physically challenged persons who visit an office. Moreover, every firm with 15 or more employees in each of 20 weeks per year—and this number includes affiliates—must make reasonable accommodation to the needs of any person with a disability who works for the firm.

If such office cannot be made accessible, the firm should have written policies on how to serve disabled customers and clients.

Workplace Discrimination [Human Relations (49B) Sections 11; 11A; 11B; 11C; 11D]

In 2007, amendments to the Human Relations Commission Article, increased the avenues of redress for employees and associates who charge their employer with workplace discrimination. They may now, under certain circumstances, individually sue the employer themselves or seek the aid of the Human Relations Commission in such a suit. Alternatively, they may make a civil complaint in which the presiding administrative law judge may make awards of $50,000, $100,000, $200,000, or $300,000, based on the number of employees of the firm. In addition to compensatory damages, back pay and attorney's fees may be awarded in these actions. Although a firm with 14 or fewer employees is not mentioned in that scale of civil awards, it is now vulnerable to private lawsuits.

Privacy of Customers' Personal Information [Commercial Law §14-3501–§14-3506]

Since 2008, it has been an unfair or deceptive trade practice for a business to fail to protect the personal information of customers—persons seeking to purchase or lease a product or to obtain a service. Personal information is defined as an individual's Social Security number, driver's license number, financial account or credit card number, or taxpayer ID number. This includes information in hard copy or unencrypted digital form that, retrieved, could easily be read. After investigation of any security breach, businesses must provide notice to those individuals that a breach has occurred that is reasonably likely to result in misuse of individuals' personal information. This is a major challenge for brokerage firms with countless documents and data to secure.

Maintenance of Records [§17-508]

The Brokers Act requires all real estate licensees to keep copies of listings and any other documents obtained in connection with a transaction involving brokerage services for at least five years starting from the date of closing, the date of listing, or the date of the end of a property management agreement. This suggests a limit on the time over which the costly, strategic storage and security plan—involving encryption of data and/or other means of secure storage—must be maintained. Nevertheless, counsel should be consulted about the firm's policy in this matter.

Office Signs [§17-519]

A real estate broker must display a sign clearly visible to the public at each office and branch office that the real estate broker maintains. The sign must include the words *Realty*, *Real Estate*, or, where authorized by the respective trade associations, *REALTOR®* or *Realtist*.

Changes in Office Location [§17-520]

Within 10 days of changing the location of any office, a real estate broker must submit:

- written notice on a form provided by the Commission of such change in the address of the principal office and any branch office of the broker;
- the license certificate and pocket card of the broker or, for the branch office, its certificate; and
- the required fee.

Upon receipt of these things, the Commission issues a new certificate and card to the broker for the unexpired period of the broker's license or branch office certificate. If a real estate broker changes the address of the principal office or a branch office and fails to submit the required notice, the license of the broker is automatically suspended until the broker submits the required notice.

Branch Offices [§17-518]

Licensed real estate brokers may maintain branch offices in the State. They must appoint managers for each branch office who are either associate brokers or salespersons with three years of active experience. However, a recent provision of the law allows salespersons with shorter periods of licensure history to be appointed as branch managers. It requires such applicants to have completed the 135 hours of broker prelicense education and have passed the state broker licensing exam. In the several years since this provision was enacted, not one applicant has taken advantage of it.

Managers must exercise reasonable and adequate supervision over the provision of real estate brokerage services by all affiliates working out of their branch offices. This responsibility is in addition to, not in lieu of, the responsibility of the broker. Licenses of all licensees registered with a branch office are retained in that branch office together with a branch office certificate that shows, among other things, the name of the broker, as registered with the Commission, and the address of the main office.

Branch office certificates and their renewals are for two-year periods. There is a $25 fee for each certificate. Applications for branch office certificates must identify the individuals appointed as managers of the branch offices and be accompanied by payment of the required fees.

■ DISCLOSURE OF LICENSEE STATUS WHEN BUYING, SELLING, OR RENTING

[COMAR 09.11.02 (d)]

Licensees may not acquire an interest in or purchase property listed with their firm for themselves or for any member of their immediate family, their firm, any member of their firm, any entity in which they have an ownership interest, any employee of their real estate brokerage, or their team or group without making their true position known to the seller. Additionally, when selling or leasing property in which the licensee, their firm, or any member of their immediate family, any entity in which they have an ownership interest, any employee of their firm or of a team or group of which they are a member, has an interest, shall reveal that interest in writing to all parties to the transaction.

■ ADVERTISING

Definition [§17-527.2]

Advertisement includes any use of

- correspondence,
- mailings,
- newsletters and brochures,
- business cards,
- sale or lease sign riders,
- promotional items,
- automobile signage,
- telephone directory listings,
- radio and television announcements,
- telephone solicitations,
- internet voice-overs, or
- websites.

Regulation .19 B states, "*Advertising* means all oral, written, and visual advertising done by the licensee or by others on behalf of the licensee including telephone solicitation by individuals or by machine. The Commission's standards apply to all advertising."

Use of Designated Names in Advertising [§17-527.1, §17-527.2, §17-527.3]

A designated name is the name that appears on the license certificate of a licensee. Whenever brokers or affiliates, or individuals acting on their behalf, advertise in any medium, the advertisement must meaningfully and conspicuously present the designated name of that broker licensee (i.e., the firm's name) as identified to the Commission. A franchise logo or a company logo, although it may appear in an advertisement, does not satisfy the requirement to identify the broker's firm. When affiliates publish their own name in an advertisement, it must be exactly as shown on their pocket card and license certificate. The ad must also meaningfully and conspicuously display the designated name of the firm with which they are affiliated.

Telephone Numbers and Email Addresses

Associate brokers and salespersons may not use their individual telephone numbers or email addresses in advertisements unless the identified telephone number of their broker or branch office manager also appears in the advertisement. There is active enforcement of these requirements. Agents who include their email address when promoting business on social media such as Facebook and Craigslist should also include a number that is identified as an office phone.

The memorandum below, from the Commission's website (www.dllr.state.md.us/license/mrec/mrecnews1.shtml), addresses this issue:

> The Commission is concerned that members of the public may be unaware of how to register any questions or concerns that may arise in their dealings with a particular associate broker or salesperson. The Commissioners believe that many issues can be resolved with the assistance of the broker or branch office manager, and that this requirement will make it easier for that assistance to be obtained.

To address this concern, it is generally agreed that when an office phone number is provided in advertising, any person or automatic answering service responding to that number must give the caller at least the choice of speaking, either with the broker or the branch office manager, or with the licensee mentioned in the advertisement.

Both the Brokers Act and COMAR require that when licensees advertise to buy, sell, or lease property for themselves, that they reveal in the advertisement the fact that they are licensees. This disclosure must be made even when the licensees are offering their own property for sale. For example, some licensees use the phrase "owner agent" in advertising their own property for sale or rent.

Licensees may not advertise the listings held by other brokerage firms without prior approval by those firms.

Broker licensees using a franchise name in any advertising are required to include, clearly and unmistakably, their own name or their firm's designated name as registered with the Commission. Both brokers and their affiliates must make clear the designated name of the brokerage in every encounter—whether face-to-face or by radio, telephone, email, or any other means.

Licensees having their own websites must be certain to present the designated name of their firm, clearly and conspicuously, whenever their own name is used. They must also show more than a franchisor name or a franchise logo to identify their particular firm. Each franchisee has a distinct name; that name should be conspicuously presented. It is not enough, for example, to show "Century Executives" (a fictional franchise name) and/or some image of an airship. Instead, "Century Executives 4000" (the fictional designated name of one of Century Executive's franchisees) must be shown. It would also be well to display, not necessarily as prominently, the firm's designated name on every page of the website. The Commission is concerned that affiliates are naming only themselves on websites and, thus, giving the impression to the public they are brokers or that a team is a licensed brokerage firm.

Signs on Ground Rent Properties [§17-606]

For Sale signs displayed by licensees on property subject to ground rent must state the amount of the annual ground rent and the full cost of capitalization if the price of the property is shown. Perhaps for that reason, the price itself is seldom shown. The lettering showing the ground rent and capitalization must be at least as large as the lettering showing the property sale price. Capitalization is the sum for which the land could be redeemed—purchased in fee—from its leasehold owner. Maryland ground rents are discussed in Chapter 13 of this book.

COMAR requires that a licensee obtain an owner's permission before placing signs on a property. Licensees should check local laws regarding the use of sale, directional, and open house signs on public property. They should also honor any restrictions imposed by cooperatives, condominiums, and homeowner associations. Licensees should familiarize themselves with the U.S. Department of Housing and Urban Development (HUD) guidelines and rules concerning the use of the Equal Housing Opportunity logo or slogan in every display ad to avoid giving even the appearance of discriminatory intent.

■ TELEMARKETING AND "BROADCAST" FAX SOLICITATION

Since 2003, the Federal Trade Commission has maintained a National Do Not Call Registry to which millions of Americans have added their home telephone numbers to avoid being disturbed. Certain categories of callers are exempt from the prohibition on calling these listed numbers: charities, surveys, political organizations, and companies with which the recipient has done business during the last 18 months. However, businesses are required to have their own registry of numbers for persons who have specifically asked them (one by one) to stop calling. Maryland has passed similar legislation. Before soliciting—live or by machine—a licensee must access and check the federal, state, and company do-not-call lists to avoid violating the restriction. The federal penalty for a pattern of violations is $11,000 per call. It is a firm's duty to inform its affiliates of the firm's policies and data resources so as to honor the law and to avoid expensive violations.

There is no "do-not-fax" list. However, faxed advertising must include on each fax page the name of the sender and the sender's phone number to call to prevent receiving more faxes from that sender. Under the Junk Fax Prevention Act of 2005, the sender of an unsolicited advertisement sent to an individual's fax machine is liable for a minimum of $500 per page; damages may also be trebled at the court's discretion upon a finding that the violation was deliberate. Since 2005, the amended law has allowed unsolicited fax advertising if the sender has an established business relationship (EBR) with the recipient and the recipient has given the fax number to the sender with permission to use it. The fax must still contain a no-cost, opt-out number to call, available 24/7.

Maryland Prohibition on Commercial Fax Solicitation [Commercial Law §14–1313]

A person may not intentionally make an electronic or telephonic transmission to a facsimile device for the purpose of commercial solicitation. Commercial solicitation means the unsolicited electronic or telephonic transmission in the State to a facsimile device to encourage a person to purchase goods, real property, or services.

There is a maximum penalty of $1,000 for each such solicitation. Commercial solicitation, however, does not include a transmission made in the course of continuing prior negotiations or one made in the course of continuing a preexisting business relationship with the person receiving the transmission.

■ FUNDS OF OTHERS HELD IN TRUST (TITLE 17, SUBTITLE V, PART I)

Trust money is defined as a deposit, payment, or other money that a person entrusts to a real estate broker to hold for the benefit of the owner or beneficial owner of that money and for a purpose that relates to a transaction involving real estate in this State.

The beneficial owner of funds in a trust account is that person—other than the owner of the trust money—for whose benefit a licensee holds the money. In summary, the owner of an earnest money deposit is the purchaser, while the beneficial owner is the seller.

Management of Trust Money [§17-504]

The Brokers Act requires that when brokers receive trust money, such as earnest money deposits, they must promptly (no later than seven business days after formation of the contract of sale) deposit those funds in a non-interest-bearing checking account, a non-interest-bearing savings account, or any combination of these accounts that they maintain for that purpose in authorized financial institutions in Maryland. The account must be exclusively for the funds of others and contain none of the broker's or firm's funds (no commingling). Real estate brokers may not use trust money for any purpose other than that for which it is entrusted to them (no conversion).

However, upon the agreement and direction of both the money's owner and its beneficial owner in the sales contract, the broker is permitted to turn the money over to a party such as an escrow company, which would later distribute and apply it at settlement.

Brokers are required to report the bank's name and the account numbers to the Commission as soon as they start depositing trust monies there. If a licensee establishes another non-interest-bearing or special escrow account, changes an escrow account number, or transfers the account to another bank, the broker must notify the Commission in writing within 10 days of such action. Trust monies from multiple transactions may be deposited in a single trust money account.

Associate real estate brokers or real estate salespersons who receive trust monies while providing real estate brokerage services shall immediately submit such money to their brokers or their brokers' designees.

Promptly should be interpreted to mean "at the earliest opportunity." Earnest money deposit checks that accompany offers to purchase are usually not transacted (deposited in the firm's trust account) until the negotiation to purchase is completed and the offer-counteroffer process has ended. At any time prior to that completion, the broker is not only free, but obliged, to return the deposit to the offeror-buyer upon that offeror's request. If the broker has deposited the offeror's check, no refund is usually made until the check clears.

Authorized Financial Institutions [§17-503]

Except when directed to the contrary in the fully signed purchase agreement, brokers must deposit all trust money in an escrow account in a financial institution located in the State whose deposits are insured by the Federal Deposit Insurance Corporation, the National Credit Union Administration, the State of Maryland Deposit Insurance Fund Corporation, or the Maryland Credit Union Insurance Corporation.

Disposition of Trust Money [§17-505]

The Brokers Act sets forth several options under which a broker may release earnest money held in trust. These choices address both situations in which the transaction goes smoothly to settlement and those where one or both parties dispute the distribution of the deposit when the transaction has collapsed.

The Brokers Act requires that real estate brokers maintain trust money in an authorized account until one of four things happens:

1. The real estate transaction is consummated or terminated, and the money paid out as intended.
2. The real estate broker receives proper written instructions from the owner and beneficial owner, agreeing on withdrawal or other disposition of the trust money.
3. A court directs disposition of funds after a broker's filing of an action of interpleader.
4. When the owner or beneficial owner of the trust money fails to complete the real estate transaction for which the trust money was entrusted, prior to distributing the trust money, the real estate broker shall notify both the owner and the beneficial owner (from here on, referred to as the buyer and the seller, respectively) of the broker's intention to distribute the trust money to the party who, in the broker's good-faith opinion, is entitled to receive it in accordance with the terms of the real estate contract. This notice must be delivered either in person or by a combination of certified mail, return receipt requested, and regular mail. It shall state whether the trust money will be paid to the buyer or the seller and tell both that either of them may prevent distribution of the trust money by submitting a formal, written, similarly delivered protest within 30 days. If neither party submits a protest within that time, the trust money is to be distributed in accordance with the real estate broker's notice. Brokers who receive a letter of protest may distribute the trust money in accordance with one of the other three alternatives or simply leave it in the firm's trust account indefinitely.

Brokers may not be held liable for exercising (or not exercising) the fourth alternative. Authority to make good-faith disbursement of funds must be granted in the purchase agreement that entrusted the funds to the broker at the time of offer and acceptance. Without such authority, the broker may not use that process to disburse the funds.

When the duty of real estate brokers to maintain trust money in an account terminates—typically at closing—they must promptly account for all trust money. Real estate brokers may invest trust money as the owners (the buyers) and beneficial owners (the sellers) of the trust money instruct in writing or as the real estate brokers, owners, and beneficial owners have set down in a written agreement.

Even though a buyer is entitled to the return of earnest money upon request during any right-of-cancellation period in the purchase of a condominium, homeowners association (HOA), and so forth, a broker holding the deposit may only return it to the deserving buyer subject to the details of §17-505. If a title/settlement company had been given the funds rather than a licensed broker, the money could be returned more expeditiously because the settlement company is not a broker licensee and, therefore, not subject to §17-505.

Records to Be Kept Secure [§17-507]

Brokers must keep, in a secured area within their office, all records of trust money. They are also required to keep copies of all real estate transaction documents formed in the course of their brokerage activities. The records of trust money activity are to be available to the Commission on demand. On reasonable notice, a licensee must allow a representative of the Commission access to other required records in the licensee's place of business during business hours.

Authority to Sign Trust Account Checks [COMAR 09.11.01.20]

The firm's real estate broker must be the signer, or at least one of the signers, on checks drawn on escrow accounts that the broker is required to maintain. The broker may designate an alternate signer to sign checks. This designated alternate signer, however, must be a licensee. A nonlicensee may be a required cosigner on the broker's escrow account, provided all checks are also signed by a licensee designated by the broker. At least one licensee must sign every check.

CHAPTER 3 QUIZ

1. What is required by law on any outdoor sign or advertisement displayed on property for sale subject to ground rent?
   1. It must, if price is shown, also show the annual ground rent but need not show any other details until an inquiry is made by a prospective purchaser.
   2. It must, if price is shown, show ground rent and cost of capitalization in lettering no smaller than the lettering used for the price.
   3. It must show only the sale price.
   4. It must show only sale price and the phrase "plus GR."

2. Which of the following is *TRUE* of ads in which licensees advertise real property they have listed?
   1. The name of the salesperson need not be included in the advertisement, but the designated name of the broker must be shown.
   2. Only the broker's name is permitted in advertisements.
   3. The price of the property must be included in all advertisements.
   4. Members of multiple listing services may advertise any of the services' listings.

3. Which of the following satisfies the requirement that a broker maintain an office?
   1. A telephone answering service
   2. A post office box
   3. A mechanical answering machine
   4. A definite place of business

4. Who may operate a real estate brokerage firm?
   1. A real estate salesperson
   2. An associate broker
   3. Any person holding a valid real estate license issued by the State Real Estate Commission
   4. A licensed real estate broker

5. When advertising, what must a broker include?
   1. The designated name of that broker as registered with the Commission
   2. The name of the broker's REALTOR® board or association or Realtist organization
   3. The legal name of the licensed real estate broker
   4. The name of the licensee who listed the property

6. In Maryland, who is the person primarily responsible for the real estate brokerage services provided through a corporation?
   1. The president of the corporation
   2. The licensed real estate broker of the firm
   3. The chairperson of the corporate board
   4. The majority stockholder of the corporation

7. Under what circumstances may salespersons use their own names and phone numbers in advertising listed property?
   1. When the designated name of their firm is clearly and meaningfully shown, as well as the firm's phone number
   2. When their office manager's name is shown in letters at least half the size of the salesperson's
   3. When different colors are used for the broker's and salespersons' names
   4. When the owner-seller gives permission

8. When there are no instructions to the contrary from their owner and beneficial owner, what does the Brokers Act require be done with earnest money deposits?
   1. They may be commingled with the broker's funds.
   2. They must be deposited in an insured and approved financial institution in Maryland.
   3. They are to be placed in an interest-bearing account.
   4. They may be withdrawn at any time prior to settlement, as long as a licensee's signature appears on the escrow check.

9. How must a check drawn on a brokerage firm's escrow (trust) account be signed?

1. By the associate broker of the firm using her designated name
2. By at least two licensees in the firm
3. It may be cosigned by an appointed non-licensee, if signed by a nondesignated licensee.
4. It does not necessarily need a second signature if signed by the broker of the firm.

10. Which of the following may an unlicensed person working in a brokerage firm *NOT* do?

1. Compute commission checks
2. Submit listings and changes to a multiple listing service
3. Conduct an open house
4. Schedule appointments for a licensee to show listed property

11. Which of the following team names would be permissible under the Brokers Act?

1. The ABC Service Team
2. The ABC Realty Service Team
3. The ABC Real Estate Expert Team
4. ABC Service Associates

12. Which of the following statements about a team leader is incorrect?

1. The team leader is designated by the firm's broker (or branch manager).
2. The team leader is responsible for reasonable and adequate supervision of the team.
3. The team leader can appoint intra-company agents (ICAs) when dual agency involves two team members.
4. The team leader can be the branch manager.

13. Which of the following is *NOT* required in advertising for a team?

1. The advertisement must contain the name of at least one licensee on the team.
2. The advertisement must contain the name of the team leader.
3. The advertisement must follow branch office and company-wide requirements.
4. The advertisement must include the phone number of the office out of which the team works.

14. Which of the following is a requirement for team advertising?

1. The name of the team must be directly connected with the full name of the brokerage firm of which it is a part.
2. The name of the team must be the same size as or smaller than the name of the firm of which it is a part.
3. The address of the office out of which the team works must be shown.
4. The phone number of the team leader must be shown.

15. Which of the following statements about teams is *FALSE*?

1. A team must have at least two licensee members.
2. Members of the team regularly work together.
3. The team identifies itself to the public with some name.
4. A salesperson cannot be a team leader.

CHAPTER 4

Listing Agreements and Buyer Representation Agreements

■ KEY TERMS

automatic renewal
   provisions
buyer representation
   agreements

completed disclosure
   form
latent defects
listings
material fact

ministerial acts
net listing agreements
owner in severalty
subagents

■ OVERVIEW

Maryland recognizes representation agreements between real estate brokers and sellers and those between real estate brokers and buyers. (References to *buyers* and *sellers* should be understood, in this book, to apply to *tenants* and *landlords* whenever appropriate.)

Listings are contracts that create agency relationships in which brokers agree to help sellers sell their realty, and the sellers agree to compensate them for their service. These agreements may be either exclusive-right-to-sell, exclusive-agency, or open listings as these terms are explained in the students' principles text.

A property owner who enters into such an agreement with a broker is listing the property. These agreements are typically arranged by affiliates (salespersons and associate brokers) on behalf of their brokers. Although this procedure may later result in compensation for affiliates, only their brokers and the client-seller are parties to the agreement. Moreover, the listing contracts belong to the brokers.

Buyer representation agreements are contracts that create an agency relationship under which, for compensation, brokers agree to help buyers find property. Despite the fact that these exclusive buyer agency agreements between their brokers and the client-buyers are typically arranged by affiliates acting for their broker, the contracts belong to their brokers and not to the affiliates.

■ RESIDENTIAL BROKERAGE AGREEMENTS

No "Standard" Form

Real estate industry boards and associations often provide listing and buyer representation agreement forms for their members' use, but no standard form is prescribed by either statute or regulation for either listing (seller representation) agreements or buyer representation agreements. Maryland law does, however, impose some specific requirements and prohibitions for whatever forms are used.

Required Provisions [§17-534]

All residential agency agreements—representing buyers or sellers, open or exclusive—must be in writing and signed by the parties to those agreements. Copies are to be given to all signers before the brokerage firm puts the listed property on the market (i.e., advertises it, enters it into a multiple listing system, or otherwise brings it to the attention of prospective purchasers).

Unless the firm's policy manual mandates that others may sign the agency agreement on behalf of the firm, only the broker may do so. Often brokers authorize branch managers to sign; rarely, some firms authorize the affiliate taking the listing to do so.

Maryland law requires that agency agreements state the duties and authority of the agent, the compensation to be paid to the agent, the performance that will call for such payment, when compensation is considered earned, and when compensation is to be paid. It also must state a definite date on which the agreement will end without further notice from either party as well as provide a provision for possible early termination. It is unlawful to include automatic renewal provisions in the agreement that would require a client to take any action to terminate representation at the end of its original term. Agency contracts may be extended but only by signed, written extension agreements.

The agreement must set forth whether the seller is giving permission for the listing firm to receive compensation from persons other than its client. It must also state whether the seller authorizes the firm to cooperate with other brokers, and the details of how commissions earned will be shared (i.e., the amount [usually expressed as a percentage] of the shared compensation with which other brokers [buyer brokers or cooperating brokers] will be compensated). The listing should also indicate whether the client is willing to participate in a dual-agency transaction. In their listings, clients may not waive any of the protections required by statute and regulation for such agreements. Listing agreements should authorize the brokerage to perform ministerial acts for prospects as part of their selling efforts on behalf of their client.

In a buyer representation agreement, the client may or may not authorize the firm (their agent) to negotiate a binding contract on their behalf.

Net Listing Forbidden [§17-322(b) and COMAR 09.11.01.01(b)]

Regarded as unethical in most states, net listings are also unlawful in Maryland. Listings may not contain agreements in which brokers retain all sale proceeds in excess of some minimum sales proceeds agreed to by sellers. This is to prevent uninformed sellers from agreeing to such an arrangement without being aware of the true value of their property.

Additional Offers: One Effect of Silence [§17-532(c)]

The Brokers Act states that when there is no express agreement to the contrary (i.e., when there is silence about these matters) in the brokerage agreement, listing brokers

- are not required to seek additional offers for a listed property that becomes subject to a contract of sale, but
- are required—unless the client directs to the contrary—to present additional written offers and counteroffers that come to the broker's firm for a property that is "under contract."

Most listing agreements provided by industry associations address these choices directly in the preprinted listing form, usually in a way that imposes the least burden on—and gives the greatest protection to—the brokerage firm. These forms typically do not require further showing and mandate no presentation of later offers (i.e., they are silent on these matters).

■ OTHER PROVISIONS

Ministerial Acts [§17-528, §17-532]

Ministerial acts are acts performed by a licensee that do not involve discretion or the exercise of expert judgment by that licensee. They may be performed both on behalf of clients and of third parties (nonclients) before, during, and after the writing of a contract to purchase. When agency agreements authorize agents to perform ministerial acts on behalf of third parties, those acts cannot be construed (interpreted) to violate the agents' duty of loyalty to their clients. Neither may they be construed to indicate an agency agreement between the nonclient and the licensee performing those acts.

If a nonclient buyer asks the seller's broker whether to order a home inspection, though, the seller's broker must refuse to give such advice because it involves providing expert judgment. Giving such guidance would constitute a magisterial (not a ministerial) act. It would open the broker to charges of undisclosed dual agency that could imperil the transaction and damage their client, the seller.

Copies of Agency Agreements [§17-322(b) 15,16; COMAR 09.11.01.12]

Licensees must give copies of agency agreements to seller-clients before beginning to carry out the tasks assigned in the agreements. Licensees must also keep copies of all such agency agreements for five years either from the date they are signed or from the scheduled date of any settlement called for by a sales contract entered into during the listing. Copies of documents creating buyer representation should also be kept for the five-year period.

Disclosure and Disclaimer Statement [§17-322(e); and COMAR 09.11.02.02(J)]

At the time of listing a residential property for sale, brokers or their affiliates are to present the Commission's Residential Property Disclosure and Disclaimer Statement (Figure 4.1) to sellers for their completion and signature. They should warn sellers that neither disclosure nor disclaimer relieves sellers of the legal requirement to make voluntary disclosure to purchasers of all material property defects. Failure by either a buyer's or seller's broker to present this form, properly completed, to the prospective buyer before presentation of the buyer's written offer opens the offending licensee to disciplinary action because that failure could result in a contract becoming void or voidable. When sellers are being asked to complete this form, they must be warned that whether they choose to "disclose" or "disclaim" the condition of the property, latent defects must always be made known to prospective purchasers. Latent defects are defined later in this chapter under "Seller Disclosure."

Licensee Responsibilities for Disclosure [§17-530(b) and §17-533(i)]

Licensees already representing either a seller or a buyer must disclose their existing agency relationship in writing not later than their first scheduled face-to-face meeting with the adverse party. This should be done using the Understanding Whom Real Estate Agents Represent (relationship information) form, which is mandated by the Commission. (See Figure 2.3 in Chapter 2 of this book.) A licensee serving in the capacity of presumed buyer-agent must orally disclose that fact to any seller or the seller's agent at first contact. When such disclosure is made orally, as permitted by § 17- 533(j) by telephone, it is advised to follow up by delivery of a properly completed Understanding Whom form at the earliest possible opportunity.

Note that the completed Understanding Whom Real Estate Agents Represent form given to the buyer shall not subsequently be used to disclose agency representation to sellers. Sellers receiving agency disclosure must be given a completed form disclosing matters to them by name and calling for their personal signatures. To give the sellers a mere copy of a form that does not apply to them amounts to complete failure to make the required disclosure.

An offer to purchase should never be presented until the purchasers have received a properly completed Maryland Residential Property Disclosure and Disclaimer Statement for the property that is the subject of the offer. (See Figure 4.1.) Many listing agents leave multiple copies of a completed form on a table in a for-sale property. However, delivery of this form must be evidenced by a properly dated receipt from the buyer. A licensee representing a seller is responsible to see that this form is presented in a timely manner and to retain proof of that presentation. If a prospective buyer submits an offer to purchase property before receiving the properly completed Understanding Whom form, the selling firm may wish to briefly delay presenting that offer to the client-sellers until the form has been given to the prospect.

FIGURE 4.1

Property Disclosure and Disclaimer Statement

MARYLAND RESIDENTIAL PROPERTY DISCLOSURE AND DISCLAIMER STATEMENT

by condition

Property Address: _____

Legal Description: _____

NOTICE TO SELLER AND PURCHASER

Section 10-702 of the Real Property Article, *Annotated Code of Maryland*, requires the owner of certain residential real property to furnish to the purchaser either (a) a RESIDENTIAL PROPERTY DISCLAIMER STATEMENT stating that the owner is selling the property "as is" and makes no representations or warranties as to the condition of the property or any improvements on the real property, except as otherwise provided in the contract of sale, or in a listing of latent defects; or (b) a RESIDENTIAL PROPERTY DISCLOSURE STATEMENT disclosing defects or other information about the condition of the real property actually known by the owner. Certain transfers of residential property are excluded from this requirement (see the exemptions listed below).

> 10-702. EXEMPTIONS. The following are specifically excluded from the provisions of §10-702:
> 1. The initial sale of single family residential real property:
>   A. that has never been occupied; or
>   B. for which a certificate of occupancy has been issued within 1 year before the seller and buyer enter into a contract of sale;
> 2. A transfer that is exempt from the transfer tax under §13-207 of the Tax-Property Article, except land installment contracts of sales under §13-207(a) (11) of the Tax-Property Article and options to purchase real property under §13-207(a)(12) of the Tax-Property Article;
> 3. A sale by a lender or an affiliate or subsidiary of a lender that acquired the real property by foreclosure or deed in lieu of foreclosure;
> 4. A sheriff's sale, tax sale, or sale by foreclosure, partition, or by court appointed trustee;
> 5. A transfer by a fiduciary in the course of the administration of a decedent's estate, guardianship, conservatorship, or trust;
> 6. A transfer of single family residential real property to be converted by the buyer into use other than residential use or to be demolished; or
> 7. A sale of unimproved real property.

Section 10-702 also requires the owner to disclose information about latent defects in the property that the owner has actual knowledge of. The owner must provide this information even if selling the property "as is." "Latent defects" are defined as: Material defects in real property or an improvement to real property that:

> (1) A purchaser would not reasonably be expected to ascertain or observe by a careful visual inspection of the real property; and
> (2) Would pose a direct threat to the health or safety of:
>   (i) the purchaser; or
>   (ii) an occupant of the real property, including a tenant or invitee of the purchaser.

MARYLAND RESIDENTIAL PROPERTY DISCLOSURE STATEMENT

NOTICE TO OWNERS: Complete and sign this statement only if you elect to disclose defects, including latent defects, or other information about the condition of the property actually known by you; otherwise, sign the Residential Property Disclaimer Statement. You may wish to obtain professional advice or inspections of the property; however, you are not required to undertake or provide any independent investigation or inspection of the property in order to make the disclosure set forth below. The disclosure is based on your personal knowledge of the condition of the property at the time of the signing of this statement.

NOTICE TO PURCHASERS: The information provided is the representation of the Owners and is based upon the actual knowledge of Owners as of the date noted. Disclosure by the Owners is not a substitute for an inspection by an independent home inspection company, and you may wish to obtain such an inspection. The information contained in this statement is not a warranty by the Owners as to the condition of the property of which the Owners have no knowledge or other conditions of which the Owners have no actual knowledge.

How long have you owned the property? _____

Property System: Water, Sewage, Heating & Air Conditioning (Answer all that apply)

Water Supply	Public	Well	Other _____		
Sewage Disposal	Public	Septic System approved for _____(# bedrooms) **Other Type** _____			
Garbage Disposal	Yes	No			
Dishwasher	Yes	No			
Heating	Oil	Natural Gas	Electric	Heat Pump Age ____	Other _____
Air Conditioning	Oil	Natural Gas	Electric Heat Pump Age ____	Other _____	
Hot Water	Oil	Natural Gas	Electric Capacity _____	Age_____	Other _____

FIGURE 4.1

Property Disclosure and Disclaimer Statement (continued)

[handwritten: — seller fill out @ listing]

[handwritten: Property Conditions → 5 days write of recision when received after offer]
[handwritten: ↳ Before offer]

Please indicate your actual knowledge with respect to the following:

1. Foundation: Any settlement or other problems?   Yes   No   Unknown
Comments:_____
2. Basement: Any leaks or evidence of moisture?   Yes   No   Unknown   Does Not Apply
Comments:_____
3. Roof: Any leaks or evidence of moisture?   Yes   No   Unknown
        Type of Roof:_____Age_____
Comments:_____
        Is there any existing fire retardant treated plywood?   Yes   No   Unknown
Comments:_____

4. Other Structural Systems, including exterior walls and floors:
Comments:_____
        Any defects (structural or otherwise)?   Yes   No   Unknown
Comments:_____
5. Plumbing system: Is the system in operating condition?   Yes   No   Unknown
Comments:_____

6. Heating Systems: Is heat supplied to all finished rooms?   Yes   No   Unknown
Comments:_____
        Is the system in operating condition?   Yes   No   Unknown
Comments:_____
7. Air Conditioning System: Is cooling supplied to all finished rooms? Yes   No   Unknown   Does Not Apply
Comments:_____
        Is the system in operating condition?   Yes   No   Unknown   Does Not Apply
Comments:_____

8. Electric Systems: Are there any problems with electrical fuses, circuit breakers, outlets or wiring?
        Yes   No.   Unknown
Comments:_____
8A. Will the smoke alarms provide an alarm in the event of a power outage? ○ Yes ○ No
Are the smoke alarms over 10 years old? ○ Yes ○ No
If the smoke alarms are battery operated, are they sealed, tamper resistant units incorporating a silence/hush button, which use long-life batteries as required in all Maryland Homes by 2018? ○Yes ○ No
Comments:_____
9. Septic Systems: Is the septic system functioning properly?   Yes   No   Unknown   Does Not Apply
        When was the system last pumped?   Date_____   Unknown
Comments:_____
10. Water Supply: Any problem with water supply?   Yes   No   Unknown
Comments:_____
        Home water treatment system: Yes   No   Unknown
Comments:_____
        Fire sprinkler system: Yes   No   Unknown   Does Not Apply
Comments:_____
        Are the systems in operating condition?   Yes   No   Unknown
Comments:_____
11. Insulation:
        In exterior walls?   Yes   No   Unknown
        In ceiling/attic?   Yes   No   Unknown
        In any other areas?   Yes   No   Where?_____
Comments:_____
12. Exterior Drainage: Does water stand on the property for more than 24 hours after a heavy rain?
        Yes   No   Unknown
Comments_____
        Are gutters and downspouts in good repair?   Yes   No   Unknown
Comments:_____

[handwritten: — is they set after offer 5 day.]

FIGURE 4.1

Property Disclosure and Disclaimer Statement (continued)

13. Wood-destroying insects: Any infestation and/or prior damage?   Yes   No   Unknown
Comments:_____
      Any treatments or repairs? Yes   No   Unknown
      Any warranties?   Yes   No   Unknown
Comments:_____

14. Are there any hazardous or regulated materials (including, but not limited to, licensed landfills, asbestos, radon gas, lead-based paint, underground storage tanks, or other contamination) on the property?
          Yes   No   Unknown
If yes, specify below
Comments:_____

15. If the property relies on the combustion of a fossil fuel for heat, ventilation, hot water, or clothes dryer operation, is a carbon monoxide alarm installed in the property?
          o Yes   o No   0 Unknown
Comments:_____

16. Are there any zoning violations, nonconforming uses, violation of building restrictions or setback requirements or any recorded or unrecorded easement, except for utilities, on or affecting the property?
          Yes   No   Unknown
If yes, specify below
Comments:_____
16A. If you or a contractor have made improvements to the property, were the required permits pulled from the county or local permitting office? ○ Yes ○ No ○ Does Not Apply ○ Unknown
Comments:_____

17. Is the property located in a flood zone, conservation area, wetland area, Chesapeake Bay critical area or Designated Historic District?
        Yes   No   Unknown   If yes, specify below
Comments:_____

18.Is the property subject to any restriction imposed by a Home Owners Association or any other type of community association?
        Yes   No   Unknown   If yes, specify below
Comments:_____

19. Are there any other material defects, including latent defects, affecting the physical condition of the property?
        Yes   No   Unknown
Comments:_____

NOTE: Owner(s) may wish to disclose the condition of other buildings on the property on a separate
RESIDENTIAL PROPERTY DISCLOSURE STATEMENT.

The owner(s) acknowledge having carefully examined this statement, including any comments, and verify that it is complete and accurate as of the date signed. The owner(s) further acknowledge that they have been informed of their rights and obligations under §10-702 of the Maryland Real Property Article.
Owner _____   Date _____

Owner _____   Date _____

The purchaser(s) acknowledge receipt of a copy of this disclosure statement and further acknowledge that they have been informed of their rights and obligations under §10-702 of the Maryland Real Property Article.

Purchaser _____   Date_____

Purchaser _____   Date_____

FIGURE 4.1

Property Disclosure and Disclaimer Statement (continued)

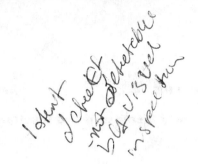

MARYLAND RESIDENTIAL PROPERTY DISCLAIMER STATEMENT

NOTICE TO OWNER(S): Sign this statement only if you elect to sell the property without representations and warranties as to its condition, except as otherwise provided in the contract of sale and in the listing of latent defects set forth below; otherwise, complete and sign the RESIDENTIAL PROPERTY DISCLOSURE STATEMENT.

Except for the latent defects listed below, the undersigned owner(s) of the real property make no representations or warranties as to the condition of the real property or any improvements thereon, and the purchaser will be receiving the real property "as is" with all defects, including latent defects, which may exist, except as otherwise provided in the real estate contract of sale. The owner(s) acknowledge having carefully examined this statement and further acknowledge that they have been informed of their rights and obligations under §10-702 of the Maryland Real Property Article.

The owner(s) has actual knowledge of the following latent defects: _____
_____
_____

Owner _____   Date_____

Owner_____   Date_____

The purchaser(s) acknowledge receipt of a copy of this disclaimer statement and further acknowledge that they have been informed of their rights and obligations under §10-702 of the Maryland Real Property Article.

Purchaser _____   Date_____

Purchaser _____   Date_____

Page 4 of 4

FORM: MREC/DLLR: Rev 8/30/2013

Licensees must also provide to buyers, on behalf of client-sellers, the federal lead-based paint disclosure form for any properties that buyers are considering that were built before January 1, 1978 (i.e., in 1977 or earlier). If the buyers are clients and the sellers are not represented by any licensee, it is then the responsibility of the buyer's agent to procure any required lead-based paint disclosure form and present it to the buyer before presenting any offer from that buyer.

There is one form required for property being rented and a different one required for property being purchased. It is of utmost importance to use the right one; use of the wrong one is regarded by federal law as utter failure to meet the disclosure requirement. That failure is subject to penalties of as much as $11,000 each for repeated, deliberate violation. Moreover, a disclosure form with any item not completed is counted as no disclosure at all.

In addition to the appropriate form, prospective purchasers and tenants must be given the government booklet *Protect Your Family From Lead in Your Home.*

■ LISTING AGREEMENT PROPERTY INFORMATION

In agency agreements for the sale of a property, the age of the house, area of the lot, zoning of the property, taxes, and other detailed property information should appear in the portion of listing agreements that will be published. If accurate data are not available from the owner, the listing licensee should obtain correct data from public records or personal inspection. Estimates of such information and educated guesses are totally unacceptable when facts are required. In preparing the listing, a licensee should take care not to accept information about the general (ad valorem) tax based on a previous year's levy. Such data seldom reflects the seller's reduction in taxes when current data is needed for the loan qualification process.

The previous year's tax may have been based on an assessment made three years earlier, and the next year's tax may be significantly different. It may also reflect homestead discounts that a prospective purchaser may not be eligible for.

Any increased tax rate should also be taken into account in projecting tax costs for a new owner. Buyer-brokers, in particular, should take great care to use the most dependable "fresh" data available.

It is suggested that listing licensees also examine any existing house location survey of the property, note what information it shows regarding property lines and improvements, and attempt to determine if it is thorough and up-to-date. Accurate information, responsibly presented in the listing, reduces chances for confusion and uncertainty when the property is shown and a contract offer prepared.

When describing the condition of the property in remarks distributed through the multiple listing service (MLS), licensees must be careful not to say anything that buyers may later consider misrepresentation. Licensees must also take care not to insert information into the MLS that betrays sellers' confidentiality. This obligation of confidentiality does not extend to material facts.

Material Facts [§17-322(b)4 and COMAR 09.11.02.01(d)]

A material fact is the extreme opposite of a trivial, unimportant one. From a buyer's point of view, a material fact is any fact that, if known by the buyer, would likely influence the buyer's decision to purchase a property, negotiate the price, and review other conditions of an offer. For a seller, a material fact is one that could influence the seller's decision to sell and the details and conditions the seller would accept in such a sale.

To prevent error and misrepresentation, the Commission's Code of Ethics requires that licensees make reasonable efforts to discover all material facts about each property they list. A material fact includes any negative condition about a property that may or may not be readily visible to or discoverable by a prudent purchaser. It is a fact that could tend to encourage (or discourage) either party in going forward with a transaction. The Brokers Act requires that licensees disclose material facts that they know, or should know, to all parties to a transaction. This is a demanding requirement.

Complicating the issue is the demand that, as an agent, the licensee is forbidden to disclose personal information about their client but must disclose matters that are material facts. Examples of things not to be disclosed are the client's motivation, urgency, and negotiating strategy.

On the other hand, the agent is required to disclose material matters their client might wish kept secret from the opposing party; such things as a history of basement leakage, foundation shifting, and septic or well problems.

Stigmatized Property [§17-322.1]

A licensee may not be held personally liable for failure to disclose that an owner or occupant of the property is, was, or is suspected of being infected with human immunodeficiency virus (HIV) or diagnosed with acquired immunodeficiency syndrome (AIDS). In fact, it is a violation of federal and state law to communicate information about the alleged presence of such diseases, even when asked.

In addition, Title 17 declares that the occurrence of a homicide, suicide, natural death, accidental death, or felony on a property is not a material fact that owners, sellers, or their agents are required to disclose. However, it is often prudent for licensees to urge their clients to give written permission to reveal to prospects the matters mentioned in this paragraph. This is because these matters are often discovered between contract and proposed settlement, prompting buyers to seek an excuse to escape the contract. If the matters were revealed to and "digested" by the buyers early in the process, they are less likely to be shocked into seeking to escape from the agreement.

The Brokers Act, § 17-322.1, states that licensees may not be charged by the Commission with failure to disclose material facts as previously described. In addition, Section 2-120 of the *Real Property* Article, Annotated Code of Maryland, also provides that the fact that a homicide, suicide, accidental death, natural death, or felony occurred on the property is not a material fact . . . relating to a property offered for sale or for lease. This same Section provides that an owner or seller of real property, or the owner's or seller's agent, shall be immune from civil liability or criminal penalty for failure to disclose such facts to a prospective buyer. Note that this Section only applies to licensees representing a seller or owner, and a buyer's agent is not given such immunity from civil and criminal penalties. A buyer's agent must reveal to their client the material information about homicide, suicide, accidental death, natural death, et cetera, that could affect the client-buyer's decisions about a property.

■ RESIDENTIAL PROPERTY DISCLOSURE AND DISCLAIMER FORM [REAL PROPERTY ARTICLE §10-702]

Seller Disclosure

The Brokers Act directs the Commission to provide a Residential Property Disclosure and Disclaimer Statement (Figure 4.1) and requires its use in most residential transactions by all brokerage firms in Maryland.

Licensees are always urged to use the most current version of this and any other required form. Failure to do so will likely expose seller-clients to the risk of rescission of sales contracts and provoke disciplinary action against a licensee. Incidentally, sellers—even when marketing their own residential property without broker assistance—are still required to present this form to purchasers before the offer to purchase is submitted.

Notice that the present form calls for the homeowner to list any latent defect in the subject property. For the purpose of this requirement, it defines *latent defects* as

> material defects in real property or an improvement to real property that: (1) A purchaser would not reasonably be expected to ascertain or observe by a careful visual inspection of the real property; and (2) Would pose a direct threat to the health or safety of: (i) the purchaser; or (ii) an occupant of the real property, including a tenant or invitee of the purchaser.

At the time a listing agreement is prepared and executed, the disclosure/disclaimer form is to be completed by the sellers. This instrument affects all parties to a sales transaction. On this form, sellers choose either to disclose or not to disclose the condition of a large number of physical features of the listed property. If they choose to make such disclosure, they should complete the disclosure form.

A completed disclosure form is one in which sellers respond to every inquiry, even if only to say "unknown" or "not applicable." By leaving even one response completely blank (or by giving contradictory answers), the sellers fail to meet the obligations imposed by Maryland law. Such failure also enables the buyers to rescind the contract in the same way as if they had not been given the Disclosure and Disclaimer Statement at all.

Disclaimer: "As Is"

If sellers choose not to disclose, they must complete the disclaimer portion of the form, the one that makes this refusal and states that they are selling the property "as is" except as otherwise provided in the sales contract.

All four pages of this form—whichever portion is completed—once signed and dated by the purchasers, is attached to and moves forward with the contract offer. Contrary to popular belief, use of the term *as is* does not free the sellers or their agents from the required affirmative (voluntary) disclosure of material facts and latent defects.

Either disclosing or disclaiming may be the more appropriate choice depending in part on market conditions, such as whether there is a buyers' market or a sellers' market, but licensees must not coach sellers in this choice. They should certainly not suggest use of the disclaimer as a means of withholding material facts. Nor should they guide the sellers' answer to any question in the disclosure portion.

If sellers need guidance in these decisions and answers, they should turn to competent legal counsel and/or other technical experts. The responses are to be the representations made by the owners, not by the licensee. The licensee, however, may generally point out the pros and cons of using the disclosure or disclaimer in given market conditions.

Listing agents should obtain from sellers the completed Maryland Residential Property Disclosure and Disclaimer Statements at the time of taking listings. Listing licensees must inform sellers of their rights and obligations arising from this form. Completion of this form is required in all sales of residential properties containing four or fewer single-family units. (There are seven situations in which the sale of single-family properties does not require the use of the form. These limited situations are listed in the preprinted Disclosure and Disclaimer Statement in its introductory paragraphs.)

Duty to Provide Purchasers with Statement

Maryland statutes even require unrepresented sellers of single-family residential real property to complete and deliver to each purchaser, upon or before entering into a contract of sale, a Disclosure and Disclaimer Statement of which either one or the other portion is completed. Both portions must be submitted, even the blank one. When sellers are represented by a licensee, it becomes the duty of that licensee to provide them with the form and explain to them their obligation to complete it for delivery to each buyer-prospect.

It is then the duty of a licensee representing client-buyers to explain their rights and obligations with respect to this form. If the buyer is not represented by a licensee, this duty falls on the licensee representing the owner-seller. The rights and obligations of all parties are listed in this form.

When listing licensees learn that prospective purchasers are planning to make an offer, they must make every effort to provide those prospects with the Disclosure and Disclaimer Statement in a timely manner. This can be done personally or through the buyers' agent.

When listing agents do not know in advance that an offer is forthcoming, they should present the completed Disclosure and Disclaimer Statement to the purchasers or their agent immediately when an offer is produced. The purchasers can then reconsider their offer in the light of the Disclosure and Disclaimer Statement before releasing the offer for presentation.

Effect of a Properly Completed Statement

When purchasers do receive the Disclosure and Disclaimer Statement before or upon entering into a contract, they are prevented from later rescinding the agreement of sale based on any information revealed in the Disclosure and Disclaimer Statement.

Purchasers who do not receive this Disclosure and Disclaimer Statement before they enter into a sales contract retain the right to rescind the contract

- until five days after they finally receive the form;
- until they apply for a loan (if the loan office gives them notice that they are losing their right of rescission); or
- until settlement or occupancy, whichever is earlier.

This means that if purchasers never get a Disclosure and Disclaimer Statement and are never warned by a lender of the loss of their right to rescind, they may rescind at any time—right up to settlement or presettlement occupancy.

■ TERMINATION OF AGENCY AGREEMENT [§17-322(10), §17-534]

Maryland law sets no minimum or maximum time periods for agency (representation) agreements for residential property. The term of such an agreement is negotiable between client and broker. However, every listing and every buyer representation agreement must contain a definite termination date on which it will end without further notice from either party. Automatic extension provisions violate this law. This prohibition is found in the part of the Brokers Act that governs residential properties, not commercial.

Unless the agency agreement states the contrary, licensees have no further obligations or duties to clients after termination, expiration, or completion of performance of the brokerage relationship, except to account for all trust monies and to keep confidential all personal and financial information about the clients or other matters that clients request be kept confidential.

Death of an owner in severalty (sole owner) would normally terminate a listing agreement by operation of law. However, death of one owner, when a married couple has held title as tenants by the entirety, may not necessarily terminate a listing. It is prudent to have the language of a listing form reviewed by a firm's legal counsel to clarify whether such an agency agreement will be binding on a deceased seller's estate. Purchasers would benefit from advice on the same matter from their own counsel.

Licensees may withdraw from representing either buyer-clients or seller-clients who refuse to consent to disclosed dual agency. The licensees may then terminate brokerage relationships with them. However, the Brokers Act states that brokers—acting as dual agents, with proper notice and appointment of an intra-company agent for each party—simply by making required disclosures of the existence of dual agency, have not thereby terminated their brokerage relationships. Persons receiving those disclosures must decide whether they want to terminate, based on the disclosures.

In this State, a trustee sale, foreclosure sale, tax sale, or condemnation proceeding that involves the listed property will generally terminate a listing.

■ DETERMINING AMOUNT AND DISTRIBUTION OF BROKERAGE FEES

Antitrust Compliance [Commercial Law Article §11-204]

Brokers (typically working through licensees affiliated with them) negotiate their compensation (brokerage fee) with the sellers in each transaction. The amount or commission rate charged in a transaction is not set by any law, regulation, association, or board. Prospective clients and brokers negotiate commission rates. Even to suggest otherwise is a violation of federal and state antitrust laws and can bring severe penalties. However, when a potential client tries to get a broker to lower the broker's commission rate and the broker refuses, this is not a "failure to negotiate." The discussion itself constitutes a negotiation.

Commission splits between and among brokers in co-brokering situations are similarly negotiable. Commission schedules for affiliates within brokerage firms are established by negotiation between brokers and the affiliates licensed under them.

Similarly, conversations among licensees from competing companies about rates and fees are regarded by federal and state governments as potential "restraint of trade," even though no change in behavior results from the conversations. Licensees serving on industry boards and associations must scrupulously avoid any discussion of members' patterns of compensation. Avoid even the very appearance of price (rate) fixing.

Agency Relationship Not Created by Payment of Fee [§17-534(d)]

The Brokers Act clearly states that payments or promises to pay compensation to licensees do not determine that brokerage (agency) relationships have been created or exist, nor do they create brokerage relationships. Contrary to a long-held notion, persons whose money goes to agents do not become clients of those agents just because of that payment.

When Fee Earned and When Paid [Real Property §14-105]

Maryland law indicates that unless there is a previous agreement to the contrary, listing brokers have earned their commissions when sellers accept and sign (what the sellers believe to be) enforceable contracts of sale. Sellers typically pay brokerage commissions at settlement, using proceeds arising from the settlement. Brokers and homeowners may, however, agree at the time of listing that if settlement does not take place, no commission is due. Such a proviso, being strongly to the disadvantage of the broker, does not appear in widely used industry listing forms.

Agency Agreement Basic to Claim [§17-516]

According to the Brokers Act, brokers performing brokerage services may not maintain an action (sue) for commission unless they had authority (derived from their then current, active license) to provide those services at the times both of offering to perform and of performing the services.

Handling Dual Agency Decisions

A licensee preparing a listing should explain to the sellers that potential buyers from a licensee's own firm may want to buy the seller's property. This would place the firm in the position of having two clients on opposing sides of a deal. To perform such dual agency, its consequences to the parties would have to be fully disclosed to both sides, their approval obtained in writing (informed consent), and two of the firm's affiliates selected by the firm's broker (or broker's designee), one to represent each side. The duties of such intra-company agents (ICAs), set forth in the Brokers Act, are described in the Understanding Whom form and should be further explained to the parties by the listing agent.

Whether a seller is willing to be served by such a dual agency arrangement, may then be indicated in the brokerage agreement (listing). Seller's willingness must be given in writing on the Consent for Dual Agency form (Figure 2.2). If a dual agency situation then arises during the listing period, and sellers are still willing to allow it, they must again give written consent. This is done by their signatures on the affirmation found at the bottom of the original Dual Agency Consent form.

This time it must show additional specific details such as property address and the would-be purchaser's signature. If, later, the negotiations collapse and another client of the seller's broker presents herself, a new consent for dual agency form with affirmation must be completed by the seller—this with the new prospective purchaser, signature, and restating the named property.

Similarly, buyer-clients agree to dual agency on the form shown in Figure 2.2 at the time of their initial listing with the broker. They must also consent again when a specific opportunity arises, this time on a consent form identifying a specific property and containing the signature of its seller. If that situation does not result in an agreement and the buyers want to make an offer on another property listed by the buyers' broker, they must complete yet another Consent for Dual Agency agreement, this one identifying the property that is the subject of the new effort and the signature of its seller.

Co-Brokerage Among Brokers [COMAR 09.11.02.03(b)]

The Code of Ethics states that brokers shall cooperate with other brokers on property listed exclusively by their firms whenever it is in the interest of their clients. The co-brokering companies may then share commissions on a previously agreed-to basis. Negotiations concerning properties that are under exclusive listings must be carried on solely through the property owners' listing brokers.

In the listing interview, as required by the Commission, brokers (or their agents) present to sellers the agency disclosure form, Understanding Whom Real Estate Agents Represent (see Chapter 2.) With the help of explanations contained in that form, sellers can decide which relationship(s) they want their listing contract to permit with co-brokering firms. Will it be cooperation (which involves subagency), or will it be buyer brokerage? Will it be whichever of the two presents itself? In this book, the term *co-broker* includes both cooperating brokers and buyer brokers. A co-broker can either be a cooperating agent or a buyer broker.

Sellers should be helped to understand that licensees from other companies who represent a purchaser will not be "on their team" but will be representing the sellers' adversary, the buyer. Sellers should also decide if, and how, the commission they pay will be shared with another company if no subagency is involved in dealing with another brokerage. Most listing forms allow sellers to authorize their broker to work with and compensate buyer brokers by sharing part of the brokerage fee.

On the listing data form that brokers submit to the MLS, they should show how sellers have decided to choose from among their representation options. They also will show the amount of the cooperating commission in the event of co-brokering. The preponderance of residential real estate transactions involves some form of co-brokering.

Listings Must Be Signed [COMAR 09.11.01.12]

When all relevant data have been entered on the listing form, all persons who have an ownership interest in the property must sign it. Alternatively, persons who have proper authorization from the owners—such as attorneys-in-fact, acting under a carefully drafted power of attorney—may sign the listing for them. Competent legal counsel should be consulted in approaching such situations. It is the responsibility of the listing agent to make sure the signatures of all required parties are on a listing. A listing becomes effective on the date of the last required signature.

When separated or divorcing couples who hold title as tenants by the entireties wish to list property, the author recommends consultation with the attorneys representing each party. Even divorced parties may each retain an interest, likely making both their signatures necessary for an enforceable listing.

When sellers are corporations, trustees, guardians of minors, or personal representatives, documentation of the authority of persons signing the listing is often required. Such documents as corporate bylaws and minutes of the meeting of the board authorizing a property to be put on the market are among usual requirements. Licensees faced with such complex situations are urged to seek competent legal guidance.

Common Source Information Companies [§17-535]

The Brokers Act states that licensees who make use of common source information companies, such as multiple listing services, are not considered to be agents of those services or companies simply by virtue of their use of data from them. So licensees who participate in the sale of multiple-listed properties are not thereby construed (considered) to be the agents or subagents of any client of another broker by reason of their participation. These information services may not restrict access to their services to licensees based on the level of their licenses (i.e., salesperson, associate broker, or broker).

Industry Forms [§17-312(17)]

The word *REALTOR®* and its related logo appear in the printed portion of many listings, area-wide contract forms, and many addenda. Licensees who use any form that bears the name of an organization of which they are not members violate the Brokers Act.

Several boards and associations of REALTORS® sponsor multiple listing services dealing with sometimes specific, and other times overlapping, geographic areas. Listing contract forms and numerous addenda are available from local real estate boards, associations, and MLSs for the exclusive use of their members. There are often special forms for different types of property: residential for sale or lease, commercial/industrial for sale or lease, income property, farms, commercial office rental, residential lots, unimproved land, condominiums, cooperatives, and businesses. Although the brokerage industry has produced forms for statewide use and regional use within the State, licensees should be alert to differences that still exist among those forms and to differences between those forms and the forms unique to certain other brokerage firms. It is misleading, incorrect, and careless to refer to an area-wide form as a "standard" form—a term that, to many consumers, implies government approval and, therefore, safety.

Certain counties require additional forms to meet local requirements. Licensees from other counties should be sure to use any forms for the county where the property being sold is located.

■ LOCAL REQUIREMENTS

Licensees should familiarize themselves with and conform to all relevant county and municipal requirements in areas where they provide real estate services. For instance, Baltimore County zoning regulations require "development plan notice and conveyances" to be provided to any purchaser of a home in any area covered by an approved development plan. In other counties, air traffic patterns are part of the information that prospective purchasers must receive. From time to time, counties severely restrict the use of signs. One county has established special licensing requirements for persons who wish to post any signs in residential areas within that jurisdiction. Client-sellers should be made aware when such requirements may affect their transaction.

■ OUT-OF-STATE LISTINGS

Maryland licensees are not authorized to show out-of-state properties, even though they are properly listed and advertised in Maryland, unless the Maryland licensees also have valid brokerage licenses for the state where the property is located and comply with all laws of that state.

CHAPTER 4 QUIZ

1. Which type of residential listing agreement is illegal for a broker to use in Maryland?
   1. Net
   2. Exclusive agency
   3. Open
   4. Exclusive right to sell

2. When using a broker to market their house, when should sellers complete the Residential Property Disclosure and Disclaimer Statement?
   1. At settlement
   2. When an offer is received
   3. When the property is being listed
   4. After a sales contract has been signed

3. What is the consequence when purchasers receive no Residential Property Disclosure and Disclaimer Statement before, at, or after entering into a purchase agreement?
   1. The contract is void by action of law after three days.
   2. The purchasers may rescind the contract before they apply for a mortgage loan.
   3. The contract is voidable by the purchaser for five days.
   4. The lender has five days to tell the purchaser of the right to void the agreement.

4. When must a licensee give a copy of the listing agreement to the sellers?
   1. When they request it
   2. Before the firm advertises the property or offers it for sale
   3. Within 15 days after acceptance by the broker
   4. When a buyer is found

5. What is required of a Maryland licensee who wishes to show a property located in Virginia that is multiple-listed by a Maryland firm?
   1. The licensee must hold a Virginia real estate license.
   2. The licensee must be a member of Maryland's multiple listing service.
   3. The licensee must hold a Maryland broker license.
   4. The licensee must hold a multiple-state license certificate.

6. Who may use a listing agreement form published by a multiple listing service?
   1. Any broker or salesperson licensed by the Commission
   2. Any member of any board or association of REALTORS®
   3. Any member of the organization that operates that listing system
   4. Any licensee

7. Which of the following is *TRUE* of a listing on Maryland residential property?
   1. It may contain an automatic renewal provision.
   2. It may be parol.
   3. It must be in writing and signed by all parties.
   4. It may leave the commission fee to be negotiated at the time an offer is made.

8. What is the affect on purchasers who have received the Residential Property Disclosure and Disclaimer Statement before signing their contract offer?
   1. They may rescind the contract at any time up to three days after signing.
   2. They may rescind the contract at any time up to five days after signing.
   3. They may rescind at any time prior to settlement or to taking occupancy.
   4. They may not rescind the contract based on any facts the statement discloses.

9. Which of the following is correct about the amount or rate of commission on a real estate sale?
   1. It must be stated in the listing agreement.
   2. It is established by the Commission.
   3. It is established by the local real estate board or association of REALTORS®.
   4. It is established by law.

10. Which of the following is *TRUE* of a Maryland residential listing agreement?
    1. It does not create an agency.
    2. It may be oral.
    3. It must be in writing.
    4. It need not contain a definite termination date.

CHAPTER 5

Interests in Real Estate

■ KEY TERMS

adverse possession   easement by prescription   mean high-water mark

■ OVERVIEW

Freehold estates, such as fee simple absolute, fee determinable, fee conditional, and life estates—as well as future interests, such as remainder and reversion—are recognized in Maryland. Leasehold estates for years, from period to period, at will, and at sufferance are also recognized. In addition, the ground rent system, as described in Chapter 13 of this book, is found in several areas.

The legal life estates—dower and curtesy—have been abolished, and there is no homestead exemption in Maryland.

◼ EASEMENT BY PRESCRIPTION AND ADVERSE POSSESSION

An easement by prescription may be acquired in Maryland when an adverse user makes use of another's land for the required period—20 years. Notice that the term *prescriptive* comes from what is prescribed by statute. Adverse possession for a similar, prescribed period (also 20 years) can also ripen into a claim for ownership. However, the occupancy must be not only open, hostile, continuous, and notorious, but also under claim of right or color of title.

By requiring such claim or color, Maryland rejects squatters' rights. Squatters acquire no claim to land merely by squatting on it; they are trespassers. Claim of right or color of title arises in a situation where an innocent buyer is deeded property by a person thought to be its owner but later proved not to be. If truly innocent, the buyer is said to be a bona fide purchaser (BFP) for value. Consult competent legal counsel in cases involving prescriptive easements and adverse possession.

◼ RIPARIAN RIGHTS

Owners of real estate bordering a navigable body of water in Maryland have the common-law right to construct a landing, wharf, or pier for their own use or for the use of the public. The right to make such an improvement is also subject to state and federal rules and regulations. The owner who makes such improvement owns the pier over the water but not the water beneath it.

Title to land above the mean (average) high-water mark of navigable waters, as well as to the waters themselves, belongs to the public. Regardless of the property descriptions in owners' deeds, they legally own their riparian property as far as the mean high-water mark. High-water mark is the highest elevation of water in the usual, regular, periodic ebb and flow of the tide, not including storms or floods.

◼ AGRICULTURAL LAND PRESERVATION EASEMENT

The Maryland Agricultural Land Preservation Foundation exists to purchase easements on land in certain areas for the purpose of restricting land to agricultural use. Details are contained in the *Agriculture* Article of the Annotated Code of Maryland. The State is actively purchasing development rights and seeking to slow residential subdivision of agricultural land. The State's purchases of these easements are funded in large part by the revenues produced by the real estate transfer tax. Further discussion is found in Chapter 14 of this book. Since 2007, a purchaser has the right, under certain conditions, to rescind a contract purchasing Maryland real estate found to be encumbered by one or more conservation easements or other restrictions held by certain entities. Sales contracts and other notice of such easements are required to control such rescission. This is described more fully in Chapter 9.

CHAPTER 5 QUIZ

1. Which government agency may purchase easements to restrict land to agricultural use?
   1. Maryland Land Development Corporation
   2. Maryland Department of Assessments and Taxation
   3. Maryland Agricultural Land Preservation Foundation
   4. Maryland Environmental Department

2. Which of the following would meet or exceed the requirement for prescriptive easement in Maryland?
   1. 15 years' continuous use
   2. 15 years' intermittent use
   3. 25 years' intermittent use
   4. 25 years' continuous use

3. Which of the following is recognized in Maryland?
   1. Dower
   2. Homestead exemption
   3. Curtesy
   4. Easement by prescription

4. Jefferson Thomas owns several acres of Maryland land located along the banks of a navigable waterway. What is an example of Thomas' riparian rights in this situation?
   1. He may build a pier out into the river, subject to State and federal laws.
   2. He may construct a dam across the river to divert the waters into an artificial lake on his property.
   3. He may construct a wharf without State approval.
   4. He may make use only of the dry land.

5. Which of the following is a source of funds with which the State can purchase agricultural easements?
   1. General (ad valorem) tax revenues
   2. Special assessments for this specific purpose
   3. Fines on developers who overdevelop agricultural land
   4. Transfer taxes imposed at the time of real estate transfers

CHAPTER 6

How Ownership Is Held

■ KEY TERMS

appurtenances	general common elements	rules
bylaws	joint tenancy	tenancy in common
common elements	limited common elements	tenants by the entirety
condominium	partition proceeding	time-share estate
council of unit owners	proprietary lease	time-share license
declaration	real estate investment trust (REIT)	units
developer		

■ OVERVIEW

Maryland law recognizes ownership in severalty and various forms of concurrent ownership: tenancy in common, joint tenancy, tenancy by the entirety, partnership, and trust—all as described in the principles text. It also provides for condominium, time-share, and cooperative ownership.

■ FORMS OF CONCURRENT OWNERSHIP (CO-OWNERSHIP)

Tenancy in Common and Joint Tenancy

Unless the deed clearly specifies otherwise, a conveyance of Maryland real estate to two or more persons normally creates tenancy in common. To create a joint tenancy, it is necessary to use such words as "to Fred Donaldson and Sam Roberts, as joint tenants and not as tenants in common." One might also add the phrase "with right of survivorship." In contrast, a deed to a husband and wife is presumed to create a tenancy by the entirety unless it specifies tenancy in common or joint tenancy.

Tenancy by the Entirety (T/E)

There are many advantages for a couple who hold real property as tenants by the entirety, but Maryland only allows legally married persons to own property as tenants by the entirety. Maryland now recognizes same-sex couples who marry in Maryland, or in another jurisdiction that recognizes same-sex marriage, as married. Common-law marriages cannot be established in Maryland but are recognized as valid if they were established in other jurisdictions that recognize and permit them.

Clients and customers of Maryland real estate brokerage licensees should be made aware of the advantages of tenancy by the entirety. Here are a few:

- Both spouses must sign a deed to convey property they hold as tenants by the entirety. Therefore, neither spouse who owns Maryland real property as a tenant by the entirety may petition a court for its partition against the will of the other tenant.
- Tenants by the entirety may join in granting their property back to themselves as either tenants in common or joint tenants, or in granting the entire property either to one spouse or the other. They can do this without having ownership pass through the hands of a third ("straw") party.
- They can also deed their property into a trust.
- Property held as a tenancy by the entirety (except in the case of federal tax liens) is not subject to forced partition to satisfy the debts of one tenant.

Since the IRS now recognizes same-sex marriage, a couple who were domestic partners may now file as "Married Filing Jointly" when reporting income to the IRS. They also pay lower, different after-death taxes and may transfer property to one another without incurring a federal gift tax, and so forth. They are now eligible for a $500,000, rather than a $250,000, exclusion from taxable capital gains tax upon the sale of their real property. Competent legal assistance and skilled tax guidance are always important in these matters.

Federal and state law impacting same-sex marriage can seem complex, contradictory, and obscure. It is also in a state of flux as it seeks to address newly identified issues. Laws vary from state tax except in matters governed by federal law. In performing real estate brokerage services for a same-sex couple, the only "legal" advice that a non-lawyer licensee should consider giving is, "An attorney and a tax expert's guidance are vital to buyers/sellers in your position."

Upon divorce or other legal termination of the marriage, tenants by the entirety become tenants in common by operation of law. When divorce occurs, causing the former couple's ownership to change to tenancy in common by action of law, a court may still delay any partition proceeding (division of the property by one against the other's will) for a period as long as three years. Normally, a tenancy in common, like joint tenancy, can be partitioned at any time by one tenant (owner) without the agreement of the other. The ban on partition after divorce can occur if the property is to be occupied as the "family home" by the spouse having custody of minor children.

Trust

The provisions of the Uniform Partnership Act apply in Maryland. The statute allows a corporation (as well as an individual) to become a member of a partnership. Also, the real estate investment trust (REIT), a form of unincorporated trust or association, is recognized. The procedures for forming or dealing with a REIT are legally complex. Brokerage licensees involved in any way with a REIT should strongly urge their clients to employ legal counsel. The licensees themselves may be required by law to hold securities licenses to engage in such activities. The Maryland Securities Act, found in the State's *Corporations and Associations* Article, requires a securities license for persons engaged in selling securities that are real estate related.

■ CONDOMINIUMS [REAL PROPERTY ARTICLE, TITLE 11]

Detailed provisions of the Maryland Condominium Act are contained in Title 11 of the *Real Property* Article of the Annotated Code of Maryland. Any licensee involved with condominium sales or development should obtain a complete copy of the law and seek competent legal advice. The Condominium Act is enforced by the Division of Consumer Protection in the Office of the Attorney General.

Definitions

A condominium is a property subject to a plan of organization called a regime. It is governed by a council of unit owners, usually through a board of directors; it may be either an unincorporated body or an incorporated nonstock corporation. Persons who subject their property to a condominium regime are called developers. Condominium units are spaces described in three dimensions in the declaration and on the condominium plat.

All the parts of a condominium other than its individual units are common elements. Limited common elements are identified in the declaration or described on the condominium plat and are reserved for the exclusive use of one or more, but fewer than all, of the unit owners. General common elements are all the common elements except the limited common elements.

Converting Property to a Condominium

To create a condominium, the property owner must expressly declare the intention to do so by recording a declaration, bylaws, and a detailed plat of the proposed site. These documents must comply with statutory requirements. When this has been done, the property is then said to be under a condominium regime, and the owner is its developer. The condominium regime must be registered with the Secretary of State before a condominium unit may be sold or even offered for sale. The declaration may subsequently be amended within certain limits only by the written consent of 80% of the unit owners at the time of amendment.

Public Offering Statement

A contract for the initial sale of a residential condominium unit to a member of the general public is not enforceable by the seller until the purchaser is given a copy of the Public Offering Statement registered with the Secretary of State. This statement contains the proposed contract for purchase of units; the declaration, bylaws, rules, and regulations; proposed property management agreements; insurance policies; maintenance agreements; and a proposed budget and financial reports. Many other items make this a very difficult package for purchasers to read, study, and understand.

Whether they read the statement or not, buyers may make written rescission of a purchase contract, without stating any reason, within 15 days of the time they receive it. Buyers who rescind within this time limit are entitled to prompt return of all deposits. There is debate as to whether this return can be automatically made by the party holding the deposit. If a deposit is held by a licensed real estate broker, and the seller objects to its return, the broker is not clearly free, under present law, to return the deposit. (The matter is being examined by the legislature at the time of publication.)

Buyers who proceed to settlement lose their rights to terminate.

A purchaser's right to rescind or cancel under the Condominium Act may not be waived in the contract of sale.

Conversion of Residential Rental Facility

Before a residential rental facility can be converted to condominium ownership, tenants must be given notice in the form prescribed by law. This notice is also registered with the Secretary of State at the same time as the Public Offering Statement. A tenant may not be required to vacate the premises prior to the expiration of 180 days from the giving of notice, except for breach of the lease. However, the tenant may terminate the lease, without penalty for termination, by providing at least 30 days' written notice to the landlord after receiving proper notice of conversion. Many other statutory requirements protect tenants during conversion of a rental property to condominium.

Ownership of Units and Interests in Common Elements

In addition to exclusive ownership of a condominium unit, each unit owner typically holds a defined, undivided percentage interest in the common elements of the property. Unit owners' undivided interests in the common elements cannot be partitioned or separated from the unit to which each percentage is assigned. Owners of every unit in a condominium are members of the council of unit owners; that council is considered a legal entity whether incorporated or not.

Organization: Declaration, Bylaws, and Rules and Regulations

In addition to federal, state, and local laws and ordinances, a condominium is governed according to its declaration, bylaws, and rules and regulations. The rules must conform to the bylaws, the bylaws must conform to the declaration, and the declaration is subject to the statute. In Maryland, the statute—in some states called a *horizontal property act*—is called the Maryland Condominium Act.

The recorded declaration must contain the name by which the condominium is to be identified, including or followed by the phrase "a condominium." It must also contain a description of the land and buildings, with a statement of the owner's intent to establish a condominium regime; a general description and number of each unit, its perimeter, location, and other identifying data; a general description of the common elements and the units to which their use is restricted initially; the percentage interest in common areas related to each unit; and the number of votes at meetings of the council of unit owners that are attached to each unit. These related common elements and voting rights are appurtenances—things of value that attach to a property.

At the least, the bylaws must express the form of administration, whether the council is to be incorporated, whether some or all of the council's duties may be delegated to a board of directors or a manager and what powers the owners have in directors' selection and removal, the council's mailing address, the procedure to be followed in council meetings, and the manner of assessing and collecting unit owners' respective shares of the common expenses. By law, the council of unit owners must be established within 60 days after the initial sale of units representing 50% of votes in the condominium (unless a smaller percentage is set forth in the declaration or bylaws). Bylaws of a condominium are recorded at the same time as its declaration. Unless higher percentages are required in the bylaws, they may be amended by a two-thirds affirmative vote by the council of unit owners.

A law passed in 2011 allows the amendment of a condominium's bylaws to require unit owners to purchase HO-6 insurance policies to pass with the approval of only 51% of the ownership votes. This is less than the usual 66⅔% vote otherwise required to amend bylaws. The statute does not require condominiums to pass such a bylaw. However, by lowering the required affirmative ratio, the law makes passage of such a change easier.

In addition to rules set forth by the developer and recorded in the Public Offering Statement, the council of unit owners (or the board of directors, if so authorized in the bylaws) can pass rules to govern the condominium by majority vote at any properly advertised meeting held for that purpose. The bylaws specify what body originates and changes rules. They also define a quorum for the meeting at which rules are voted upon. A simple majority of those present and voting adopts rules.

The Maryland Condominium Act was amended in 2013 to allow condominium boards to meet in closed session to consider the terms of a business transaction in the negotiation stage if disclosure would adversely affect the economic interests of the condominium. This amendment extended to condominiums the "business transaction" exemption already available to homeowners associations.

Termination of Regime

Unless taken by eminent domain, a condominium regime may be terminated only by agreement of at least 80% of the unit owners (more if so specified in the declaration).

Common Expenses, Taxes, Assessments, and Liens

Unit owners are responsible for their percentage share of the common expenses of the council of unit owners. Assessments against each unit owner for common expenses are unrecorded liens on their units. Such a lien may be foreclosed in the same manner as a mortgage or deed of trust if it is recorded and action to foreclose is brought within three years.

In 2013, the Maryland Contract Lien Act was amended to limit the ability of condominium and homeowners associations to foreclose on liens that include charges other than assessments and reasonable costs and attorney's fees "directly related to the filing of the lien and not exceeding the amount of the lien." A lien that includes late fees, interest, fines, collection costs, and attorney's fees not directly related to filing the lien is no longer subject to foreclosure. However, the new law expressly states that a condominium or homeowners association is still free to seek collection of those charges by means other than foreclosure.

The priority assessment lien law of 2011 aids condominium and homeowner associations when there is a lender foreclosure. The law allows a four-month priority lien up to $1,200 for condominium and homeowner association assessments. When there is a lender foreclosure sale, up to $1,200 of assessments will be paid before the mortgage debt is paid. This applies to loans obtained after October 1, 2011. In lender foreclosure, though, municipal liens still have priority over such unpaid assessments.

Each unit is taxed as a separate and distinct entity on the county tax records. A delinquent tax on a specific unit will not affect the title to other units on which all taxes and assessments have been paid.

Under the Consumer Protection Act of the *Commercial Law* Article of the Annotated Code of Maryland, certain condominium disputes will be investigated by the Division of Consumer Protection of the Office of the Attorney General, which is authorized to administer a program of voluntary mediation of condominium disputes involving unit owners, boards of directors, and/or councils of unit owners.

Resale of Unit

A contract for the resale of a unit by a unit owner other than a developer is not enforceable unless that contract contains, in conspicuous type, a notice in the form specified in the Condominium Act (Section 11-135). The unit owner is required to furnish four things to the purchaser no fewer than 15 days prior to the closing:

- A copy of the declaration (other than the plat)
- The bylaws
- The rules or regulations of the condominium
- A certificate containing statements concerning such things as monthly expenses, proposed capital improvements, fees payable by unit owners, financial statements of the condominium, insurance coverage, and much more

Once resale purchasers receive all these condominium documents ("condo docs"), they have seven days to give written notice rescinding their contract to purchase without stating any reason. This right is waived if they proceed to closing before the seven-day period ends.

Condominium resale contracts must contain the required clauses and disclosures to ensure compliance with the act. Local real estate boards and associations usually offer their members a Condominium Contract of Sale and Condominium Listing Contract.

Renting a Condominium Unit in Montgomery County

In Montgomery County, before a tenant executes a lease for an initial term of 125 days or more, the owner of any residential rental property within any condominium or development is required to provide to the prospective tenant—to the extent applicable—a copy of the rules, declaration, and recorded covenants and restrictions that limit or affect the use and occupancy of the property or common areas and under which the owner and the tenant are also obligated.

The State Securities Commission requires that anyone offering part ownership or interest in condominiums must disclose the inherent risks of such an investment. Limited-use resort securities must comply with the registration and antifraud requirements of the State Securities Act.

■ TIME-SHARE OWNERSHIP

In Maryland there are two principal forms of time-sharing: the right-to-use (called time-share license) and the purchase-of-fractional-interest (called a time-share estate).

In the time-share license, owners of interests in vacation properties, including condominiums, hotels, motels, marinas, and boats, may trade their vacation periods and facilities either directly or indirectly through space banks that are maintained by firms established to help time-sharers swap vacation facilities.

In the time-share estate, widely used in Maryland in both the Eastern Shore and the western areas, customers buy fractional interests for designated time periods in a resort condominium, either on a rental (estate for years) or permanent (fee simple) basis. The fee simple buyer receives a deed for a share of the property.

The Maryland Real Estate Time-Sharing Act [*Real Property* Article, Title 11A]

The Maryland Real Estate Time-Sharing Act provides for the creation, sale, lease, management, and termination of time-share interests; registration of certain documents; registration of time-share developers with the Commission; and certain bonding requirements. Certain advertising and promotional practices are prohibited. Developers are required to prepare Public Offering Statements describing time-share projects and are regulated by the Secretary of State. Certain protections for purchasers are provided, such as sales contract cancellation periods and disclosures of information, warranties, and exchange programs. Any licensee involved in time-share sales or development should obtain a complete copy of the act or seek competent legal advice. Time-share developers and persons selling time-share estates are also subject to the provisions of the Brokers Act.

Public Offering Statement   Upon or before the signing of a sales contract, the developers must deliver to each purchaser a Public Offering Statement. The requirements for disclosure under the Time-Sharing Act differ substantially from those required under the Condominium Act.

Conversions   A developer who desires to convert a building more than five years old into a time-share project is required to include an engineer's report in the Public Offering Statement and to give any tenant or subtenant at least 120 days' notice of the intention to convert the building to a time-share project.

Cancellation rights   First purchasers of time-shares have the right to cancel the sales contract until midnight of the 10th calendar day following the latest of (1) the contract date, (2) the day on which the time-share purchaser received the last of all documents required as part of the Public Offering Statement, or (3) the date on which either the time-share unit meets all building requirements and is ready for occupancy or the developer obtains a payment and performance bond and files the bond with the Commission. This right of cancellation cannot be waived.

Unlike the law concerning condominiums, no closing on a time-share can occur until the purchaser's cancellation period has expired. If closing is held prior to the cancellation period, the closing is voidable at the option of the purchaser for a period of one year after the expiration of the cancellation period.

Resale disclosures   Owners selling their time-share are required to furnish to the purchaser, before execution of the contract or transfer of title or use,

- a copy of the time-share instrument, and
- a resale certificate containing the information required by the Time-Sharing Act.

The resale purchaser may cancel the contract to purchase at any time within seven days after receipt of the resale certificate without reason and without liability and is then entitled to the return of any deposits made under the contract.

Deposits   All purchase money received by a developer from a purchaser must be deposited in an escrow account designed solely for that purpose with a financial institution whose accounts are insured by a government agency. The funds remain there until the end of the 10-day cancellation period or any later time provided for in the contract. Purchase money may then be released to the developer, provided the developer maintains a surety bond. No claim can be made against the Real Estate Guaranty Fund if a loss is covered by that bond.

Warranties   All time-share units sold by developers have implied warranties of three years for common elements and one year for units with respect to structural components and heating and cooling systems. In addition, the developer must warrant to a purchaser of a time-share that any existing use of the time-share unit that will continue does not violate any law.

Sales contract   The statute requires contracts for the first sale of time-shares to use specific language to disclose cancellation rights. Contracts must also show the estimated completion date of each unit and each common element as well as estimates of the time-share expenses and facility fees. All this is intended to disclose the total financial obligation being incurred by purchasers.

Exchange programs   The Time-Sharing Act requires detailed information concerning each exchange program a developer makes available for purchasers' use.

Registration   The Time-Sharing Act requires that developers, with certain exceptions, register with the Commission. A developer may not offer a time-share to the public until the developer has received from the Commission a certificate of registration as a time-share developer. The developer is required to file certain documents and material with the Commission. The Time-Sharing Act gives the Commission the authority to

- issue regulations and orders consistent with the act;
- investigate possible violations of the act and subpoena witnesses and documents in connection with the investigations;
- bring suit against violators;
- order violators to correct conditions resulting from the violation; and
- revoke the registration of any developer who is convicted of violating the act.

In addition, the Secretary of State is authorized to adopt regulations necessary to implement and enforce the provisions of the act pertaining to Public Offering Statements. A violation of the act could provide grounds for the suspension or revocation of a broker's or salesperson's license under the Brokers Act.

Project broker   Developers are required to designate a licensed real estate broker as the project broker for each time-share project. Each time-share project is considered a separate real estate office for purposes of the Brokers Act. Any person who sells, advertises, or offers for sale any time-share must be a licensed broker, an associate broker, or a salesperson or be exempt from licensure under Title 17. An unlicensed person may be employed by a developer or project broker to contact, but not solicit, prospective buyers so long as the unlicensed person

- performs only clerical tasks,
- schedules only those appointments induced by others, or
- prepares or distributes only promotional materials.

Time-Share Regulations [COMAR 09.11.04]

Regulations governing time-shares require that records be maintained of names and addresses of all personnel retained for sale of time-share estates, including agents, employees, and licensees, whether employees or independent contractors. Records must also be made and kept of all sales transactions, of estates conveyed and encumbrances on them, and of amounts of purchase money held for such sales. The Commission may require certification of such amounts by a Certified Public Accountant. Developers must also maintain bonding in prescribed amounts for deposit monies being held.

Time-share marketing statements about the characteristics of the time-share project or estate may not be false, inaccurate, or misleading. A developer may not indicate that an improvement will be placed in a time-share project unless the developer has sufficient finances and bona fide intentions to complete the improvement. Statements used in the marketing of time-share estates located in Maryland may not induce a prospective purchaser to leave the State for the purpose of executing a contract for sale when to do so would circumvent the provisions of Maryland law. No one may advertise or represent that the Commission has approved or recommended any time-share project or estate offered for sale.

■ MARYLAND COOPERATIVE HOUSING CORPORATION ACT [CORPORATIONS AND ASSOCIATIONS ARTICLE, TITLES 5–6B]

The Maryland Cooperative Housing Act provides for conditions, contracts, rights, and requirements relative to the development and sale of interests in cooperatives. Detailed provisions are contained in statutes. A member of the cooperative receives a proprietary lease, an agreement with the cooperative housing corporation that gives the member an exclusive possessory interest in a unit and a possessory interest in common with other members in that portion of a cooperative project not constituting units. It creates a legal relationship of landlord and tenant between the corporation and the member.

■ MARYLAND HOMEOWNERS ASSOCIATION ACT [REAL PROPERTY ARTICLE §11B]

This act sets forth conditions, rights, and requirements regulating homeowners associations (HOAs) in the State.

For sales contracts to be binding on purchasers, sellers must disclose that the property is subject to an HOA; must list the rights, responsibilities, and obligations of purchasers; and must disclose purchasers' rights of rescission in the event that information required by the Maryland Homeowners Association Act is not provided to them by sellers in a timely manner. This information recites factual details pertaining to disclosures, which must include liability, warranties, meetings, books, and records. Time periods for rescission vary in relation to the number of lots in the HOA. The rescission period in initial sales is different from that in resales.

Any violation of the Maryland Homeowners Association Act that affects a consumer falls under the enforcement duties and powers of the Division of Consumer Protection of the Office of the Attorney General of the State, thus giving such homeowners associations protections similar to those afforded condominiums and cooperatives.

■ CANCELLATION PERIODS

Because it is important for real estate licensees to know the cancellation periods allowed by law for various types of condominium and time-share sales contracts, they are summarized in Figure 6.1.

In each of the instances in Figure 6.1, immediate refund of a deposit without the written agreement of the parties, is subject to §17-505 of the Brokers Act when the deposit is held by a real estate brokerage firm. On the other hand, when a deposit is held by a settlement company rather than a brokerage licensee, the money may be refunded immediately by its holder without going through the steps in §17-505.

F I G U R E   6.1

Cancellation Periods in Various Sale Situations

Type of Sale	Period for Cancellation	After
Condominium by developer	15 days	Receipt of Public Offering Statement
Condominium by developer	5 additional days	Receipt of any later amendments to Public Offering Statement
Condominium by resale	7 days	Receipt of Resale Certificate (This certificate must also be received no fewer than 15 days prior to closing.)
Time-share by developer	10 days	Contract, receipt of last required disclosure document, or receipt of occupancy permit, whichever is last. A settlement performed before the end of a cancellation period is unlawful and voidable by purchaser.
Time-share by resale	7 days	Receipt of Certificate
HOA	Varies by number of lots and whether original or resale	n/a

CHAPTER 6 QUIZ

1. Which of the following forms of ownership is *NOT* usually recognized in Maryland?
   1. Tenancy in common
   2. Community property
   3. Trust
   4. Ownership in severalty

2. What form of ownership is created in Maryland by a deed that conveys ownership to "Karen and David Muñoz, husband and wife," but does *NOT* specify the form of ownership?
   1. This language will create a tenancy in common.
   2. The deed must be redrawn to specify the form of ownership before the deed is recorded.
   3. This language will be construed to create tenancy by the entirety.
   4. This language will be construed to create ownership in severalty.

3. In Maryland, which of the following is *FALSE* concerning tenancy by the entirety?
   1. It may be held only by a married couple.
   2. It continues after the death of one of the owners.
   3. It gives each individual possession of the entire estate.
   4. It may not be partitioned by one owner.

4. What is the license or registration requirement for a developer wishing to create a Maryland time-share?
   1. Register with the State Real Estate Commission
   2. Register with the State Treasurer
   3. Register with the local Board or Association of REALTORS®.
   4. Be a licensed real estate broker.

5. What is required for amending the bylaws of a Maryland condominium?
   1. The management company has this authority.
   2. It requires affirmative vote by two-thirds of the unit owners.
   3. It requires affirmative vote of a majority vote of the council of unit owners.
   4. It requires affirmative vote by a simple majority of unit owners.

6. With what Maryland government agency must a developer register when converting a residential rental facility to a condominium regime?
   1. Office of the Attorney General
   2. Local Board of REALTORS®
   3. Secretary of State
   4. Maryland Real Estate Commission

7. Which of the following is *TRUE* of developers who wish to sell newly built Maryland condominium units to original purchasers?
   1. For five years after the sale, they are liable to their purchasers for damages that result from misleading statements.
   2. If the developers fail to deliver Public Offering Statements to them, they are subject to their purchasers' voiding their contracts.
   3. They are protected from liability for misleading statements to purchasers by the doctrine of caveat emptor.
   4. They must register Public Offering Statements with the Real Estate Commission.

8. When purchasers contract with developers to purchase new time-shares, which of the following is *TRUE* of their rights and responsibilities?
   1. They have the right to cancel the contract only if the seller has misrepresented material facts.
   2. They have the right, for 10 days, to cancel the sale for any or no reason.
   3. They must close the sale within 10 days after signing the sales contract.
   4. They must obtain a "payment and performance" bond to ensure developers' compliance with their contracts.

9. To protect the contract's enforceability, what must the owner of a condominium unit (other than its developer) furnish to purchasers not later than 15 days before closing when reselling the property?
   1. A copy of the declaration
   2. The bylaws, rules, and regulations
   3. A statement regarding monthly expenses, proposed capital improvements, other fees, financial statements of the condominium, and insurance details
   4. All of the above

10. Should a dispute develop between or among Maryland condominium unit owners, the board of directors, and/or council of unit owners, to whom may the parties apply for mediation?
   1. The local Board of REALTORS®
   2. The Office of the County State's Attorney
   3. The Office of the Maryland Attorney General
   4. The local Board of Development and Planning

CHAPTER 7

Legal Descriptions

boundary survey

location drawing

metes and bounds

misdemeanor

recorded plat of
subdivision

system of coordinates

■ **OVERVIEW**

Two of the methods of property description presented in the student's principal text are most frequently used in Maryland real estate brokerage. They are the metes and bounds and recorded plat of subdivision methods. In addition, Baltimore City has its own map coordinates system used by the city's Bureau of Plans and Surveys. Baltimore also describes property by using a system based on city blocks. Maryland has still another method—a system of coordinates it shares with the rest of the United States, Canada, Mexico, and nations in Central America. It is based upon precise indication of longitude, latitude, and elevation.

Maryland Coordinate System [Real Property §14-401–§14-406]

While not a part of the federal rectangular survey system, this system is based on the North American Datum (starting plane) established in 1927 and known as NAD27. Modified in 1983 as NAD83, it was adopted by the Maryland legislature, taking effect from 1987 to 1992. Based on satellite technology and observations, the 1983 data removed distortions associated with NAD27. Also, NAD83 fit the size, shape, and center-of-mass location of the earth more accurately. These data are reflected in the sometimes puzzling numbers and tick marks appearing at the edges of the street book maps so frequently used by real estate licensees. Licensees may never have to use this data but may want to be aware of their existence and purpose.

At the very least, a description that identifies land with reasonable certainty is required in a contract for its sale. Postal address alone is usually not an adequate legal description except for short residential leaseholds as one or two years.

■ EXAMPLES OF LEGAL DESCRIPTIONS USED IN CONTRACTS

Metes and Bounds

■ **FOR EXAMPLE** "Beginning at an iron pipe set on the northeast side of Annapolis Street at a point located South 38° 45' East, 200 feet from where the northeast side of Annapolis Street intersects the southeast side of Giddings Avenue—all as shown on Aldridge's Revised and Corrected Plat of West Annapolis recorded among the Land Records of Anne Arundel County in JCB Liber 4, Folio 297; and running thence and at right angles to Annapolis Street, North 51° 15' East, 150 feet to a pipe; thence South 38° 45' East 50 feet to a pipe; thence South 51° 15' West, 150 feet to a pipe on the northeast side of Annapolis Street; thence with same, North 38° 45' West, 50 feet to the place of beginning."

■ **FOR EXAMPLE** "That certain parcel of real estate located in Worcester County, Maryland, being on the east side of Farm Lane, north of Jerry Road, being further known as the Arthur R. Jackson property, consisting of one acre, more or less, with the improvements thereon, previously conveyed by deed of Robert Allen, grantor, recorded in FWH Liber 29, Folio 1312, the exact boundaries and acreage to be determined by means of a survey, which has been ordered to be prepared by Johnson and Landsman, Surveyors, Snow Hill."

Recorded Plat of Subdivision

■ **FOR EXAMPLE** "Lot #16, Block #3 of the Plat of Melville Development Corporation as surveyed by John Walmer, Catonsville, Maryland, August 15, 1968, as recorded in FWH Liber 295, Folio 1720, in the County of Ridge, State of Maryland."

■ SURVEY MARKERS

Surveyors are governed by the Maryland Professional Land Surveyors Act and licensed by the State Board for Professional Land Surveyors. Among other requirements, the board specifies the use of specific types of stakes, markers, monuments, and other landmarks in their work.

It is a misdemeanor (a crime less than a felony) intentionally to move, damage, or obliterate any markers on property belonging to another person if the marker was put in place by a civil engineer, surveyor, real estate appraiser, or members of their teams. The exception is when the marker interferes with proper use of the land. A fine of not more than $500 can be imposed upon conviction.

If there is a dispute over any boundary line or if the bounds mentioned in a document are lost, the circuit court of the county where the property is located may be petitioned to establish the boundary lines or the location of the missing bounds. These experts' fees are considered costs in the proceeding.

A person may file suit against a land surveyor for errors in a survey no more than 15 years after the survey was made or within three years after the discovery of the error, whichever occurs first.

■ LOCATION DRAWINGS AND BOUNDARY SURVEYS

The Office of the Secretary of Licensing and Regulation, through its Board for Professional Land Surveyors, requires that surveyors have a signed election form requesting either a location drawing or a boundary survey from the party ordering the survey. This election (choice) should be made by purchasers at the time of forming their agreement to purchase. A description of each and a list of its uses, limitations, and costs appear on the election form. The form electing which survey is being ordered is typically submitted by the title, settlement, or law office preparing for settlement.

The boundary survey identifies property boundary lines and corners sufficiently well to establish the physical position and extent of the boundaries, including visible indications of rights that may arise from prescription or adverse possession. It is needed for an owner having a fence placed or other improvements erected. It reports that monuments have either been located or placed on the property.

A location drawing provides a plat of the property that shows the location of any improvements. It costs less than a boundary survey but is sufficient for most residential resales and refinancing situations.

■ SUBDIVISION PLATS

Subdividers must have plats of proposed subdivisions prepared by a licensed surveyor and approved and recorded by local authorities before offering them for sale. Reference to a recorded subdivision plat may be part of a sufficient legal description. No distances on a subdivision plat may be marked "more or less" except those lines that begin, terminate, or bind on a body of water.

CHAPTER 7 QUIZ

1. Real estate sales agreements and listings use property descriptions. Which of the following is *TRUE* about the use of lot, block, section—and similar references to a subdivision plat—for such descriptions?
   1. They are sufficient if the plat referred to was properly recorded.
   2. They must be prepared by licensed real estate brokers.
   3. They are not sufficient for sales agreements but are good enough for listings.
   4. They are sufficient for listings but not for sales agreements.

2. Which is *TRUE* of location drawings?
   1. They are essentially the same as boundary surveys.
   2. They are appropriate for typical residential resales.
   3. They cost more than boundary surveys.
   4. They can properly be used for placing fences and other improvements.

3. Which of the following is MOST likely to be a sufficient legal description for the sale of land?
   1. "142 Pinehurst Road, Ocean Pines"
   2. "That lot fronting 100 feet on Pinehurst and being 250 feet deep"
   3. "That two acres, shown on attached plat of subdivision survey as prepared by Landsman & Co., Surveyors of Catonsville, Maryland"
   4. "1776B Liberty St., Snow Hill, Md., being the northern half of a duplex"

4. "Beginning at the intersection of the east line of Goodrich Boulevard and the south line of Jasmine Lane and running south along the east line of Goodrich Boulevard a distance of 230 feet; thence easterly parallel to the north line of Wolf Road, a distance of 195 feet; thence northeasterly on a course of N 22°E, a distance of 135 feet; and thence northwesterly along the south line of Jasmine Lane to the point of beginning." What kind of legal description is this an example of?
   1. Block
   2. Rectangular survey
   3. Subdivision
   4. Metes-and-bounds

5. Which of the following is *TRUE* of property descriptions used in most Maryland real estate transfers?
   1. They refer to the government rectangular survey system.
   2. They consist of the street or mailing addresses of the properties.
   3. They are based on recorded plats of subdivision or metes-and-bounds data.
   4. They consist of post office box numbers.

CHAPTER 8

Real Estate Taxes and Other Liens

◼ OVERVIEW

Maryland property taxes are levied by and for the support of state, county, and city governments, as well as local special taxing districts. A number of counties also impose impact fees on developers in addition to property taxes on owners. The impact fees are levied on new residential units to pay for additional public facilities and services that will be needed by residents in the newly constructed homes. Of course, such fees increase the purchase price of housing as developers pass this cost along to purchasers.

■ ASSESSMENT

Real estate taxes are based on the amount at which the property is assessed. Residential real property is assessed for tax purposes by the State Department of Assessments and Taxation. That department has local offices in Baltimore City and in each Maryland County. Maryland's general (ad valorem) tax assessment is 100% of the market value indicated by triennial assessment. In addition to state-wide taxes, ad valorem, transfer, and recordation taxes are imposed by counties at their own rates (See Figure 8.1).

The procedure for assessing property in Maryland, the triennial assessment, is based on a threeyear cycle in which onethird of all properties are revalued for tax purposes each year. Each county has been organized into three principal assessing areas to coincide with the years of the assessment cycle. The areas generally have similar density and other common characteristics and are reviewed on a rotating basis. By the end of a threeyear period, all properties have been physically reviewed and valued once; then a new cycle commences.

Upon completion of the triennial review, if the value of a property is found to have changed, the owner is sent a notice of reassessment that shows the property's assessment for the next three years; no other notice is sent until the new cycle begins three years later. Taxpayers who believe that their assessments are improper may appeal within 45 days of receiving their notice of assessment.

Exterior inspection of premises is part of each reassessment. If changes in zoning or use occur, or if additions or extensive improvements to property are discovered, the property may be revalued without regard to the three-year sequence.

Real property assessment is further controlled by a phasein provision that was designed to take some of the financial sting out of swiftly rising property values. For that onethird of real properties reassessed in a particular year, the first onethird of any increase in value is added for that year, and the balance is added in equal increments over the next two years. For example, a property increasing in value from $200,000 to $260,000 would be assigned a value of $220,000 the first tax year, $240,000 the second, and $260,000 the third.

■ PAYMENT

Taxes on residential property are paid in two equal installments. The first payment is *due* July 1 but can be *paid* as late as September 30 without penalty. The second, *due* January 1, can be *paid* without penalty as late as January 31. One of the purposes of the two-payment arrangement is to reduce the amount of ad valorem tax "set asides" needed by purchasers at settlement. The statute requires counties to prepare their data-processing systems for quarterly payments, which may be authorized by future legislation.

Lenders who accept responsibility to forward property taxes on the mortgaged properties, accumulate the required funds in expense (escrow/trust/impound) accounts. They are required to pay those taxes within 45 days after the earlier of the following: (1) the first due date after their receipt of the tax bill or (2) after funds collected by the lender are sufficient to pay the amount of taxes and interest due. Lenders who fail to forward escrowed taxes as provided must bear any additional costs of penalties and interest.

FIGURE 8.1

County Tax Rates

	2013–2014 (Fiscal 2014) County Tax Rates		
Municipality	***Real Property Tax Rate in Dollars per $100 of Assessment**	**†Transfer Tax is the Consideration Payable Multiplied by this Rate**	**Recordation Tax Quoted in Dollars per $500 of Transaction Amount**
Allegany	0.98	0.50%	0.005	3.25
Anne Arundel	0.95	1.00%	0.010	3.50
Baltimore City	2.248	1.50%	0.015	5.00
Baltimore County	1.100	1.50%	0.015	2.50
Calvert	0.892	0.00%	0.000	5.00
Caroline	0.94	0.50%	0.005	5.00
Carroll	1.018	0.00%	0.000	5.00
Cecil	0.9907	0.00%	0.000	4.10
Charles	1.025	0.00%	0.000	5.00
Dorchester (first $30,000 exempt for residential)	0.976	0.75%	0.0075	5.00
Frederick	1.064	0.00%	0.000	6.00
Garrett (first $50,000 is exempt for owner-occupied)	0.99	1.00%	0.010	3.50
Harford	1.042	1.00%	0.010	3.30
Howard	1.014	1.00%	0.010	2.50
Kent	1.022	0.50%	0.005	3.30
Montgomery	0.759	1.00%	0.010	3.45
Prince George's	0.960	1.40%	0.014	2.50
Queen Anne's	0.8471	0.50%	0.050	4.95
St. Mary's	0.857	1.00%	0.010	4.00
Somerset	0.915	0.00%	0.000	3.30
Talbot (first $50,000 is exempt for owner-occupied)	0.512	1.00%	0.010	3.30
Washington	0.948	0.50%	0.005	3.80
Wicomico	0.9086	0.00%	0.000	3.50
Worcester	0.77	0.50%	0.050	3.30

* To this assessment, add any municipal tax and state tax of 0.112.
† This is in addition to the State Transfer Tax Rate of 0.500%.
This information is found at www.dat.state.md.us/sdatweb/taxrate.html.

■ PROPERTY TAX RELIEF PROGRAMS

The Homestead Tax Credit Program

This program is designed to protect owneroccupied residence assessments from the effects of rapid inflation. It automatically provides a credit against the real estate tax if the assessment on a dwelling increases over the previous year by more than a certain percentage. That percentage is determined by the Maryland Legislature. The credit equals the amount by which the reassessment exceeds the established percentage and applies if certain other conditions were met during the previous calendar year. Homeowners are required to submit—even if they have done so before—a tax credit application, which is included in the assessment notices sent to one-third of property owners.

Homeowners' Property Tax Credit Program

Because the Homestead Tax Credit Program does not take into account homeowners' ability to pay, the State legislature created the Homeowners' Property Tax Credit Program, popularly known as the "circuit breaker." After taking into account homeowners' net worth, gross annual income, and assessed value of their property, this program, for homeowners of all ages, sets limits on the amount of residential property tax due. Application for this relief must be made each year. Under this program, there is also a tax credit for renters who meet various income and asset requirements when the assessed value of their property does not exceed $250,000. This tax credit can be as much as $750 per year.

Property Tax Deferral

This program allows property owners age 65 or older to elect to defer the increase in their property tax bill. Each local government must first adopt the program. The local government then has the authority under State law to impose income restrictions and interest rate amounts. The deferred taxes become a lien on the property and must be repaid when the property is transferred. Montgomery County makes this relief available to homeowners of all ages who meet certain residency and income requirements.

Other Relief

Owners of unsold or unrented single-dwelling units or newly constructed or substantially rehabilitated commercial properties may be entitled to tax credits not exceeding the property taxes on the improvements. The credit applies for no more than one year immediately following construction or substantial rehabilitation.

Special provision has also been made for senior tenants age 60 or older to receive as much as $600 from the State to offset property taxes. Asset and income limits are among certain restrictions that apply.

The residential property owned by a veteran with a permanent, 100%, service-connected disability is exempt from property tax. The 100% disability may result from blindness or some other disabling cause. This benefit is retained by the unremarried surviving spouse of the deceased disabled veteran as well. Application for this benefit must be accompanied by documentation of veteran status, of 100% disability, and of ownership of the property.

Assessment on a residence owned by an individual who is legally blind is reduced by $15,000. The property must be the individual's legal residence and not be occupied by more than two families. The unremarried surviving spouse of a blind individual receives the same benefit. No individual may claim both the exemption for being blind and the exemption for being a disabled veteran.

■ TRANSFER AND RECORDATION TAXES

Except as discussed in the following paragraph, in every written or oral agreement for the sale or other disposition of property, it is presumed, in the absence of any contrary provision in the agreement or the law, that the parties to the agreement intended that the cost of any recordation tax or any State or local transfer tax be shared equally between the grantor and grantee. This presumption does not apply to mortgages or deeds of trust. (Refer to Figure 8.1.)

First-Time Maryland Homebuyers

The law provides that first-time homebuyers who will occupy the property as their principal residence will not pay the State transfer tax. In a transfer involving such a buyer, the State transfer tax of 0.5% is reduced to 0.25% and must be paid by the seller. Furthermore, unless the parties in such a transaction agree to the contrary, the recordation taxes and local transfer taxes are to be paid by the seller. *First-time homebuyer* is defined in the law as "an individual who has never owned in the State residential real property that has been the individual's principal residence."

■ CORPORATE FRANCHISE TAX

Most corporations are taxed annually on their franchise, or right, to do business in the State. The annual tax becomes a general lien on the property of the corporation and can be enforced against it. When a broker files for a real estate license and the brokerage is a corporation, the Commission requires that a copy of the brokerage's Articles of Incorporation be filed.

■ PROPERTY TAX ASSESSMENTS, AGRICULTURAL USE

Lands that are actively devoted to farm or agricultural uses are favorably assessed on the basis of those uses rather than on their probably more intensive, highest and best use.

Agricultural Use Assessment

The State Department of Assessments and Taxation establishes criteria for the purpose of determining whether land qualifies for assessment as agricultural use. The State's purpose is to slow the conversion of farm lands into more intensive, nonfarm uses.

Agricultural Transfer Tax

The Agricultural Transfer Tax, ranging from 3% to 5% of the consideration, funds the State's Agricultural Land Preservation Program. The tax is based on multiple factors: the size of the tract, improvements that may be in place, and the value of the land reflected in the consideration. The tax is waived in a transfer in which the purchaser promises to keep the land in agricultural use for five tax years. The tax is more fully discussed in Chapter 10 of this book.

The Agricultural Transfer Tax is calculated by the Assessments Office and is payable at the time the property transfer to a nonagricultural user takes place. Negotiation about which party will pay should be reflected in the contract of sale. A full discussion of this tax is found at the Maryland State Department of Assessment and Taxation website: www.dat.state.md.us/sdatweb/agtransf.html.

AD VALOREM TAX DELINQUENCY AND REDEMPTION

The residential property taxes are due in two payments: one on July 1 and the other on January 1 each year. Taxes that are not paid by September 30 and by January 31 under the two-payment system are considered delinquent, bear interest as provided by law, and are subject to a real estate tax sale held by the county treasurer.

The dates and rules regarding such sales are made by each county. Taxdelinquent properties sold at a tax sale are not conveyed immediately to the buyer. During a sixmonth statutory period of redemption, the delinquent taxpayer may redeem the property by paying the county treasurer the amount of the delinquent tax plus the accumulated interest on penalties and related legal fees. The annual interest rate for redemption—from 6% to 24%—is set by the various jurisdictions. If no redemption is made during the sixmonth period, the tax sale buyer may apply to the court for the issuance of a deed to the property. Unpaid taxes create a priority (first) lien on real property.

Ad valorem taxes on a parcel of property that remain unpaid for longer than three years—perhaps because the lien on the property did not sell at three successive tax sales—are no longer collectible. There is a three-year limitation of actions on this tax. Only the most recent three years' taxes remain a lien on any property. A number of tax program pamphlets are available in each county's Tax Assessment Office.

MECHANICS' LIENS

Mechanics' liens, as discussed in the main textbook, are authorized by law in many states to protect the rights of contractors, suppliers, and other persons engaged to improve real estate. In addition to mechanics and materialmen, Maryland allows architectural, engineering, land surveying, and landscaping service providers to file mechanics' liens. Work on Maryland real estate that improves a property by 15% of its previous value qualifies for a mechanic's lien. Contractors or suppliers have six months after completion of such work to record a notice of their lien. They then have one year from the date of recording to petition the courts to enforce the lien in the event such petition was not included when the lien was recorded.

It is unlawful for executory (as yet unperformed) contracts between contractors and subcontractors relating to construction, alteration, or repair of a building, structure, or improvement, to contain a provision that waives or requires that the subcontractor waive the right to file a mechanic's lien.

Buyers purchasing recently constructed or improved properties should seek protection against possible outstanding mechanics' liens. In the usual purchase of real estate, the buyer's attorney has responsibility to ascertain that the property being purchased is free from unpaid taxes, mechanics' liens, or other outstanding liens.

A building, or the land on which the building is erected, may not be subjected to a lien under this subtitle if, prior to the establishment of the lien, legal title has been granted to a bona fide purchaser for value.

Release of Lien

When a lien on real property is satisfied, lienholders are required to mail or deliver a release of the lien within seven days after receipt of payment. The release may be in the form of the original note, marked "paid" or "canceled." If lienholders fail to provide such a release after demand by the payor, the payor may bring action in the circuit court. In such an action, the lienholders or their agent may be liable for delivery of the release, as well as for all costs and expenses of the action.

CHAPTER 8 QUIZ

1. In Maryland, what entity or entities can levy (impose) real estate taxes?
   1. Cities
   2. Special taxing districts
   3. Counties
   4. All of the above

2. Which is *TRUE* of Maryland residential real property assessment?
   1. It is performed each year.
   2. It is based on each property's full market value.
   3. It occurs every other year.
   4. It is done after each resale.

3. Nyla Mack owns a contracting firm in Maryland. On February 1, Arch Chandler hired the Mack firm to construct a large addition to his fivebedroom house. Mack finished work on the project on March 15. It is now April 15, and Mack has not yet been paid. Based on this situation, which of the following is correct?
   1. Mack has until August 1 to record a notice of lien.
   2. Mack has until August 1 to enforce the mechanic's lien.
   3. Mack has until September 15 to record a mechanic's lien.
   4. Mack has until October 15 to enforce a mechanic's lien.

4. Pierre Andre makes semiannual real estate tax payments on the lot beneath his house. Which of the following statements is *TRUE*?
   1. Andre's taxes are due July 1 of each year.
   2. Andre's taxes are due September 30 of each year.
   3. Andre's first semiannual payment is late if not paid before September 1.
   4. Andre's second semiannual payment is late if not paid before December 15.

5. Ted Bolton has never before owned and occupied a principal residence in Maryland. He will settle on the purchase of a $400,000 home to occupy here in April. How will the State transfer tax (usually 0.5% of the consideration) be apportioned at settlement?
   1. Bolton will pay $0, and sellers will pay $1,000.
   2. Bolton will pay $1,000, and sellers will pay $1,000.
   3. Bolton will pay $0, and sellers will pay $2,000.
   4. The apportionment will be whatever Bolton and the sellers agree in the contract of sale.

CHAPTER 9

Real Estate Contracts

■ KEY TERMS

attorneys-in-fact
equitable title
executory contract
installment contracts

lease purchase option
  agreement
lease with option to renew
new home warranty

option price
parol transfer
powers of attorney

■ OVERVIEW

Maryland real estate contracts are used for, among other things, sales, rentals, options, and installment sales. This chapter discusses various contract issues, including age requirements for valid contracts, the Statute of Frauds, mandatory clauses for residential resales, and limitation of actions on contract enforcement in Maryland. It also presents the industry-created statewide sales contract now available for REALTORS® use throughout Maryland. Students who go on to practice real estate brokerage as REALTORS® are advised to always use the latest version of such contracts and their appropriate addenda.

■ GENERAL CONTRACT RULES: COMPETENCY, STATUTE OF FRAUDS, AND LIMITATION OF ACTIONS

Competency

Under Maryland law, a person reaches the age of majority and has the capacity to enter into a valid real estate contract at age 18. However, minors married to persons who have reached the age of majority may enter into valid real estate contracts jointly with their spouses. Generally, competency has three requirements: age (majority), state of mind, and authority to act.

Statute of Frauds

To be legally enforceable under Maryland's Statute of Frauds, all contracts for the transfer of any interest in real property for more than one year must be in writing and signed by the parties. Any parol (oral) transfer of an interest in real property for more than one year conveys no more than a tenancy at will. While Maryland laws require a 30-day notice to vacate under a tenancy at will, various counties require longer periods.

The Maryland Statute of Frauds does not require a lease for a term of one year or less to be in writing to be enforceable. That year is measured from the date the lease is entered into rather than the date on which occupancy begins. Regardless of this interesting fact, all licensees are required by Commission regulations to reduce to signed, written form all agreements, including leases of any length, they help prepare.

Limitation of Actions (Statute of Limitations)

Suits to enforce a simple contract must be filed within three years. For contracts signed "under seal," however, the time limit is 12 years. A statement in the body of a contract that it is made "under seal" and/or uses the phrase "witness my seal" above the signature block creates a contract under seal. Such a contract is called a specialty contract and is subject to action for enforcement for 12 years.

■ CONTRACTS FOR THE SALE OF REAL ESTATE

Real estate sales contracts and other contract forms must always be drafted (drawn up "from scratch") by attorneys. Licensees are authorized only to insert required information into forms that attorneys have drafted. Licensees who draft even clauses or phrases on their own could be accused of the misdemeanor unauthorized practice of law. Under Maryland statutes, the maximum penalty for such unauthorized practice is a fine of not more than $5,000 and/or imprisonment for not more than one year.

Although licensees, unless otherwise licensed to do so, cannot act as attorneys in their brokerage activities, they should nevertheless emphasize to buyers and sellers that a signed sales contract is legally binding. Buyers and sellers should obtain legal counsel to interpret and approve the provisions of contracts. It is grossly misleading, and probably an example of the unauthorized practice of law, to give false assurance to the parties, such as, "Don't worry; there will be an attorney at settlement," or, "An attorney can always find a way to get you out of it," as if that would protect them from their own errors in judgment.

To reduce confusion that can arise from use of a variety of contract forms, the Maryland Association of REALTORS® (MAR), working with its member associations and boards throughout the State, makes a contract form available to its members for use in residential sale transactions statewide. The MAR, with the aid of its legal counsel, also provides contract language for 20 or more addenda. All these forms are copyrighted by the MAR and may not be altered or modified without the prior written express consent of that association. MAR member-brokers are free either to use the statewide forms—as long as they make no changes in their wording—or to have attorneys draft forms for each particular firm's use. Non-member-brokers may not use the MAR forms.

Beside the statewide (MAR) form, several trade groups within the state have their own locally used forms. Licensees must be familiar with more than one contract used in their area. In every case, the parties (buyer and seller) can demand to use an agreement other than the ones most common in an area.

In Maryland, a contract may lawfully be drafted by one of the parties or by an attorney. Anyone else attempting to draft (write from scratch) an agreement is engaging in the unauthorized practice of law. Such a practice is contrary to Maryland law. However, it is acceptable for a licensee to "complete" a form contract, pre-drafted by a local board or association. Even filling in the blanks requires the greatest care. Nonetheless, licensees' drafting their own contingencies and addenda could lead to the unauthorized practice of law.

When presenting a state- or area-wide contract for approval by the parties, avoid the cliché, "This is our standard contract." Such a statement subtly implies that it cannot be modified by the parties as part of their negotiations. There is no standard contract; to say there is one is patently unethical.

A sample of the MAR's Residential Sales Contract is shown in Figure 9.1.

FIGURE 9.1

Maryland Association of REALTORS® Residential Sales Contract

RESIDENTIAL CONTRACT OF SALE

This is a Legally Binding Contract; If Not Understood, Seek Competent Legal Advice.
THIS FORM IS DESIGNED AND INTENDED FOR THE SALE AND PURCHASE OF IMPROVED SINGLE FAMILY RESIDENTIAL REAL ESTATE LOCATED IN MARYLAND ONLY. *FOR OTHER TYPES OF PROPERTY INCLUDE APPROPRIATE ADDENDA.*

> **TIME IS OF THE ESSENCE.** Time is of the essence of this Contract. The failure of Seller or Buyer to perform any act as provided in this Contract by a prescribed date or within a prescribed time period shall be a default under this Contract and the non-defaulting party, upon written notice to the defaulting party, may declare this Contract null and void and of no further legal force and effect. In such event, all Deposit(s) shall be disbursed in accordance with Paragraph 19 of this Contract.

1. DATE OF OFFER: _____ .

2. SELLER: _____

3. BUYER: _____

4. PROPERTY: Seller does sell to Buyer and Buyer does purchase from Seller, all of the following described Property (hereinafter "Property") known as _____
located in _____City/County, Maryland, Zip Code _____,
together with the improvements thereon, and all rights and appurtenances thereto belonging.

5. ESTATE: The Property is being conveyed: _____ in fee simple or _____ subject to an annual ground rent, now
existing, in the amount of _____ Dollars ($_____)
payable semi-annually, as now or to be recorded among the Land Records of _____City/County, Maryland.

6. PURCHASE PRICE: The purchase price is _____ Dollars
   ($_____).

7. PAYMENT TERMS: The payment of the purchase price shall be made by Buyer as follows:
(a) An initial Deposit by way of _____ in the amount of _____ Dollars
($_____) at the time of this offer.
(b) An additional Deposit by way of _____ in the amount of _____ Dollars
($_____) to be paid _____
_____.
(c) All Deposits will be held in escrow by: _____.
   (If not a Maryland licensed real estate broker, the parties may execute a separate escrow deposit agreement.)
(d) The purchase price less any and all Deposits shall be paid in full by Buyer in cash, wired funds, bank check, certified
check or other payment acceptable to the settlement officer at settlement.
(e) Buyer and Seller instruct broker named in paragraph (c) above to place the Deposits in: **(Check One)**
    ☐ A non-interest bearing account;
OR ☐ An interest bearing account, the interest on which, in absence of default by Buyer, shall accrue to
    the benefit of Buyer. Broker may charge a fee for establishing an interest bearing account.

8. SETTLEMENT: Date of Settlement _____or sooner if agreed to in writing by the parties.

9. FINANCING: Buyer's obligation to purchase the Property is contingent upon Buyer obtaining a written commitment for a
loan secured by the Property as follows:
(Check) ☐ Conventional Loan as follows: ☐ FHA Financing Addendum
    Loan Amount $ _____ ☐ Gift of Funds Contingency Addendum
    Term of Note _____ Years ☐ Owner Financing Addendum
    Amortization _____ Years ☐ VA Financing Addendum
    Interest Rate _____ % ☐ Assumption Addendum
    Loan Program _____ ☐ OTHER: _____
    Loan Origination/Discount Fees (as a % of loan amount):
    Buyer agrees to pay _____%; ☐ No Financing Contingency
    Seller agrees to pay _____%.
    Buyer shall receive the benefit of any reduction in fees.

Buyer_____/_____ Page 1 of 10 10/13 Seller_____/_____

F I G U R E   9.1

Maryland Association of REALTORS® Residential Sales Contract (continued)

10. FINANCING APPLICATION AND COMMITMENT: Buyer agrees to make a written application for the financing as herein described within _____ (_____) days from the Date of Contract Acceptance. If such written financing commitment is not obtained by Buyer within _____ (_____) days from the Date of Contract Acceptance: (1) Seller, at Seller's election and upon written notice to Buyer, may declare this Contract null and void and of no further legal effect; or (2) Buyer, upon written notice to Seller, which shall include written evidence from the lender of Buyer's inability to obtain financing as provided in Paragraph 9 of this Contract, may declare this Contract null and void and of no further legal effect. In either case, the deposit shall be disbursed in accordance with the Deposit paragraph of this Contract. If Buyer has complied with all of Buyer's obligations under this Contract, including those with respect to applying for financing and seeking to obtain financing, then the Release of Deposit agreement shall provide that the deposit shall be returned to Buyer.

11. ALTERNATE FINANCING: Provided Buyer timely and diligently pursues the financing described in Paragraph 9 **"Financing"**; Paragraph 10 **"Financing Application and Commitment"**; and the provisions of Paragraph 28 **"Buyer Responsibility"**, Buyer, at Buyer's election, may also apply for alternate financing. If Buyer, at Buyers sole option, obtains a written commitment for financing in which the loan amount, term of note, amortization period, interest rate, down payment or loan program differ from the financing as described in Paragraph 9, or any addendum to this Contract, the provision of Paragraph 10 or any addendum to this Contract shall be deemed to have been fully satisfied. Such alternate financing may not increase costs to Seller or exceed the time allowed to secure the financing commitment as provided in Paragraph 10, or any addendum to this Contract.

12. HOME AND/OR ENVIRONMENTAL INSPECTION: Buyer acknowledges, subject to Seller acceptance, that Buyer is afforded the opportunity, at Buyer's sole cost and expense, to condition Buyer's purchase of the Property upon a Home Inspection and/or Environmental Inspection in order to ascertain the physical condition of the Property or the existence of environmental hazards. If Buyer desires a Home Inspection and/or Environmental Inspection contingency, such contingency must be included in an addendum to this Contract. Buyer and Seller acknowledge that Brokers, agents or subagents are not responsible for the existence or discovery of property defects.

Inspection(s) Addenda Attached _____ _____ Inspection(s) Declined _____ _____
                              Buyer   **Buyer**   **Buyer**   **Buyer**

13. INCLUSIONS/EXCLUSIONS: Included in the purchase price are all permanently attached fixtures, including all smoke detectors. Certain other **now existing items** which may be considered personal property, whether installed or stored upon the property, are included if box below is checked.

INCLUDED	INCLUDED	INCLUDED	INCLUDED
□ Alarm System	□ Exist. W/W Carpet	□ Satellite Dish	□ Window Fan(s) #____
□ Built-in Microwave	□ Fireplace Screen Doors	□ Screens	□ Wood Stove
□ Ceiling Fan(s) # ___	□ Freezer	□ Shades/Blinds	
□ Central Vacuum	□ Furnace Humidifier	□ Storage Shed(s) # ____	
□ Clothes Dryer	□ Garage Opener(s) #_____	□ Storm Doors	
□ Clothes Washer	w/remote(s) #_____	□ Storm Windows	
□ Cooktop	□ Garbage Disposer	□ Stove or Range	
□ Dishwasher	□ Hot Tub, Equip. & Cover	□ T.V. Antenna	
□ Drapery/Curtain Rods	□ Intercom	□ Trash Compactor	
□ Draperies/Curtains	□ Playground Equipment	□ Wall Oven(s) #_____	
□ Electronic Air Filter	□ Pool, Equip. & Cover	□ Water Filter	
□ Exhaust Fan(s) # ____	□ Refrigerator(s) #_____	□ Water Softener	
	□ w/ice maker	□ Window A/C Unit(s) #____	

ADDITIONAL INCLUSIONS (SPECIFY): _____

ADDITIONAL EXCLUSIONS (SPECIFY): _____

14. AGRICULTURALLY ASSESSED PROPERTY: The Property, or any portion thereof, may be subject to an Agricultural Land Transfer Tax as imposed by Section 13-301 et seq. of the Tax-Property Article, Annotated Code of Maryland, by reason of the Property's having been assessed on the basis of agricultural use. Agricultural taxes assessed as a result of this transfer shall be paid by _____ .

15. FOREST CONSERVATION AND MANAGEMENT PROGRAM: Buyer is hereby notified that this transfer may be subject to the Forest Conservation and Management Program imposed by Section 8-211 of the Tax-Property Article, Annotated Code of Maryland. Forest Conservation and Management program taxes assessed as a result of this transfer shall be paid by

_____
_____ .

16. LEAD-BASED PAINT:
A. FEDERAL LEAD-BASED PAINT LAW: Title X, Section 1018, the Residential Lead-Based Paint Hazard Reduction Act of 1992 (the "Act"), requires the disclosure by Seller of information regarding lead-based paint and lead-based paint hazards in

FIGURE 9.1

Maryland Association of REALTORS® Residential Sales Contract (continued)

connection with the sale of any **residential** real property on which a residential dwelling was constructed prior to 1978. Unless otherwise exempt by the Act, the disclosure shall be made on the required federal Disclosure of Information on Lead-Based Paint and/or Lead-Based Paint Hazards form. **Seller and any agent involved in the transaction are required to retain a copy of the completed Lead-Based Paint Disclosure form for a period of three (3) years following the date of settlement. A Seller who fails to give the required Lead-Based Paint Disclosure form and EPA pamphlet may be liable under the Act for three times the amount of damages and may be subject to both civil and criminal penalties.**

Buyer acknowledges by Buyer's initials below that Buyer has read and understands the provisions of Paragraph 16.A.
_____/_____ **(BUYER)**

B. RENOVATION, REPAIR AND PAINTING OF PROPERTY: In accordance with the Lead Renovation, Repair and Painting Rule ("RRP") as adopted by the Environmental Protection Agency ("the EPA"), effective April 22, 2010, if the improvements on the Property were built before 1978, contractor(s) engaged by Seller to renovate, repair or paint the Property must be certified by the EPA where such work will disturb more than six square feet of paint per room for interior projects; more than 20 square feet of paint for any exterior project; or includes window replacement or demolition ("Covered Work"). Before and during any Covered Work project, contractor(s) must comply with all requirements of the RRP.

A Seller who personally performs any Covered Work on a rental property is required to be certified by the EPA prior to performing such Covered Work. No certification is required for a Seller who personally performs Covered Work on the Seller's principal residence. However, Seller has the ultimate responsibility for the safety of Seller's family or children while performing such Covered Work. For detailed information regarding the RRP, Seller should visit http://www2.epa.gov/lead/renovation-repair-and-painting-program.

Buyer acknowledges by Buyer's initials below that Buyer has read and understands Paragraph 16.B.
_____/_____ **(BUYER)**

C. MARYLAND LEAD POISONING PREVENTION PROGRAM: Under the Maryland Lead Poisoning Prevention Program (the "Program"), any residential dwelling constructed prior to 1950 that is leased for residential purposes is required to be registered with the Maryland Department of the Environment (MDE). Any residential dwelling constructed between 1950 and 1978 that is leased for residential purposes may be registered with the MDE at the election of the owner. If the property was built prior to 1979 and is now or has been a rental property or may become a rental property in the future, a separate Maryland Lead-Based Paint Disclosure form should be completed.

Buyer acknowledges by Buyer's initials below that Buyer has read and understands Paragraph 16.C.
_____/_____ **(BUYER)**

17. ADDENDA/DISCLOSURES: The Addenda checked below, which are hereby attached, are made a part of this Contract:

- ☐ Affiliated Business Disclosure Notice
- ☐ As Is
- ☐ Cash/Conventional Financing Appraisal Contingency
- ☐ Condominium Resale Notice
- ☐ Conservation Easement
- ☐ Disclosure of Licensee Status
- ☐ First-Time Maryland Home Buyer Transfer & Recordation Tax
- ☐ Homeowners Association Notice
- ☐ Kickout
- ☐ Lead-Based Paint Hazard Inspection
- ☐ Federal Lead-Based Paint and Lead-Based Hazards Disclosure of Information
- ☐ Maryland Lead-Based Paint Disclosure
- ☐ Local City/County Certifications/Registrations
- ☐ Local City/County Notices/Disclosure

- ☐ MD Non-Resident Seller Transfer Withholding Tax
- ☐ Notice to Buyer and Seller – Maryland Residential Real Property Disclosure/Disclaimer Act
- ☐ On-Site Sewage Disposal System Inspection
- ☐ Property Subject to Ground Rent
- ☐ Property Inspections
- ☐ Purchase Price Escalation
- ☐ Short Sale
- ☐ Sale, Financing, Settlement or Lease of Other Real Estate
- ☐ Seller's Purchase of Another Property
- ☐ Third Party Approval
- ☐ Water Quality
- ☐ Seller Contribution Addendum

☐ Other Addenda/Special Conditions:

_____
_____.

18. WOOD DESTROYING INSECT INSPECTION: Buyer, at Buyer's expense, (if VA, then at Seller's expense) is authorized to obtain a written report on the state regulated form from a Maryland licensed pest control company that, based on a careful visual inspection, there is no evidence of termite or other wood-destroying insect infestation in the residence or within three (3) feet of the residence; and damage due to previous infestation has been repaired. The provisions of this paragraph also shall

FIGURE 9.1

Maryland Association of REALTORS® Residential Sales Contract (continued)

apply to: (1) the garage or within three (3) feet of the garage (whether attached or detached); (2) any outbuildings located within three feet of the residence or garage; and (3) a maximum of ten (10) linear feet of the nearest portion of a fence on Seller's Property within three feet of the residence or garage. If there is evidence of present infestation as described above, or if damage caused by present or prior infestation is discovered, Seller, at Seller's expense, shall repair any damage caused by present or prior infestation and have the present infestation treated by a licensed pest control company. If the cost of treatment and repair of such damage exceeds 2% of the purchase price, Seller may, at Seller's option, cancel this Contract, unless Buyer, at Buyer's option should choose to pay for the cost of treatment and repairs exceeding 2% of the purchase price, then this Contract shall remain in full force and effect. If such report reveals damage for which the cost of treatment and repair exceeds 2% of the purchase price, Seller's decision regarding treatment and repair of damage shall be communicated in writing to Buyer within five (5) days from receipt of the report, after which Buyer shall respond to Seller in writing with Buyer's decision within three (3) days from receipt of Seller's notification of Seller's decision. If Seller does not notify Buyer in writing of Seller's decision within five (5) days from receipt of report, Buyer may, at Buyer's option, pay for the cost of treatment and repairs exceeding 2% of the purchase price. If Buyer does not want to pay for the cost of treatment and repairs exceeding 2% of the purchase price, Buyer may terminate this Contract upon written notice delivered to Seller. In the event this Contract is terminated under the terms of this paragraph, the Deposit(s) shall be disbursed in accordance with the Deposit paragraph of this Contract.

19. DEPOSIT: If the Deposit is held by a Broker as specified in Paragraph 7(c) of this Contract, Buyer hereby authorizes and directs Broker to hold the Deposit instrument without negotiation or deposit until the parties have executed and accepted this Contract. Upon acceptance, the initial Deposit and additional Deposits (the "Deposit"), if any, shall be placed in escrow as provided in Paragraph 7(e) of this Contract and in accordance with the requirements of Section 17-502(b)(1) of the Business Occupations and Professions Article, Annotated Code of Maryland. If Seller does not execute and accept this Contract, the initial Deposit instrument shall be promptly returned to Buyer. The Deposit shall be disbursed at settlement. In the event this Contract shall be terminated or settlement does not occur, Buyer and Seller agree that the Deposit shall be disbursed by Broker only in accordance with a Release of Deposit agreement executed by Buyer and Seller. In the event Buyer and/or Seller fail to complete the real estate transaction in accordance with the terms and conditions of this Contract, and either Buyer or Seller shall be unable or unwilling to execute a Release of Deposit agreement, Buyer and Seller hereby acknowledge and agree that Broker may distribute the Deposit in accordance with the provisions of Section 17-505(b) of the Business Occupations and Professions Article, Annotated Code of Maryland.

20. DEED AND TITLE: Upon payment of the purchase price, a deed for the Property containing covenants of special warranty and further assurances (except in the case of transfer by personal representative of an estate), shall be executed by Seller and shall convey the Property to Buyer. Title to the Property, including all chattels included in the purchase, shall be good and merchantable, free of liens and encumbrances except as specified herein; except for use and occupancy restrictions of public record which are generally applicable to properties in the immediate neighborhood or the subdivision in which the Property is located and publicly recorded easements for public utilities and any other easements which may be observed by an inspection of the Property. Buyer expressly assumes the risk that restrictive covenants, zoning laws or other recorded documents may restrict or prohibit the use of the Property for the purpose(s) intended by Buyer. In the event Seller is unable to give good and merchantable title or such as can be insured by a Maryland licensed title insurer, with Buyer paying not more than the standard rate as filed with the Maryland Insurance Commissioner, Seller, at Seller's expense, shall have the option of curing any defect so as to enable Seller to give good and merchantable title or, if Buyer is willing to accept title without said defect being cured, paying any special premium on behalf of Buyer to obtain title insurance on the Property to the benefit of Buyer. In the event Seller elects to cure any defects in title, this Contract shall continue to remain in full force and effect; and the date of settlement shall be extended for a period not to exceed fourteen (14) additional days. If Seller is unable to cure such title defect(s) and is unable to obtain a policy of title insurance on the Property to the benefit of Buyer from a Maryland licensed title insurer, Buyer shall have the option of taking such title as Seller can give, or terminating this Contract and being reimbursed by Seller for cost of searching title as may have been incurred not to exceed 1/2 of 1% of the purchase price. In the latter event, there shall be no further liability or obligation on either of the parties hereto; and this Contract shall become null and void; and all Deposit(s) shall be disbursed in accordance with the Deposit paragraph of this Contract. In no event shall Broker(s) or their agent(s) have any liability for any defect in Seller's title.

21. CONDITION OF PROPERTY AND POSSESSION: At settlement, Seller shall deliver possession of the Property and shall deliver the Property vacant, clear of trash and debris, broom clean and in substantially the same condition as existed on the Date of Contract Acceptance. All electrical, heating, air conditioning, plumbing (including well and septic), and any other mechanical systems and related equipment, appliances and smoke detector(s) included in this Contract shall be in working condition. Buyer reserves the right to inspect the Property within five (5) days prior to settlement. **EXCEPT AS OTHERWISE SPECIFIED IN THIS CONTRACT, INCLUDING THIS PARAGRAPH, THE PROPERTY IS SOLD "AS IS"**. The obligations of Seller as provided in this paragraph shall be in addition to any Disclosure and Disclaimer Statement as required by Section 10-702, Real Property Article, Annotated Code of Maryland and any provision of any inspection contingency addendum made a part of this Contract (See Property Inspections and Condition Notice).

22. ADJUSTMENTS: Ground rent, homeowner's association fees, rent and water rent shall be adjusted and apportioned as of date of settlement; and all taxes, general or special, and all other public or governmental charges or assessments against the Property which are or may be payable on a periodic basis, including Metropolitan District Sanitary Commission, Washington Suburban Sanitary Commission, or other benefit charges, assessments, liens or encumbrances for sewer, water, drainage,

FIGURE 9.1

Maryland Association of REALTORS® Residential Sales Contract (continued)

paving, or other public improvements completed or commenced on or prior to the date hereof, or subsequent thereto, are to be adjusted and apportioned as of the date of settlement and are to be assumed and paid thereafter by Buyer, whether assessments have been levied or not as of date of settlement if applicable by local law. Any heating or cooking fuels remaining in supply tank(s) at time of settlement shall become the property of Buyer.

23. SETTLEMENT COSTS: Buyer agrees to pay all settlement costs and charges including, but not limited to, all Lender's fees in connection herewith, including title examination and title insurance fees, loan insurance premiums, all document preparation and recording fees, notary fees, survey fees where required, and all recording charges, except those incident to clearing existing encumbrances or title defects, except if Buyer is a Veteran obtaining VA financing, those prohibited to be paid by a Veteran obtaining VA financing, which prohibited charges shall be paid by Seller.

24. TRANSFER CHARGES:
       A. IN GENERAL. Section 14-104(b) of the Real Property Article, Annotated Code of Maryland provides that, unless otherwise negotiated in the contract or provided by State or local law, the cost of any recordation tax or any State or local Transfer Tax shall be shared equally between the Buyer and Seller.
       B. FIRST-TIME BUYER. Under Section 14-104(c) of the Real Property Article, the entire amount of recordation and local transfer tax shall be paid by the Seller of property that is sold to a first-time Maryland homebuyer, unless there is an express agreement that the recordation tax or any state or local transfer tax will not be paid entirely by the Seller.
RECORDATION AND LOCAL TRANSFER TAX. If the Buyer is a first-time Maryland homebuyer, Buyer and Seller <u>expressly agree</u>, in accordance with Section 14-104(c) of the Real Property Article, Annotated Code of Maryland, that payment of recordation tax and local transfer tax shall be shared equally between the Buyer and Seller unless a "First-time Maryland Homebuyer Transfer and Recordation Tax Addendum" is attached, which contains a different express agreement.
STATE TRANSFER TAX: Under Section 13-203(b) of the Tax-Property Article, Annotated Code of Maryland, the amount of state transfer tax due on the sale of property to a first-time Maryland homebuyer is reduced from 0.50% to 0.25% and shall be paid entirely by the Seller. Buyer is hereby notified that to ensure receipt of the above reduction, Buyer should so indicate on Page 9 of this Contract and complete the required affidavit at settlement indicating that the Buyer is a first-time Maryland homebuyer.

25. BROKER LIABILITY: Brokers, their agents, subagents and employees do not assume any responsibility for the condition of the Property or for the performance of this Contract by any or all parties hereto. By signing this Contract, Buyer and Seller acknowledge that they have not relied on any representations made by Brokers, or any agents, subagents or employees of Brokers, except those representations expressly set forth in this Contract.

26. BROKER'S FEE: All parties irrevocably instruct the settlement officer to collect the fee or compensation and disburse same according to the terms and conditions provided in the listing agreement and/or agency representation agreement. Settlement shall not be a condition precedent to payment of compensation.

27. SELLER RESPONSIBILITY: Seller agrees to keep existing mortgages free of default until settlement. All violation notices or requirements noted or issued by any governmental authority (including without limitation, any permit violation notices), or actions in any court on account thereof, against or affecting the Property at the date of settlement of this Contract, shall be complied with by Seller and the Property conveyed free thereof. The Property is to be held at the risk of Seller until legal title has passed or possession has been given to Buyer. If, prior to the time legal title has passed or possession has been given to Buyer, whichever shall occur first, all or a substantial part of the Property is destroyed or damaged, without fault of Buyer, then this Contract, at the option of Buyer, upon written notice to Seller, shall be null and void and of no further effect, and the deposits shall be disbursed in accordance with the Deposit paragraph of this Contract.

28. BUYER RESPONSIBILITY: If Buyer has misrepresented Buyer's financial ability to consummate the purchase of the Property, or if this Contract is contingent upon Buyer securing a written commitment for financing and Buyer fails to apply for such financing within the time period herein specified, or fails to pursue financing diligently and in good faith, or if Buyer makes any misrepresentations in any document relating to financing, or takes (or fails to take) any action which causes Buyer's disqualification for financing, then Buyer shall be in default; and Seller may elect by written notice to Buyer, to terminate this Contract and/or pursue the remedies set forth under the Default paragraph of this Contract.

29. HOMEOWNER'S ASSOCIATION: The Property is not part of a development subject to the imposition of mandatory fees as defined by the Maryland Homeowner's Association Act, unless acknowledged by attached addendum.

30. GROUND RENT: If the Property is subject to ground rent and the ground rent is not timely paid, the ground lease holder (i.e., the person to whom the ground rent is payable) may bring an action under Section 8-402.3 of the Real Property Article, Annotated Code of Maryland. As a result of this action, a lien may be placed upon the property. If the Property is subject to ground rent, Sections 14-116 and 14-116.1 of the Real Property Article provide the purchaser, upon obtaining ownership of the Property, with certain rights and responsibilities relative to the ground rent. (If the Property is subject to ground rent: See Property Subject to Ground Rent Addendum.)

FIGURE 9.1

Maryland Association of REALTORS® Residential Sales Contract (continued)

31. SALE/SETTLEMENT OR LEASE OF OTHER REAL ESTATE: Neither this Contract nor the granting of Buyer's loan referred to herein is to be conditioned or contingent in any manner upon the sale, settlement and/or lease of any other real estate unless a contingency for the sale, settlement and/or lease of other real estate is contained in an addendum to this Contract. Unless this Contract is expressly contingent upon the sale, settlement and/or lease of any other real estate, Buyer shall neither apply for nor accept a financing loan commitment which is contingent upon or requires as a pre-condition to funding that any other real estate be sold, settled and/or leased.

32. LEASES: Seller may neither negotiate new leases nor renew existing leases for the Property which extend beyond settlement or possession date without Buyer's written consent.

33. DEFAULT: Buyer and Seller are required and agree to make full settlement in accordance with the terms of this Contract and acknowledge that failure to do so constitutes a breach hereof. If Buyer fails to make full settlement or is in default due to Buyer's failure to comply with the terms, covenants and conditions of this Contract, the initial Deposit and additional Deposits (the "Deposit") may be retained by Seller as long as a Release of Deposit Agreement is signed and executed by all parties, expressing that said Deposit may be retained by Seller. In the event the parties do not agree to execute a Release of Deposit Agreement, Buyer and Seller shall have all legal and equitable remedies. If Seller fails to make full settlement or is in default due to Seller's failure to comply with the terms, covenants and conditions of this Contract, Buyer shall be entitled to pursue such rights and remedies as may be available, at law or in equity, including, without limitation, an action for specific performance of this Contract and/or monetary damages. In the event of any litigation or dispute between Buyer and Seller concerning the release of the Deposit, Broker's sole responsibility may be met, at Broker's option, by paying the Deposit into the court in which such litigation is pending, or by paying the Deposit into the court of proper jurisdiction by an action of interpleader. Buyer and Seller agree that, upon Broker's payment of the Deposit into the court, neither Buyer nor Seller shall have any further right, claim, demand or action against Broker regarding the release of the Deposit; and Buyer and Seller, jointly and severally, shall indemnify and hold Broker harmless from any and all such rights, claims, demands or actions. In the event of such dispute and election by Broker to file an action of interpleader as herein provided, Buyer and Seller further agree and hereby expressly and irrevocably authorize Broker to deduct from the Deposit all costs incurred by Broker in the filing and maintenance of such action of interpleader including but not limited to filing fees, court costs, service of process fees and attorneys' fees, provided that the amount deducted shall not exceed the lesser of $500 or the amount of the Deposit held by Broker. All such fees and costs authorized herein to be deducted may be deducted by Broker from the Deposit prior to paying the balance of the Deposit to the court. Buyer and Seller further agree and expressly declare that all such fees and costs so deducted shall be the exclusive property of Broker. If the amount deducted by Broker is less than the total of all of the costs incurred by Broker in filing and maintaining the interpleader action, then Buyer and Seller jointly, and severally, agree to reimburse Broker for all such excess costs upon the conclusion of the interpleader action.

34. MEDIATION OF DISPUTES: Mediation is a process by which the parties attempt to resolve a dispute or claim with the assistance of a neutral mediator who is authorized to facilitate the resolution of the dispute. The mediator has no authority to make an award, to impose a resolution of the dispute or claim upon the parties or to require the parties to continue mediation if the parties do not desire to do so. Buyer and Seller agree that any dispute or claim arising out of or from this Contract or the transaction which is the subject of this Contract shall be mediated through the Maryland Association of REALTORS®, Inc. or its member local boards/associations in accordance with the established Mediation Rules and Guidelines of the Association or through such other mediator or mediation service as mutually agreed upon by Buyer and Seller, in writing. Unless otherwise agreed in writing by the parties, mediation fees, costs and expenses shall be divided and paid equally by the parties to the mediation. If either party elects to have an attorney present that party shall pay his or her own attorney's fees.

Buyer and Seller further agree that the obligation of Buyer and Seller to mediate as herein provided shall apply to all disputes or claims arising whether prior to, during or within one (1) year following the actual contract settlement date or when settlement should have occurred. Buyer and Seller agree that neither party shall commence any action in any court regarding a dispute or claim arising out of or from this Contract or the transaction which is the subject of this Contract, without first mediating the dispute or claim, unless the right to pursue such action or the ability to protect an interest or pursue a remedy as provided in this Contract, would be precluded by the delay of the mediation. In the event the right to pursue such action, or the ability to protect an interest or pursue a remedy would be precluded by the delay, Buyer or Seller may commence the action only if the initial pleading or document commencing such action is accompanied by a request to stay the proceeding pending the conclusion of the mediation. If a party initiates or commences an action in violation of this provision, the party agrees to pay all costs and expenses, including reasonable attorneys' fees, incurred by the other party to enforce the obligation as provided herein. The provisions of this paragraph shall survive closing and shall not be deemed to have been extinguished by merger with the deed.

35. ATTORNEY'S FEES: In any action or proceeding between Buyer and Seller based, in whole or in part, upon the performance or non-performance of the terms and conditions of this Contract, including, but not limited to, breach of contract, negligence, misrepresentation or fraud, the prevailing party in such action or proceeding shall be entitled to receive reasonable attorney's fees from the other party as determined by the court or arbitrator. In any action or proceeding between Buyer and Seller and/or between Buyer and Broker(s) and/or Seller and Broker(s) resulting in Broker(s) being made a party to such action or proceeding, including, but not limited to, any litigation, arbitration, or complaint and claim before the Maryland Real Estate

F I G U R E   9.1

Maryland Association of REALTORS® Residential Sales Contract (continued)

Commission, whether as defendant, cross-defendant, third-party defendant or respondent, Buyer and Seller jointly and severally, agree to indemnify and hold Broker(s) harmless from and against any and all liability, loss, cost, damages or expenses (including filing fees, court costs, service of process fees, transcript fees and attorneys' fees) incurred by Broker(s) in such action or proceeding, providing that such action or proceeding does not result in a judgment against Broker(s).

As used in this Contract, the term "Broker(s)" shall mean: (a) the two (2) Brokers as identified on Page 10 of this Contract; (b) the two (2) named Sales Associates identified on Page 10 of the Contract; and (c) any agent, subagent, salesperson, independent contractor and/or employees of Broker(s). The term "Broker(s)" shall also mean, in the singular, any or either of the named Broker(s) and/or Sales Associate(s) as identified or, in the plural, both of the named Brokers and/or Sales Associates as identified.

This Paragraph shall apply to any and all such action(s) or proceeding(s) against Broker(s) including those action(s) or proceeding(s) based, in whole or in part, upon any alleged act(s) or omission(s) by Broker(s), including, but not limited to, any alleged act of misrepresentation, fraud, non-disclosure, negligence, violation of any statutory or common law duty, or breach of fiduciary duty by Broker(s). The provision of this Paragraph shall survive closing and shall not be deemed to have been extinguished by merger with the deed.

36. NOTICE OF BUYER'S RIGHT TO SELECT SETTLEMENT SERVICE PROVIDERS: Buyer has the right to select Buyer's own title insurance company, title lawyer, settlement company, escrow company, mortgage lender or financial institution as defined in the Financial Institutions Article, Annotated Code of Maryland. Buyer acknowledges that Seller may not be prohibited from offering owner financing as a condition of settlement.

37. LIMITED WARRANTY: NOTICE TO BUYER: IF A WARRANTY PLAN IS BEING OFFERED WITH THE PURCHASE OF THE PROPERTY, IT MAY BE A LIMITED WARRANTY. SINCE SUCH WARRANTY PLANS DO NOT COVER STRUCTURAL DEFECTS AND MAY NOT COVER PRE-EXISTING DEFECTS, BUYER SHOULD REQUEST THE REAL ESTATE AGENT TO PROVIDE BUYER WITH ANY BROCHURE WHICH DESCRIBES THE PLAN IN ORDER TO DETERMINE THE EXTENT OF COVERAGE PROVIDED BY THE WARRANTY.

38. PROPERTY INSURANCE BROCHURE: An informational brochure published by the Maryland Association of REALTORS®, Inc. titled "The New Reality of Property Insurance – What You Should Know" is available to explain current issues relative to obtaining insurance coverage for the Property to be purchased.

39. GUARANTY FUND: NOTICE TO BUYER: BUYER IS PROTECTED BY THE REAL ESTATE GUARANTY FUND OF THE MARYLAND REAL ESTATE COMMISSION, UNDER SECTION 17-404 OF THE BUSINESS OCCUPATIONS AND PROFESSIONS ARTICLE OF THE ANNOTATED CODE OF MARYLAND, FOR LOSSES IN AN AMOUNT NOT EXCEEDING $50,000 FOR ANY CLAIM.

40. SINGLE FAMILY RESIDENTIAL REAL PROPERTY DISCLOSURE NOTICE: Buyer is advised of the right to receive a "Disclosure and Disclaimer Statement" from Seller (Section 10-702 Real Property Article, Annotated Code of Maryland).

41. MARYLAND NON-RESIDENT SELLER: If the Property is not the Seller's principal residence and the Seller is a non-resident individual of the State of Maryland or is a non-resident entity which is not formed under the laws of the State of Maryland or qualified to do business in the State of Maryland, a withholding tax from the proceeds of sale may be withheld at the time of settlement except as otherwise provided by Maryland law. (See Maryland Non-Resident Seller Transfer Withholding Tax Addendum.)

42. INTERNAL REVENUE SERVICE FILING: Buyer and Seller each agree to cooperate with the settlement officer by providing all necessary information so that a report can be filed with the Internal Revenue Service, as required by Section 6045 of the IRS Code. To the extent permitted by law, any fees incurred as a result of such filing will be paid by the Seller.

43. NOTICE TO BUYER CONCERNING THE CHESAPEAKE AND ATLANTIC COASTAL BAYS CRITICAL AREA: Buyer is advised that all or a portion of the property may be located in the "Critical Area" of the Chesapeake and Atlantic Coastal Bays, and that additional zoning, land use, and resource protection regulations apply in this area. The "Critical Area" generally consists of all land and water areas within 1,000 feet beyond the landward boundaries of state or private wetlands, the Chesapeake Bay, the Atlantic Coastal Bays, and all of their tidal tributaries. The "Critical Area" also includes the waters of and lands under the Chesapeake Bay, the Atlantic Coastal Bays and all of their tidal tributaries to the head of tide. For information as to whether the property is located within the Critical Area, Buyer may contact the local Department of Planning and Zoning, which maintains maps showing the extent of the Critical Area in the jurisdiction. Allegany, Carroll, Frederick, Garrett, Howard, Montgomery and Washington Counties do not include land located in the Critical Area.

44. WETLANDS NOTICE: Buyer is advised that if all or a portion of the Property being purchased is wetlands, the approval of the U.S. Army Corps of Engineers will be necessary before a building permit can be issued for the Property. Additionally, the future use of existing dwellings may be restricted due to wetlands. The Corps has adopted a broad definition of wetlands which

FIGURE 9.1

Maryland Association of REALTORS® Residential Sales Contract (continued)

encompasses a large portion of the Chesapeake Bay Region. Other portions of the State may also be considered wetlands. For information as to whether the Property includes wetlands, Buyer may contact the Baltimore District of the U.S. Army Corps of Engineers. Buyer may also elect, at Buyer's expense, to engage the services of a qualified specialist to inspect the Property for the presence of wetlands prior to submitting a written offer to purchase the Property; or Buyer may include in Buyer's written offer a clause making Buyer's purchase of the Property contingent upon a satisfactory wetlands inspection.

45. FOREST CONSERVATION ACT NOTICE: If the Property is a tract of land 40,000 square feet or more in size, Buyer is notified that, unless exempted by applicable law, as a prerequisite to any subdivision plan or grading or sediment control permit for the Property, Buyer will be required to comply with the provisions of the Maryland Forest Conservation Act imposed by Section 5-1601, et seq. of the Natural Resources Article, Annotated Code of Maryland, including, among other things, the submission and acceptance of a Forest Stand Delineation and a Forest Conservation Plan for the Property in accordance with applicable laws and regulations. Unless otherwise expressly set forth in an addendum to this Contract, Seller represents and warrants that the Property is not currently subject to a Forest Conservation Plan, Management Agreement or any other pending obligation binding the owner of the Property under said Act; further, Seller represents and warrants that no activities have been undertaken on the Property by Seller in violation of the Forest Conservation Act.

46. NOTICE CONCERNING CONSERVATION EASEMENTS: If the Property is encumbered by a Conservation Easement as defined in Section 10-705 of the Real Property Article, Annotated Code of Maryland, the contract must contain a notice concerning the easement, which is contained in an attached addendum. This Paragraph does not apply to the sale of property in an action to foreclose a mortgage or deed of trust. (If the Property is encumbered by a Conservation Easement: See Conservation Easement Addendum.)

47. FOREIGN INVESTMENT TAXES-FIRPTA: Section 1445 of the United States Internal Revenue Code of 1986 provides that a Buyer of residential real property located in the United States must withhold federal income taxes from the payment of the purchase price if (a) the purchase price exceeds Three Hundred Thousand Dollars ($300,000.00) and (b) the seller is a foreign person. Unless otherwise stated in an addendum attached hereto, if the purchase price is in excess of Three Hundred Thousand Dollars ($300,000.00), Seller represents that Seller is not a non-resident alien, foreign corporation, foreign partnership, foreign trust or foreign estate (as those terms are defined by the Internal Revenue Code and applicable regulations) and agrees to execute an affidavit to this effect at the time of settlement.

48. CRIMINAL ACTIVITY AND SEXUAL OFFENDERS. Buyer may contact the state, county or municipal police departments in which the Property is located or check the "Sex Offender Registry" at the Maryland Department of Public Safety and Correctional Services website in order to ascertain criminal activity in the vicinity of the Property or the presence of registered sexual offenders who live or work within the vicinity of the Property. Buyer acknowledges that Buyer is solely responsible to inquire of such matters before signing this Contract. Buyer shall have no right to cancel this Contract based upon criminal activity or the presence of registered sexual offenders in the vicinity of the Property. Buyer further acknowledges that no real estate licensee involved in the sale or purchase of the Property, whether acting as the agent for Seller or Buyer, has any duty nor assumes any duty or responsibility to ascertain criminal activity or the presence of registered sexual offenders in the vicinity of the Property.

49. MILITARY INSTALLATIONS: This Section does not apply in Allegany, Carroll, Frederick, Garrett, Howard, Montgomery, and Washington Counties. Buyer is advised that the Property may be located near a military installation that conducts flight operations, munitions testing, or military operations that may result in high noise levels.

50. NOTICE TO THE PARTIES:
  (A) NO REPRESENTATIONS: Brokers, their agents, subagents and employees, make no representations with respect to: (1) Water quantity, quality, color, or taste or operating conditions of public and/or private water systems;
  (2) Location, size or operating condition of on-site sewage disposal systems;
  (3) The extensions of public utilities by local municipal authorities, existence or availability of public utilities, and any assessments, fees or costs for public utilities which might be imposed by local municipal authorities or private entities, should public utilities be extended or available to the subject Property. (Buyer should consult the Department of Public Works to determine the availability of proposed future extensions of utilities.);
  (4) Lot size and exact location. If the subject Property is part of a recorded subdivision, Buyer can review the plat upon request at the Record Office. If the subject Property is not part of a recorded subdivision, Buyer may verify exact size and location through a survey by a licensed engineer or land surveyor, at Buyer's expense;
  (5) Existing zoning or permitted uses of the Property, including, without limitation, whether any improvements to the Property required permit(s) and, if so, whether such improvements, were completed pursuant to permit(s) issued and/or whether any permit(s) issued were complied with. Buyer should contact the appropriate local government agency and/or a licensed engineer to verify zoning, permit issuance/status, and permitted uses; or
  (6) Whether properly licensed contractors have been used to make repairs, renovations and improvements to the Property.

F I G U R E   9.1

Maryland Association of REALTORS® Residential Sales Contract (continued)

(B) NO ADVISING: Brokers/agents are not advising the parties as to certain other issues, including without limitation: soil conditions; flood hazard areas; possible restrictions of the use of property due to restrictive covenants, subdivision, environmental laws, easements or other documents; airport or aircraft noise; planned land use, roads or highways; and construction materials and/or hazardous materials, including without limitation flame retardant treated plywood (FRT), radon, radium, mold spores, urea formaldehyde foam insulation (UFFI), synthetic stucco (EIFS), asbestos, polybutylene piping and lead-based paint. Information relating to these issues may be available from appropriate governmental authorities. This disclosure is not intended to provide an inspection contingency.

(C) COMPENSATION OF VENDORS: Buyer and Seller each assume full responsibility for selecting and compensating their respective vendors.

(D) PROTECTION OF HOMEOWNERS IN FORECLOSURE ACT NOTICE: BUYER AND SELLER ACKNOWLEDGE THAT, UNDER SECTION 7-310 OF THE REAL PROPERTY ARTICLE OF THE ANNOTATED CODE OF MARYLAND, IF THE MORTGAGE ON THE PROPERTY IS AT LEAST 60 DAYS IN DEFAULT ON THE DATE OF CONTRACT ACCEPTANCE, SELLER HAS THE RIGHT TO RESCIND THE CONTRACT WITHIN 5 DAYS AFTER THE DATE OF CONTRACT ACCEPTANCE. ANY PROVISION IN THIS CONTRACT OR OTHER AGREEMENT THAT ATTEMPTS OR PURPORTS TO WAIVE ANY OF THE SELLER'S RIGHTS UNDER SECTION 7-310 IS VOID.

51. PROPERTY TAX NOTICE - 60 DAY APPEAL: If any real property is transferred after January 1 and before the beginning of the next taxable year to a new owner, the new owner may submit a written appeal as to a value or classification on or before 60 days after the date of the transfer.

52. NON-ASSIGNABILITY: This Contract may not be assigned without the written consent of Buyer and Seller. If Buyer and Seller agree in writing to an assignment of this Contract, the original parties to this Contract remain obligated hereunder until settlement.

53. PARAGRAPH HEADINGS: The Paragraph headings of this Contract are for convenience and reference only, and in no way define or limit the intent, rights or obligations of the parties.

54. COMPUTATION OF DAYS: As used in this Contract, and in any addendum or addenda to this Contract, the term "days" shall mean consecutive calendar days, including Saturdays, Sundays, and holidays, whether federal, state, local or religious. A day shall be measured from 12:00:01 a.m. to and including 11:59:59 p.m. E.S.T. For the purposes of calculating days, the count of "days" shall begin on the day following the day upon which any act or notice as provided in this Contract, or any addendum or addenda to this Contract, was required to be performed or made.

55. ENTIRE AGREEMENT: This Contract and any addenda thereto contain the final and entire agreement between the parties, and neither they nor their agents shall be bound by any terms, conditions, statements, warranties or representations, oral or written, not herein contained. The parties to this Contract mutually agree that it is binding upon them, their heirs, executors, administrators, personal representatives, successors and, if permitted as herein provided, assigns. Once signed, the terms of this Contract can only be changed by a document executed by all parties. This Contract shall be interpreted and construed in accordance with the laws of the State of Maryland. It is further agreed that this Contract may be executed in counterparts, each of which when considered together shall constitute the original Contract.

56. ELECTRONIC DELIVERY: The parties agree that this Contract offer shall be deemed validly executed and delivered by a party if a party executes this Contract and delivers a copy of the executed Contract to the other party by telefax or telecopier transmittal, or delivers a digital image of the executed document by email transmittal.

_____   _____   _____   _____
Buyer's Signature   Date   Seller's Signature   Date

_____   _____   _____   _____
Buyer's Signature   Date   Seller's Signature   Date

DATE OF CONTRACT ACCEPTANCE: _____

□ **Check if First-Time Maryland Homebuyer**

FIGURE 9.1

Maryland Association of REALTORS® Residential Sales Contract (continued)

Contact Information:

BUYER / NAME(S): _____

MAILING ADDRESS: _____

_____

SELLER / NAME(S): _____

MAILING ADDRESS: _____

_____

Information provided for reference only:

LISTING BROKER: _____   BRANCH OFFICE: _____

OFFICE PHONE: _____ FAX: _____ BROKER/AGENT MLS ID:_____

OFFICE ADDRESS: _____

SALES ASSOCIATE: _____ E-Mail: _____ PHONE: _____

ACTING AS: □ LISTING BROKER AND SELLER AGENT; OR
              □ INTRA - COMPANY AGENT WITH BROKER AS DUAL AGENT

SELLING BROKER: _____   BRANCH OFFICE: _____

OFFICE PHONE: _____ FAX: _____ BROKER/AGENT MLS ID:_____

OFFICE ADDRESS: _____

SALES ASSOCIATE: _____ E-Mail: _____ PHONE: _____

ACTING AS: □ SELLER AGENT (WHETHER "COOPERATING AGENT" OR "SELLING AGENT"); OR
              □ BUYER AGENT; OR
              □ INTRA - COMPANY AGENT WITH BROKER AS DUAL AGENT

■ INFORMATION REQUIRED IN CONTRACTS

In certain circumstances, Maryland statutes require that licensees include specific information in contracts. Other information is required in all contracts of sale, even when the sellers are not licensees and are simply selling their own property. Unless otherwise specifically agreed, a contract of sale is generally not made invalid by the omission of required disclosures, such as those discussed here.

Deferred Water and Sewer Charges

All contracts for the sale of improved residential real property must disclose the estimated cost of any deferred water and sewer charges for which the purchaser may become liable. Violation of this disclosure requirement entitles the initial purchaser of the improved property to recover from the seller twice the amount of deferred charges the purchaser would be obligated to pay during the five years of payments following the sale.

Disclosure of Licensee Status

When licensees themselves are either the sellers or purchasers of real estate, they must notify the other party they are licensees. This notification must be in writing and is typically made within the contract itself.

Presence of Ground Rent

A real estate sales contract must disclose any ground rent or leasehold interest involved in the sale. If the ground rent is presently irredeemable, this fact must be indicated. If the ground rent is to be redeemed at the time of settlement, responsibility for notice, costs of redemption, and so forth should be fixed as part of the written agreement.

A contract for the sale of real property subject to a ground rent must contain a notice of the existence of the ground rent and a warning that if ground rent is not paid on time, the reversionary owner of the ground rent may have a lien for unpaid ground rent placed on the property and then bring an action to foreclose the lien and seek possession. If these actions are successful, a ground landlord can become the fee simple owner of both the land and all improvements (houses) on it.

Allocation of Recordation Fees and Transfer Tax

The Brokers Act requires that every contract for use in the sale of residential property that is used as a dwelling place for one or two single-family units must contain the following statement in conspicuous type or handwritten: "Section 14-104 of the Real Property Article of the Annotated Code of Maryland provides that, unless otherwise negotiated in the contract or provided by local law, the cost of any recordation tax or any state or local transfer tax shall be shared equally between the buyer and seller."

Notwithstanding this statement, the *First-Time Home Buyers Closing Cost Reduction Act* of 1995 reduces the State transfer tax from 0.5% to 0.25% in transactions involving first-time homebuyers, with that entire amount to be paid by the seller. In such a transaction, the seller must also pay the entire amount of recordation and local transfer tax unless there is an express agreement between the parties to the contrary. Other details on this matter appeared in Chapter 8 of this book.

Notice of HOA Fees

If the property is subject to a homeowners association (HOA) and to the imposition of mandatory HOA fees, this fact must be disclosed to purchasers in the purchase agreement, usually by reference to the public record. Similar reference should be included about a residential property within a condominium regime.

Limit on Buyer Protection from Guaranty Fund

Contracts for the sale of real estate must contain a notice of purchaser protection by the Real Estate Guaranty Fund for actual losses in an amount not to exceed $50,000 for any one transaction.

Handling of Earnest (Deposit) Monies

A real estate broker must promptly place all earnest (deposit) monies in a special non-interest-bearing account, unless directed to do otherwise by both buyer and seller. Contracts in which a licensee holds an earnest deposit should also authorize that broker to disperse the deposit according to the rules now contained in Section 505 of the Brokers Act (Title 17). Details of these rules are found in Chapter 3, under "Disposition of Trust Money."

Choice of Settlement and Similar Service Providers

The Brokers Act mandates that contracts state that a licensee may not require buyers of single-family dwellings to employ specific title insurance, settlement, or escrow companies or title attorneys; buyers may choose their own. (See Chapter 1.)

Agricultural Land Transfer Tax

Every seller is required to notify the purchaser when land being transferred may be subject to agricultural land transfer tax. The statewide MAR Residential Contract of Sale provides that sellers who fail to notify buyers in accordance with this requirement are liable to those buyers for the agricultural land transfer tax that the buyers will have to pay. This provision can, of course, be removed from the contract language by negotiation before it is signed.

Conservation Easements Disclosure

The purchaser has a right to rescind a contract encumbered by a conservation easement if:

- the seller fails to give, on or before entering into the contract of sale, or within 20 days afterward, a copy of all conservation easements encumbering the property; and
- the contract of sale fails to contain a statement with specified /information about the conservation easement and the purchaser's rights and responsibilities, in conspicuous type to the effect that:

    this property is encumbered by one or more conservation easements or other restrictions limiting or affecting uses of the property and owned by the Maryland Environmental Trust, the Maryland Historical Trust, the Maryland Agricultural Land Preservation Foundation, the Maryland Department of Natural Resources, or a land trust (the "Conservation

Easements"). Maryland law requires that the seller deliver to the buyer copies of all Conservation Easements, ...

and notice of the requirement that, within 30 calendar days after the property is sold, the purchaser must give notice of the transfer, including specified information, to the owner of the conservation easement.

"Critical Areas"

All contracts for sale of property suitable for one or two single-family units are required to contain the following language:

> ### *Notice to Buyer Concerning the Chesapeake and Atlantic Coastal Bays Critical Area*
>
> Buyer is advised that all or a portion of the property may be located in the "Critical Area" of the Chesapeake and Atlantic Coastal Bays, and that additional zoning, land use, and resource protection regulations apply in this area. The "Critical Area" generally consists of all land and water areas within 1,000 feet beyond the landward boundaries of state or private wetlands, the Chesapeake Bay, the Atlantic Coastal Bays, and all of their tidal tributaries. The "Critical Area" also includes the waters of and lands under the Chesapeake Bay, the Atlantic Coastal Bays, and all of their tidal tributaries to the head of tide. For information as to whether the property is located within the Critical Area, buyer may contact the local Department of Planning and Zoning, which maintains maps showing the extent of the Critical Area in the jurisdiction. Allegany, Carroll, Frederick, Garrett, Howard, Montgomery, and Washington Counties do not include land located in the Critical Area.

Note that the previous paragraph must be used in contracts for all counties, even those that are not included in the critical area.

Notice of Possible High Noise Levels Due to Military Installations

A notice using the following wording must appear in residential sales transactions in all areas of the State except Allegany, Carroll, Frederick, Garrett, Howard, Montgomery, and Washington counties. However, all local laws requiring a statement or notice substantially similar to this statement shall prevail over this requirement: "Buyer is advised that the property may be located near a military installation that conducts flight operations, munitions testing, or military operations that may result in high noise levels."

Other Required Clauses

The *Real Property* Article requires that contracts of sale must also include the following notices and disclosures, where applicable:

- Notice pertaining to sale of real property in Prince George's County creating subdivision
- Notice pertaining to resale of condominium unit
- Notice pertaining to initial sale of lot in development containing more than 12 lots
- Notice pertaining to resale of any lot or initial sale of lot in development containing 12 or fewer lots

- Notice pertaining to initial sale of lot not intended to be occupied or rented for residential purposes
- Notice pertaining to initial sale of cooperative interests
- Notice of liability for agricultural land transfer tax
- Notice to purchaser pertaining to sale of certain land in Prince George's County if the land being sold is subject to a development impact fee and the unpaid amount of that fee
- Notice pertaining to sale of certain agriculturally assessed land in St. Mary's and Charles counties

Baltimore City and most counties have various additional contract requirements unique to their jurisdictions. Information about these requirements is available from local boards or associations for use by their members. For example, contracts for the sale of multiple-dwelling property in Baltimore City must contain a clause whereby the seller guarantees that the property being purchased complies with the Baltimore City Multiple-Dwelling Code and that the license will be delivered to the buyer at the time of settlement.

Property in Maryland not served by public sewerage and water systems is subject to the State Department of Health and Mental Hygiene laws and regulations pertaining to individual sewerage disposal systems and wells. The licensee must provide the buyer of unimproved land with a notice that if the property being purchased is to be used for residential purposes, the buyer, before signing the contract, should ascertain the status of sewerage and water facilities and, if required, whether the property will be approved for installation of a well and/or private sewerage system.

The U.S. Department of Veterans Affairs (VA), the Federal Housing Administration (FHA), and many private lenders require an evaluation by the local health department of the sewerage system and the water supply on residential property prior to settlement. When this is required, a bacteriologic sample must be collected from the well and analyzed by the health department. Consequently, licensees involved in such a transaction must allow sufficient time for these procedures when estimating a settlement date. Assistance and information are available from the Department of Health and Mental Hygiene, O'Connor Building, 201 W. Preston Street, Baltimore, MD 21201 or from local health boards.

Although the law requires such notices, the absence of one or more does not make a sales agreement unenforceable or voidable. However, certain elements are material to the formation of an enforceable contract. The absence of one or more of them would make a contract unenforceable. For examples, signatures of all parties, clear statement of mutual consideration, legal description of the property sufficient to identify it with reasonable certainty, illegality of purpose, time of settlement, and so forth.

Contingency and Other Clauses

To express the exact agreement of the parties to a contract and to protect the best interests of their clients, licensees often employ contingency and other addenda. Licensees should avoid drafting the language of such clauses themselves but rather make use of forms with wording drafted by competent legal counsel. Such forms are typically available from realty boards and associations of which licensees are members. Additional disclosure clauses and contingency language often address such matters as the following:

- Details of financing
- Impact of appraisal
- Buyer's prompt loan application and receipt of lender's commitment
- Lenders' fees and charges and who will receive the benefit of any favorable changes due to market conditions
- Home inspections and their impact
- Sale of purchasers' home and any release (kickout) clause
- Existence and extent of any leasehold interests
- Disposition of any agricultural crops
- Party to pay fees for IRS filing
- Requirements for mediation
- Limitations on participating brokers' (and their affiliates') liability for any untoward happening
- Agreement to following English Rule for payment of attorneys after a dispute is decided
- Placing the risk of casualty loss upon the seller until such time as the purchaser occupies or settlement is held
- Assurance that the seller will deliver the property free from municipal (or similar) code violations of which the seller has been notified
- Seller's commitment to deliver possession upon settlement or other specified date
- Details of any presettlement occupancy agreement
- Various inspection contingencies
- Presence of any financial contingencies

Survival

A statement in a contract asserting that the entire contract (or specific portions) shall survive and not be merged into the deed allows enforcement of unperformed portions of that contract after settlement for either 3 or 12 years from the date of the contract. If no "survival" language appears in a contract, its terms are merged into the deed at settlement (i.e., they are no longer subject to suits for enforcement after delivery of deed at settlement). To be "merged" could better be thought of as "submerged"—as in "drowned."

Release from Contract of Sale

When one party is unable or unwilling to consummate a contract of sale, and the other party agrees to release that party, the broker should provide a competently drafted release form for signatures of both parties. If, on the other hand, the parties do not agree, upon release, as to how any deposits are to be distributed, the broker is free to follow the statutory procedure contained in § 17-505 of the Brokers Act as described in Chapter 3.

■ OPTION AGREEMENTS

In Maryland, a lease purchase option agreement is a lease agreement containing a clause that gives the tenant some power to purchase the landlord's interest in real property. No lease option purchase of improved residential property is valid in Maryland unless it contains the statement in capital letters "THIS IS NOT A CONTRACT TO BUY" and a clear statement of the option agreement's purpose and effect with respect to the purchase of the property that is the subject of the option.

Even though details of times, prices, dates, financing, prorations, settlement expenses, and so forth—everything needed for a contract of sale—are clearly set forth in the option, it still "IS NOT A CONTRACT TO BUY." It is, rather, a unilateral contract that would become bilateral and binding on both parties only if option rights are exercised by the optionee.

Similarly a lease with an option to renew is not a contract to renew but still should contain all details of the situation created should the optionee decide to exercise the option and renew (e.g., recitation of any changes in rent or other significant matter and reiteration, by reference to the original agreement, of other details that would not change).

In every option, an option price (consideration for the option itself) must be recited in addition to the price or rental to be paid were the option to be exercised. Enforceability does not depend upon the size of the amount paid for the option price—only the fact that some amount was paid.

■ CONSTRUCTION CONTRACTS

Maryland law now requires automatic fire sprinklers in the construction of new town homes and new one- and two-family unit residential units. There are exemptions for new construction not connected to any electrical utility (Amish exemption); and—until 2016—any properties with building permits issued for properties on lots subject to existing public works utility agreements executed before March 1, 2012; or for building permits on lots served by existing water service lines that are less than one inch and installed by March 1, 2012.

■ NEW HOME WARRANTIES AND DEPOSITS

Before entering into contracts for sale or construction of new homes, builders must disclose to purchasers on a State-mandated form whether they participate in a new home warranty security plan and the extent of that plan. If builders do not participate in a new home warranty plan, they must disclose, among other things, that without a new home warranty, the purchaser may be afforded only certain limited (statutory) warranties.

The disclosure must also state that builders of new homes, although registered, are not required to be licensed by the State and are not required to be licensed by most local jurisdictions. Purchasers who acknowledge by their signature that they have been so informed then have five working days to rescind their contract and recover all money paid for their purchases. Contracts for purchase or construction of new homes that do not contain this notice are voidable by the buyers. Builders are required to register with the Home Builder and Home Builder Sales Representative Registration Unit in the Consumer Protection Division of the Office of the Maryland Attorney General, thus bringing some oversight of that industry under State government influence. If builders' registrations are revoked, they are no longer allowed to sell homes they have built. Salespersons selling a registered builder's new homes need to be similarly registered but do not need to hold real estate sales licenses. The fee for their registration for a two-year period is $200. Builders pay a $600 fee.

Any person knowingly misrepresenting the existence of a new home warranty is subject to a fine not exceeding $50,000, imprisonment for not more than two years, or both, in addition to other penalties provided by the *Real Property* Article.

In connection with the sale and purchase of new, single-family residential units, including condominiums that are not completed at the time of contracting the sale, if the vendor or builder obligates purchasers to pay any sum of money before units have been completed and the realty has been granted to the purchaser, the builder or vendor is required to

- deposit or hold those sums in an escrow account to ensure their return to purchasers who are entitled to them, or
- obtain and maintain a corporate surety bond to provide return of deposits to purchasers who are entitled to them.

The Maryland Custom Home Protection Act, found in the *Real Property* Article, provides certain protections for buyers of newly constructed homes. This law sets standards for contract payments, surety bonds, contract requirements, mortgage loans, and sales by licensed real estate brokers. Detailed provisions govern brokers' handling of deposit monies.

■ INSTALLMENT CONTRACTS

Maryland statutes provide protections for purchasers of residential property under installment contracts, which are stronger than the protections provided by common law. Some Maryland requirements for sale of residential property by installment contract are presented in Chapter 12. The principles text presents general information on installment contracts in its chapters on contracts and finance.

■ DISCLOSURE REQUIREMENTS OF INITIAL SALES OF CONDOMINIUMS

A contract for the initial sale or resale of a condominium unit requires the disclosure of certain information to the purchaser before the execution of the contract. The buyer of a condominium unit has 15 days (for initial sale) or 7 days (for resale) from the signing of such a contract within which to freely rescind the agreement without stating any reason. Looking at the law's requirements from another perspective, the developer must deliver all required papers to condominium purchasers 15 days prior to settlement. Purchasers cannot waive this requirement in a sales contract. However, they are permitted to proceed to settlement without having received the required papers. If they do so, they still retain the right to rescind the transaction for up to one year. A contract for the initial sale of a residential condominium unit to a member of the public must also contain notice of the developer's warranties.

■ RESIDENTIAL PROPERTY DISCLOSURE AND DISCLAIMER STATEMENT

The required use of the Residential Property Disclosure and Disclaimer Statement is presented in Chapter 4. Failure to present the statement to purchasers in a timely fashion may enable them to rescind the contract as late as the day when settlement is to take place—or at least until they apply for the loan required for the purchase.

Use of the Disclosure and Disclaimer Statement is not required in:

- the initial sale of a single-family residential real property that has never been occupied or for which a certificate of occupancy has been issued within one year before the seller and buyer enter into a contract;
- the transfer of properties exempt from transfer tax under the *Tax-Property* Article (land installment contracts and certain options to purchase require the use of the statement);
- sale by a lender, an affiliate, or a subsidiary of a lender of property acquired by foreclosure or by deed in lieu of foreclosure;
- a sheriff's sale, tax sale, or sale by foreclosure, partition, or court-appointed trustee;
- a transfer by a fiduciary in the course of the administration of a decedent's estate, guardianship, conservatorship, or trust;
- the transfer of a single-family residential real property to be converted by the buyer into use other than residential use or to be demolished; or the sale of unimproved real property.

■ RETENTION OF AGENCY DISCLOSURE FORMS

Even if the transaction to which they are related never reaches settlement, all agency disclosure form originals— Understanding Whom Real Estate Agents Represent—should be retained in the relevant property file by the licensee who presented them. These forms can help firms and individual licensees defend against undisclosed dual agency charges when parties may seek to attack a contract. A copy of each of these forms was initially given to the customer, client, and so forth, to whom it was originally presented for signature.

Unsigned forms must also be retained in situations where original recipients refused to sign them.

■ POWERS OF ATTORNEY

An attorney-in-fact (now called an "Agent") is a person to whom authority is granted by a document, called a power of attorney, to perform in place of its grantor (the principal) certain actions, such as selling or conveying property on behalf of the owner who granted the power.

In the following paragraphs, the capitalized word Agent does not refer to real estate licensees involved in a transaction.

Maryland law requires that a power of attorney document be signed by the principal in the presence of a notary public and two witnesses, all of who must sign in each other's presence. The notary public may serve as one of the witnesses.

Maryland has two statutory forms of power of attorney: A 20-page general personal financial power of attorney and a six-page limited power of attorney. The limited power of attorney is typically used for real estate purposes. Maryland has a statutory Agent's Certification, which title underwriters are requiring Agents to sign, have notarized, and record along with the original power of attorney prior to recording any documents they signed as Agent. This requires the Agent to certify that, to their knowledge, the principal is alive and that the principal has not revoked the power of attorney—that Agent's authority to act.

The law imposes a duty on the Agent to act loyally, avoid conflicts of interest, and keep a record of all receipts, disbursements, and transactions made on behalf of the principal unless otherwise provided for in the power of attorney.

If, acting under the authority of a valid power of attorney document, Joe Garcia were to sign on behalf of Mary Garcia, he should sign as "Joe Garcia, as attorney-in-fact for Mary Garcia."

It is prudent, in all cases involving powers of attorney, for licensees preparing for settlement to check with closing and title officers well before the scheduled closing to make sure such powers of attorney are in a form acceptable to the settlement officers and to the lending institutions involved.

DUTIES AND OBLIGATIONS OF LICENSEES

The Regulations of the Commission set forth a number of duties and obligations that real estate licensees have to clients, the public, and fellow licensees with respect to contracts. These include

- prompt presentation of all written offers and counteroffers,
- reduction of all agreements to a written form that clearly sets forth all the obligations of the parties,
- obtaining proper signatures on all forms, and
- giving and retaining copies of all signed agreements.

EQUITABLE TITLE AND RISK OF LOSS

When a contract of sale has been signed by all parties, the buyers receive equitable title. This is called the doctrine of equitable conversion. Under Maryland common law, possession of equitable title places the risk of loss due to accidental damage to the premises on the buyers who hold an executory contract—one that exists between contract signing and closing. This is true unless the sellers cause the damage or the buyers have taken presettlement, physical possession of the premises. To offset this possibility, most contracts in Maryland include a provision that the sellers will bear any casualty losses until settlement or occupancy, whichever occurs first. Licensees should see that this issue is addressed in any contract they negotiate.

RESIDENTIAL SALES CONTRACT PROVIDED FOR MARYLAND REALTORS®

The residential sales contract form (Figure 9.1) is provided to members of the Maryland Association of REALTORS® for their exclusive use. The association also provides an array of addenda for specific situations and to meet certain legal requirements. Examples are the "Lead-Based Paint Hazard Inspection Addendum," required by federal law in residential sales of structures built before 1978, and the "First-Time Maryland Home Buyer Transfer and Recordation Tax Addendum."

CHAPTER 9 QUIZ

1. Which of the following is a requirement in Maryland for a valid real estate sales contract?
   1. It must be in writing.
   2. It must be on a standard printed form.
   3. It needs to be signed only by the seller.
   4. It needs to be signed only by the buyer.

2. What is *TRUE* of oral contracts for the sale of real estate in Maryland?
   1. They are valid.
   2. They are called parol agreements.
   3. They are usually enforceable in a court of law.
   4. They are against the law.

3. What is a duty of licensees buying or selling real property on their own account?
   1. Advise the other party of the fact that they are real estate licensees
   2. Advise lending institutions of their licensure
   3. Write to the Real Estate Commission
   4. Advise the Attorney General

4. Which of the following is *NOT* required to be disclosed in a Maryland real estate sales contract?
   1. That a leasehold interest is involved in the sale
   2. That the owner/seller is a real estate licensee
   3. The existence of possible tax charges for agricultural land development
   4. The name of the title insurance company

5. In what counties must the "Critical Areas" notice be included in real estate sales contracts?
   1. All counties with major waterways
   2. Only counties bordering on Atlantic or Chesapeake waterways
   3. All counties, regardless of whether they are affected by such regulation
   4. All except Allegany, Carroll, Frederick, Garrett, Howard, Montgomery, and Washington counties

Transfer of Title

■ KEY TERMS

adverse possession	donor	legatees
attested	elective share	nominate
beneficiaries	grantor	notorious
constructive notice	heirs	nuncupative wills
custodian	holographic wills	pretermitted
deed	hostile	residue
devise	intestate	surviving issue
devisees	issue	transfer tax
documentary stamp tax	legacy	

■ OVERVIEW

Title to land in Maryland, as elsewhere, can pass by descent, devise, adverse possession, gift, grant, escheat, eminent domain, erosion, accretion, reliction, foreclosure, and tax and sheriff's sales. This chapter deals with transfers of title by descent, action of law, will, and deed.

■ TRANSFER OF TITLE BY DESCENT

Surviving spouses are provided for by the Maryland Law of Descent and Distribution, which abolished dower and curtesy. This statute also names other classes of heirs who inherit property owned by decedents who die intestate (without a valid will). An example of situations involving intestacy that the law addresses is that of a surviving spouse and

- a minor child: each gets half;
- no minor children but with surviving issue (adult children and perhaps their children): spouse gets $15,000 and half of the residue (rest);
- no issue (children) but surviving parents: spouse gets $15,000 and half of the remainder;
- no surviving issue or parents: spouse takes all.

When the decedent is not intestate but leaves a will that gives the spouse less than the portions provided in each situation previously listed, perhaps as little as nothing, the spouse may renounce the will and elect (choose) to claim the larger amount that may be authorized by statute. This is called the survivor's elective share.

Title to real property of decedents passes immediately to their personal representatives (formerly called administrators) in situations without a valid will. These individuals pay decedents' debts and estate taxes and then distribute the remainder of the estate according to statute under supervision of the court.

Persons who receive property by descent are called heirs. Persons who receive property through a will are called beneficiaries. Beneficiaries are of two types: devisees, who receive real property (a devise), and legatees, who receive personal property (a legacy).

If the decedent was both intestate and entirely without heirs, the estate is converted to cash, and that cash is paid to the Maryland Medical Assistance Program if the decedent received long-term care benefits from that program. If that is not the case, the cash is paid to the board of education in the county in which the personal representative was granted authority to administer the estate.

■ TRANSFER OF TITLE BY ACTION OF LAW

To obtain title to real estate through adverse possession, an adverse user must be in actual possession of the property, and that possession—alone or combined with that of a sequence of previous adverse owners—must have been continuous for at least 20 years. The possession also must be or have been open, notorious (known to others), exclusive, hostile (without permission), and—because Maryland law does not recognize "squatters' rights"—under claim of right or color of title. Each of those terms has a very specific legal meaning. Situations involving adverse possession can be very complex and should always be handled with guidance from competent legal counsel.

■ TRANSFER OF TITLE BY WILL

There are statutory requirements for a valid will. Persons age 18 or older, who are of sound mind and are legally competent, may make a will. A will should be prepared carefully by the testator's (maker's) attorney, signed by the maker, and witnessed by two persons as required by law. While surviving spouses can contest wills that grant them less than what would have been their intestate share, other potential beneficiaries—such as the testator's children—may not.

Omitted Children

Children born after a testator's will is signed and before the testator's death are said to be pretermitted (omitted). This category also includes children of the decedent who had not yet been born at the time of the decedent's death. Under common law, pretermitted children do not have a share in the decedent's estate. However, Maryland statute has set aside this aspect of common law and treats pretermitted children as if they were born before the will was signed.

Nuncupative (oral) wills are not recognized in Maryland. Holographic wills (those in the handwriting of the testator) are recognized if they are properly attested (witnessed).

■ TRANSFER OF TITLE BY DEED

Maryland statutes also set forth requirements for a valid deed. A deed must be prepared in writing by an attorney or by one of the parties, give a legally sufficient property description, be executed by a competent grantor at least 18 years of age, state the actual consideration or be accompanied by an affidavit that states the actual amount.

Deeds must be typewritten and in English to be recorded, although an accompanying official consular translation into English satisfies this requirement for a deed written in another language.

A deed signed only by the grantor (the one granting the property) is effective if delivered and accepted by the grantee. It is called a deed poll. In contrast, transfer of property belonging to a minor, or of property involving a corporate seller or purchaser, are situations in which both grantee and grantor must sign.

Recordation of Deeds and Mortgages

Maryland law specifies that the transfer of any fee or freehold estate, any declaration or limitation of use, and any estate extending beyond seven years (such as a deed or a long-term lease) shall be effective only if the deed is executed and recorded. Chapter 13 of this book also points out that leases for more than seven years must be recorded. Title to property passes, as between the parties, upon delivery and acceptance of a valid deed. Consequently, unrecorded deeds are valid between grantors and grantees and also against third parties but only those third parties with actual notice. Grantees under unrecorded deeds are subject to having their equitable title interests extinguished if their grantor subsequently grants the property to others who are unaware of the earlier transfer. The law requires that deeds be recorded to alert potential purchasers of land to the possible interests of others. Recording deeds can also protect grantees against third persons who do not have actual notice. The recording of a deed constitutes constructive notice as of date of recording. Deeds are recorded in the county where the land lies. For land lying in more than one county, the deed must be recorded in each of the counties.

Recordation requires acknowledgment before a notary or other authorized public officer and payment of all required transfer taxes, ad valorem taxes, and special assessments. The deed is considered made (done) on the date it is signed, sealed, and delivered, even though it is acknowledged later and recorded still later.

Mortgages or deeds of trust (but not deeds) are exempt from the recordation tax if they secure home loans made for the initial purchase or for renovation of the mortgagor's (borrower's) principal residence.

■ TAXES ON CONVEYANCES

The documentary stamp tax (so-called because, historically, its payment was indicated by attaching actual revenue stamps to the deed) is a Maryland State tax levied at the rate of $0.55 per $500 or fraction thereof on the full sales price of the property. Several cities and counties have added their own stamp tax.

Another State tax is the Maryland transfer tax. It is 0.5% of the full consideration except for transfers to a first-time Maryland homebuyer, as explained in Chapter 8. Cities and counties collect additional transfer taxes.

■ AGRICULTURAL TRANSFER TAX

The agricultural transfer tax is calculated by the Assessments Office and is payable at the time of property transfer. It is imposed when land subject to agricultural ad valorem tax assessment is sold with nonagricultural use in view. The student is referred to the full discussion and resources given in Chapter 8.

■ MARYLAND UNIFORM TRANSFERS (GIFTS) TO MINORS ACT

This law authorizes a donor (one who gives a gift) to nominate (name) a custodian to act on behalf of the minor beneficiary (the one receiving the gift). The designation, powers, and responsibilities of a custodian and procedures for transfers of custodial property and claims against such property are set forth in the statute. Use of legal counsel is important in such a transfer.

CHAPTER 10 QUIZ

1. Which of the following is a requirement for claiming adverse possession?
   1. Claimant must post a sign on the subject property.
   2. Claimant must notify the original owner in writing.
   3. Claimant must have been in possession of the property at least 20 years.
   4. Claimant must own the adjoining land.

2. Which of the following can the Maryland Law of Descent and Distribution affect?
   1. Estates of those not leaving a valid will
   2. Surviving spouses
   3. The estates of both those leaving a valid will and those dying intestate.
   4. All of the above

3. Which of the following is NOT required for the validity of a deed that transfers title between parties?
   1. It must be voluntarily delivered during the lifetime of the grantor.
   2. It must be in writing and signed.
   3. It must be signed by a grantor who is competent.
   4. It must be recorded.

4. Which of the following is a requirement for recordation of a Maryland real estate deed?
   1. That nominal consideration be shown
   2. That it be in the handwriting of the grantee
   3. That it was drafted by an attorney or by one of the parties
   4. That is was signed as witnesses by two persons not mentioned in the deed

5. In Maryland, which of the following is required for a valid will?
   1. Delivery during the lifetime of the testator/testatrix
   2. Signature of at least one of the beneficiaries
   3. Acknowledgement before an officer of the court (notary public)
   4. A minimum of two witnesses

CHAPTER

Title Records

■ **OVERVIEW**

According to Maryland State law, deeds, mortgages, ground leases, and other instruments creating an estate in real estate for longer than seven years must be recorded. This practice benefits owners, prospective purchasers, and lenders. Recording benefits buyers, who need to know who claims to own the property they are considering. It protects grantees by giving constructive notice to the world of their claim of interest in a property. It also enables lenders to know if a mortgage loan applicant is the "owner of record" of the property being mortgaged and if there are any financial encumbrances against the property of which they have not been told.

■ DETAILS OF RECORDATION

Deeds and Mortgages

To be eligible for recordation, a deed must state the full consideration actually paid for the property. If that information is not shown in the deed, it must be stated in an affidavit attached to the deed. Only deeds acknowledged before a notary public or similar official may be recorded.

Deeds and mortgages on real estate are recorded by the clerk of circuit court in each county and Baltimore City. Recording must take place in the county or city where the land is located. If property is located in two counties, it must be recorded in both, with each county receiving a recording fee proportional to the amount of land located in the county, as shown by the tax assessment. Occasionally, recordings are made in a county other than that in which the property is located.

It should be noted that Maryland has one basic system of recording. In it, real estate records are sorted into two indices: grantor and grantee. Both deeds and mortgages convey title and so are recorded in these indices. Because Maryland law regards mortgages as conveying legal title to the lender/mortgagee (or to the trustees in the cases of deeds of trust), the mortgagor's (borrower's) name is recorded in the grantor index, and the mortgagee's (trustee's) name in the grantee index.

No deed conveying real estate may be recorded in any county of Maryland until all taxes and other public assessments or charges on the property have been paid and the record of ownership has been transferred on the tax assessment books to the grantee that is named in the deed to be recorded. If the deed transfers all of the real estate owned by the grantor in the county, then, in many counties, all of the grantor's personal property tax (if any) must also be paid prior to recording.

In Baltimore City, a deed conveying real estate may not be recorded if there is an outstanding unpaid water bill of more than $50. In Harford County, no deed conveying real estate may be recorded if any water bill is unpaid. Licensees preparing for settlement should check for such requirements imposed by the property's county or municipality.

In addition to transfer taxes, fees are charged for recording deeds and other documents. For example, counties may set such fees as $3 per page, or portion thereof, plus $1 for each name to be recorded in the grantor-grantee index. One who records a document takes it to the office of the clerk of court, pays the proper amount of documentary stamps and transfer tax stamps, pays the recording fee, and leaves the document with the clerk. The clerk's staff then reproduces the document in the public record, stamps the original to indicate where the information has been recorded, and returns it to the person designated to receive it.

Leases

Recording a lease for a period longer than seven years may protect the tenants if a mortgage/lender forecloses on their landlord. It also provides protection against certain persons to whom the landlord is indebted and for whom judgment was already rendered. Lease recordation costs are often as great as the costs for recording deeds. However, most leases of seven years or less are not subject to the recordation tax.

Plats of Subdivision

The law requires that subdividers have plats of subdivision approved by state and local authorities before recording those plats. Documents such as listings, sales contracts, and deeds typically refer to recorded plats by liber and folio (book and page). Such reference to the properly recorded plat in a later document can satisfy the need for exact property description. No lot within a subdivision can be offered for sale until the plat of subdivision has been recorded.

Plat recordation and the development of individual lots in a subdivision are regulated on a local level by the county where the property is located. Licensees should always be sure that the deeds to the individual lots for sale in a subdivision have been properly recorded and that all local laws regarding recordation have been met before advertising the lots for sale. Failure to do so could result in a judicial injunction, which would halt the marketing of the property. In addition, depending on the situation, the licensees may also be in violation of the State license law and, thus, subject to suspension or revocation of their real estate licenses.

■ TITLE EVIDENCE

In Maryland, it is customary for buyers in a real estate transaction to authorize the ordering of title evidence at their expense, although this, like so many other things, is negotiable. Generally, buyers will choose a title (settlement) company whose legal staff will (among other things):

■ order an abstract of title to be prepared and, based on that abstract, prepare a report (opinion) of title as to whether the present condition of the title, as contained in the public record, is marketable; or

■ acting as licensed representatives of a title insurance company, issue a preliminary title insurance policy (a title insurance binder) based on favorable abstract data.

The person performing settlement is required by statute to explain owner's title insurance at the closing meeting and make it available (offer to sell it) to residential purchasers. A policy of title insurance is the most frequently used form of title evidence in Maryland.

Note that Maryland law requires that the following notice be given to buyers, printed in bold type in the body of each sales contract presented by licensees: **YOU ARE ENTITLED TO SELECT YOUR OWN TITLE INSURANCE COMPANY, SETTLEMENT COMPANY, ESCROW COMPANY, OR TITLE ATTORNEY.**

Although a licensee may not require a purchaser to use a particular title insurance company, settlement or escrow company, or title attorney, the purchaser is, of course, free to use a company recommended by the seller. Moreover, a seller could make the buyer's use of a particular title company as a condition of entering into the sales agreement.

■ PREREQUISITES TO RECORDING

No fee simple deed, mortgage, or deed of trust may be recorded, unless it bears a certification that the instrument has been prepared by attorneys admitted to practice before the Maryland Court of Appeals, under the supervision of such attorneys, or by one of the parties to the instrument. Various localities impose other requirements.

■ UNIFORM COMMERCIAL CODE

The Uniform Commercial Code (UCC) is in effect in Maryland. Two provisions of this code may affect real estate practices:

- The use of chattel mortgages on fixtures or contents has been replaced by use of security agreements and financing statements.
- The bulk sales provision applies when a person sells all of the stock in trade when selling a business.

The principles text contains more information about the UCC.

CHAPTER 11 QUIZ

1. Where should a deed conveying title to land that lies in two counties be recorded?
    1. In the county with the larger portion
    2. In the county with the smaller portion
    3. At the State capital
    4. In both counties

2. When a parcel of Maryland real estate is being sold, on whose behalf is the title search customarily ordered?
    1. Seller
    2. Buyer
    3. Broker
    4. Seller and broker together

3. Where are deeds and mortgages recorded in each county?
    1. Office of the County Clerk of Circuit Court
    2. Torrens System Office
    3. Personal property tax office
    4. Office of Municipal Planning and Zoning

4. Which of the following is *FALSE* regarding recorded deeds and mortgages?
    1. They are indexed under the names of grantors.
    2. They are indexed under the names of grantees.
    3. They are indexed under the names of selling brokers.
    4. They contain references to previously recorded conveyances.

5. Which of the following is *FALSE* concerning requirements for recording a deed?
    1. It may have been be drafted (prepared) by one of the parties.
    2. It may have been witnessed (attested) rather than notarized.
    3. It may have been drafted (prepared) by an attorney.
    4. It must have been notarized (acknowledged).

CHAPTER 12

Real Estate Financing

■ KEY TERMS

balloon clause	maturity date	surplus money action
deed in trust	mortgagee	tax and insurance expense account
deed of release	mortgagor	
deed of trust	notice of sale	title theory
deed of trust financing	power-of-sale clause	trustee's sale
judicial mortgage foreclosure	satisfaction of mortgage	trustee's deed
	secondary mortgage	vendees
junior lenders		

■ OVERVIEW

Most real estate is purchased using borrowed funds. Both the traditional mortgage and the deed of trust are common in Maryland and are used in both lender financing and owner financing. The State allows, but stringently regulates, another form of owner financing—the installment land contract.

■ NOTE TO STUDENT

The deed of trust—also called a *trust deed*—is different from a deed in trust, which is used to place property into a trust. Both are different from a trustee's deed, by which property is transferred out of a trust by the trustee. The student should review the discussion of these terms in the principles text.

■ MORTGAGE AND DEED OF TRUST LOANS

Maryland is considered a title theory state, as defined in the main text. A lender who records a properly signed and delivered mortgage or deed of trust holds naked legal title to the real estate pledged. Nevertheless, Maryland's mortgage and deed of trust foreclosure and sale laws are similar to those of a lien theory state with this exception: lenders, rather than the delinquent landlords, are allowed to collect rents on investment properties during the foreclosure process.

Deeds of trust are used throughout the state as financing instruments for real estate. Deed of trust financing is a three-party arrangement involving borrower (the trustor), trustee, and lender (beneficiary). This arrangement is so popular in Maryland that it has been called a Potomac Mortgage.

The deed of trust forms used in Maryland have a power-of-sale clause, which gives the trustee authority to sell pledged property in the event of a borrower's default. In such a case, there is no court action. After giving adequate public notice, the trustee has the property sold at a trustee's sale (a public auction). Some mortgages contain a clause that gives the mortgagee (the lender) this power—to sell without court action.

The money from the trustee's sale is applied to accrued interest and the legal cost caused by the sale, and then the principal of the mortgage is paid. The remainder, the amount over and above what is due any lienholder, is returned to the defaulted borrower.

In Maryland, a corporation or a partnership may not serve under a deed of trust and sell the property in case of default under the provisions of the document's power-of-sale clause. Only an individual (a natural person) may do this. In some other states, any form of "person" (corporation, partnership) may have this right.

■ DEFAULT, FORECLOSURE, AND DEFICIENCY

The parties to a mortgage are the mortgagor (borrower) and the mortgagee (lender). If the borrower defaults, the lender who wishes to foreclose seeks a court order to sell the mortgaged property at public auction, unless there is a power-of-sale clause in the mortgage. When the funds from a judicial (court-ordered) mortgage foreclosure sale are insufficient to satisfy the debt, a judgment may be issued against the borrower for the deficiency. However, when a deficiency occurs after a nonjudicial foreclosure, either by a trustee or by the mortgagee under a power-of-sale clause, no such judgment is entered. Deficiency actions are not allowed in Federal Housing Administration (FHA) loans, and the U.S. Department of Veterans Affairs (VA) is reluctant to allow them.

■ AVOIDING FREQUENT FUTURE FORECLOSURES

Emergency legislation in 2008 was designed to reduce the likelihood of future waves of foreclosure like the one in the first decade of the 21st century. Based on the premise that borrowers had been lured into debt beyond their means and lenders had turned a blind eye to applicants' poor credit history, the legislation sought to require understandable explanations so that the terms of every mortgage agreement would be understandable to borrowers. People who sign off on application information at every level must be identified, and severe penalties are specified for failing to follow the new guidelines. Additionally, lenders will be penalized for pressuring appraisers to inflate appraisals to fit unrealistic offers, and so on.

■ REDUCING RESIDENTIAL MORTGAGE DEFAULTS AND FORECLOSURES

Preventive Legislation

In 2008, the Protection of Homeowners in Foreclosure Act was passed forbidding mortgage fraud, defined as[1]

- ■ knowingly making any deliberate misstatement, misrepresentation, or omission (or using such misrepresentations by others) during the mortgage lending process with the intent that they be relied on by a mortgage lender, borrower, or any other party to the mortgage lending process;
- ■ receiving any proceeds or any other funds related to the closing of a mortgage loan involving such misstatements and misrepresentations;
- ■ conspiring to do either of the above; or
- ■ recording any document related to a mortgage loan that the filer knows to contain such misstatements.

Violation of this law can bring felony convictions and maximum penalties of $5,000 and imprisonment for not more than one year, $15,000 and 15 years if the victim is a vulnerable adult, and $100,000 and 20 years for a pattern of violation of mortgage fraud.

Other Preventive Legislation

Identifying lenders and originators when mortgages first recorded   Under rules set by the Commissioner of Financial Regulation, to be accepted for recordation, a mortgage must contain the names of, and other information about, both the mortgage originator and the mortgage lender.

Remedial legislation: slowing the foreclosure process   With certain exceptions, an action to foreclose a mortgage on residential property may not be filed until either 90 days after default or 45 days after notice of intent to foreclose is sent to the delinquent borrower and the owner of the property, whichever is later.

Curbing misleading practices of faux "consultants"   Maryland law imposes heavy penalties on unauthorized persons who offer or attempt to perform foreclosure "rescue." During the recent wave of mortgage difficulties, predatory "rescuing" behavior by parties who actually intend to be foreclosure purchasers rather than rescuers has included misleading representations that the so-called "rescuers"

- ■ will "save" a homeowner's house (or similar language),
- ■ are acting as "advisors" to the delinquent homeowner, and/or
- ■ hold certifications or licenses they do not actually hold.

Such representations and many other promises often persuaded unwary ho‧ owners to agree to actions resulting in loss of their home, being stripped c equity they had in it, and forfeiture of their good credit.

---

[1]   General Assembly of Maryland, "Statute §7–401: Article Real Property," ᴦ
   Assembly of Maryland, http://mgaleg.maryland.gov/2013RS/Statute_Weᴸ
   (accessed April 30, 2014).

Real estate licensees, when involved in so-called "short sales," are permitted to contact lenders on the subject property only as conduits for documents and information. They may act only within the scope of the services listed in the Brokers Act. They may not engage in any negotiations with the lender.

The Maryland Mortgage Fraud Protection Act [*Criminal Procedures*, Title 13, Subtitle 4] requires foreclosure consultants, except attorneys and certain others, to be licensed as real estate brokers and to provide homeowners with their research on values related to a defaulting property. It also requires that contracts and agreements with—and notices and disclosures to—defaulting borrowers during foreclosure consulting, be in the language of the defaulting borrowers—that language used in the interviews with them. It makes a violation of the act an unfair or deceptive trade practice under the Maryland Consumer Protection Act, punishable by fines of as much as $10,000 and three years' imprisonment.

■ SHORT SALES AND REAL ESTATE LICENSEES

Note: The following information is provided by the Maryland Real Estate Commission (www.dllr.state.md.us/license/mrec/mrecshortsales.pdf).

Increasingly, real estate licensees are involved in short sales, where the sales price agreed upon is less than that owed to lenders by the seller. The listing agent is often called upon to communicate between the lender/servicer and the seller regarding financial obligations. Licensees need to be fully aware of the Maryland laws that regulate the activities of those who assist homeowners under these circumstances; laws that go beyond those that govern real estate brokerage activities.

The Maryland Credit Services Businesses Act (MCSBA) requires that a person who advises a consumer with regard to the extension of credit must be licensed by the Commissioner of Financial Regulation. There is a licensing exemption for a person licensed as a Maryland real estate broker, associate broker, or salesperson when that person is acting within the course and scope of that license.

Since the scope of a real estate license is limited by definition to assisting in the purchase or sale of property, the exemption would not extend to negotiation of a deficiency note that is independent of the sale of the property.

Maryland's Protection of Homeowners in Foreclosure Act (PHIFA) applies where a homeowner's mortgage is at least 60 days in default. The law sets forth the activities that constitute foreclosure-consulting services offered to a homeowner in that situation. An individual who engages in those activities must follow specific requirements regarding written agreements with the consumer. PHIFA provides an exemption (or "safe harbor") for real estate licensees where they are engaged in an activity for which they are licensed by the Real Estate Commission.

For example, one of the activities defined in the PHIFA law as a foreclosure consulting service is "arranging or facilitating the purchase of a homeowner's equity of redemption or legal or equitable title." This activity is one included in the definition of the provision of real estate brokerage services, and therefore may be provided by a real estate licensee without the need for compliance with PHIFA (or additional licensing under MCSBA).

The PHIFA law requires, among other provisions, that:

- the homeowner and the foreclosure consultant enter into a foreclosure consulting contract that includes all the specific terms set out in Section 7-306 of the *Real Property* Article;
- the foreclosure consultant refrain from engaging in any of the prohibited activities set forth in Section 7-307, including charging or collecting any compensation until all the foreclosure consulting services have been performed;
- a real estate licensee who provides real estate brokerage services under a foreclosure consultant license must present the homeowner with a copy of the real estate license no later than when the foreclosure consulting contract is signed; and
- the foreclosure consultant may not receive a commission, regardless of how it is described, for the sale of a residence in default that exceeds 8% of the sales price.

The difficulty arises when the licensee is called upon to be the go-between for the lender and the seller, and/or where the transaction results in a new debt being incurred by the seller in the form of a deficiency note. If one or both of these circumstances arises, the licensee must take great care in not crossing the line between the provision of real estate brokerage services and activities that would require additional licensing.

At a minimum, in order to qualify for the statutory "safe harbor" protection under PHIFA, the licensee must ensure that the residence in default:

- is listed in the multiple list service, and
- is sold or transferred through a settlement, including the conveyance or transfer of deed, title, or establishment of equitable interest.

If those basic requirements are met, a licensee may work with a seller under a valid listing agreement to request a short sale or other foreclosure alternative from a lender or servicer under PHIFA. The seller must voluntarily sign the appropriate authorization for the lender, indicating that the listing agent may submit the required short sale or loss mitigation documentation on the seller's behalf. With that authorization, the agent may transmit documentation by computer in a format specified by the lender.

Beyond submitting the requested documentation to the lender or services, the licensee's conduct must meet the following standards in order to comply with the applicable laws.

As a real estate licensee, one *may* do these things:

- May conduct a Comparative Market Analysis (CMA), which an out-of-state lender/servicer may refer to as a Broker's Price Opinion (BPO).
- Must refer a client to an individual licensed under the Credit Services Businesses Act, or otherwise exempt under that law, to negotiate on issues such as deficiencies and relocation allowances as soon as those issues arise. The licensee may serve as a conduit of information from the MCSBA licensed individual to the seller, but may not negotiate on those issues with the lender/servicer.
- Must refer a client to an accountant to explain to the seller the potential income tax consequences of a short sale and the applicability of the Mortgage Forgiveness Debt Relief Act of 2007.

- Must refer a client to a housing counselor for discussions about alternatives available to avoid foreclosure. Free housing counseling is available through the Maryland HOPE Program at 1-877-462-7555.
- Must refer any requests from the lender/servicer for reductions in real estate brokerage commissions on a short sale to the licensee's broker.

As a real estate licensee, one *may* not do these things:

- Collect any monies in addition to the real estate brokerage services commission from a client unless the licensee holds an additional license under the MCSBA.
- Assist a seller in negotiating with the lender/servicer to obtain a loan modification or a promissory note for the deficiency amount, or to otherwise prevent foreclosure.
- Use direct mail solicitations or advertisements targeted to a homeowner in default (or imminent default or "underwater" on the mortgage) that indicate that the licensee (1) can assist in preventing foreclosure; (2) is an "expert" in short sales; (3) can arrange refinancing; or (4) will contact creditors on the owner's behalf.
- Make representations to a homeowner that the licensee can save the owner's home, stop foreclosure, or obtain a short sale.
- Provide advice to a homeowner regarding the benefits of a strategic default.
- Predict or suggest credit score consequences of one loss mitigation strategy over another.
- Make any predictions with regard to the likelihood of the waiver of deficiency judgments or the payment of relocation costs in a short sale.

A licensee who serves as more than a conduit of information between the seller and the lender/servicer regarding deficiencies, or who engages in any of the "Don't" activities, no longer has the protection of the "safe harbor" provision, and must follow the strict terms of the PHIFA law, if the mortgage is in default, as well as obtain a license from the Commissioner of Financial Regulation under the MCSBA.

▥ MORTGAGE INTEREST RATE LIMITS AND PREPAYMENT

In Maryland, there is no limit on the rate of interest lenders may charge in first mortgage loans. The state interest ceiling on second mortgage loans and land installment contracts is 24%. The written agreement between mortgagor and mortgagee must specify the rate of interest.

If the agreement between mortgagor and mortgagee does not expressly limit prepayment and/or impose a penalty for it, a mortgage debt can be prepaid at any time without penalty. However, when such a penalty has been agreed to, it may not exceed two month's advance interest on the total of all amounts prepaid within a 12-month period that are more than one-third of the original loan.

▥ FOR EXAMPLE:

Original loan: $90,000 for 10 years at 8%

Partial prepayments made in Year 3: $25,000 + $15,000 = $40,000

This $40,000 is $10,000 more than ⅓ of the original loan.

Therefore, two months' interest on $10,000 at 8% = $133.33 prepayment charge.

If a bank pays various expenses of a borrower (closing expenses) and the borrower later prepays the loan, the bank may then recover from the borrower—at any time before the end of the loan's term—all the costs it had incurred on the borrower's behalf and the amount will not be regarded as prepaid interest or a "prepayment penalty." The procedure merely makes the borrower repay the closing costs that the lender had previously advanced on the borrower's behalf.

Banks' ability to recover such costs has been the subject of sharp controversy, pitting Maryland courts against federal regulators, who hold that federal powers preempt powers of states in regulating nationally related banks and their subsidiaries. In short, Maryland's restrictions were stricter than federal ones on banks' recovering borrowers' settlement costs that the banks had paid.

A lender who violates the usury ceiling for second mortgages, except for a bona fide error of computation, may collect only the principal amount of the loan and may not collect any interest, costs, or other charges with respect to the loan. In addition, a lender who knowingly violates any provision of this portion of the law shall forfeit to the borrower three times the amount of interest and charges already collected in excess of that authorized by law, or $500, whichever is greater.

■ MORTGAGE EXPENSE ACCOUNTS

Under Maryland law, lending institutions (banks, savings banks, and savings associations) that require a tax and insurance expense account for first mortgage loans must pay interest on these funds at passbook rate but not less than 3%. The interest is computed on the average monthly balance in the escrow account and paid annually by crediting the borrower's account with the amount of interest due. This payment is reported to the IRS on a Form 1099. The requirement to pay interest continues even when loans are sold into the secondary market, if the original lending institution continues to service them.

■ DISCRIMINATION

Under Maryland law, a lender may not refuse loans to any person based solely on geographic area, neighborhood, race, religion, color, age, sex, disability, marital status, familial status, or national origin. However, a lender may refuse to make a loan based on higher than normal risks connected with the loan.

■ GROUND RENT: FHA/DVA LOANS

The U.S. Department of Veterans Affairs will guarantee loans only on properties subject to ground rent that are located in Anne Arundel County, Baltimore City, Baltimore County, and the Joppatowne subdivision in Harford County. If a veteran purchases leasehold property located in another part of the State using such financing—formerly called a GI loan—the ground rent must be redeemed on or prior to the date of closing.

For Federal Housing Administration (FHA) loans on Maryland property held subject to a ground rent, the residential mortgage limit must be reduced by the capitalization value of the annual ground rent. Ground rents are discussed in Chapter 13 of this book.

■ RELEASE OF MORTGAGE LIEN

When a mortgage note has been fully repaid by the borrower, the lender must prepare and provide to the borrower a release of lien document. This may be either a satisfaction of mortgage or a deed of release. Although the lender will often record this instrument, it is the borrower's responsibility to ensure that the document actually does get recorded.

In some instances, a mortgagee simply enters the statement of release directly in the margin of the recorded mortgage instrument; that document is then rerecorded so that the public record will indicate the release. Recording the release provides public notice that the original mortgage lien has been canceled.

■ MORTGAGE PRESUMED PAID

Sometimes a mortgage is paid off, and the release of the lien document does not get recorded. Years later, when the owner of the property seeks to pledge the property for another loan, the old lien still appears on record. To address this, Maryland law presumes the old lien to have been satisfied if a period of 12 years has elapsed since the last payment date called for in the instrument (its maturity date). Alternatively, if the maturity date cannot be ascertained and 40 years have elapsed since the date of the lien's original recording, the mortgage will be presumed paid and the lien extinguished.

■ FORECLOSURES AND TRUSTEE SALES

The mortgage or deed of trust (but not the note) must be recorded before a lender may start foreclosure proceedings in case of borrower default. State law requires that to record a residential mortgage or deed of trust, a lender must execute and attach an affidavit to each mortgage stating

■ that the mortgage document accurately sets forth the amount of the loan, and
■ that the entire amount was disbursed when the mortgage was executed or delivered to the lender by the borrower.

When a mortgage does not contain a provision giving the mortgagee the power of sale, a foreclosure sale ordered and supervised by the court is the lender's final remedy for default by the borrower.

Because there is no statutory right of redemption in Maryland, a defaulted borrower has to make redemption by paying the necessary funds to the mortgagee before the sale has been completed—that is, before the court officer delivers the sale deed to the foreclosure purchaser.

Mortgagees or trustees are permitted to purchase properties in default at their sale rather than selling them to satisfy debts, provided they have diligently attempted to obtain the best possible price for each property on the market.

Holders of subordinate interests in real property, such as equity credit lines or second mortgages, may record a request for a notice of sale. This action would require holders of superior interests in property to give notice in the event of an impending foreclosure sale. Holders of subordinate interests must then file a surplus money action to receive any of the proceeds of a scheduled foreclosure sale that are not used to satisfy superior liens. If holders of such junior liens fail to do these things, their liens will be extinguished, no matter how large the proceeds from the sale.

Residential Tenants in Possession When Foreclosure Occurs

The foreclosure purchaser of a residential property must give formal, dated, written notice to tenants in that property of the date by which they must surrender possession. That date must be at least 90 days after the date of the notice. The notice must advise the tenants on which of the following is the basis of their termination:

■ Expiration of the term of the lease
■ Sale of the property to a purchaser who will occupy the property as the purchaser's primary residence Termination of a month-to-month or other terminable-at-will tenancy.

Required contents of this notice—several pages in length—can be found at §7-105.6 in the *Real Property* Article of the Maryland law. The protections for tenants provided by this law are at least as great as those provided by federal law.

■ LAND INSTALLMENT CONTRACTS

The State law regarding land installment contract sales of real estate is found in Title 10 of the *Real Property* Article, Annotated Code of Maryland. Note that this law applies only to the sale of improved properties, occupied or to be occupied by the purchaser for a dwelling, or of an unimproved, subdivided lot or lots intended to be improved for residential purposes. In other cases, common-law rules apply with fewer protections for vendees (purchasers).

Land installment contracts should be prepared and processed by attorneys. The purchaser may rescind the contract and demand that all sums paid be returned if the vendor does not record the contract within 15 days of its being signed by all parties. Land installment contract financing also requires cumbersome ongoing reporting by the vendor for protection of the purchaser.

■ JUNIOR FINANCING

The maximum interest rate a lender may charge in Maryland for a secondary mortgage (the term Maryland statutes use for a mortgage other than a first mortgage) is 24%; the maximum loan origination fee that may be charged is $250 or 10% of the proceeds of the loan, whichever is less. Only an actual cost, such as a recording fee or title insurance, may be charged in addition to the origination fee. A lender may refinance a junior loan not more than once in any 12-month period and not more than twice during any five-year period. The *Commercial Law* Article of the Maryland Annotated Code sets forth the details.

Maryland law permits all fees, discounts, and points allowed or required under federally related second mortgage purchase programs. However, the points and the contract interest rate combined may not exceed an annual percentage rate (APR) of 24%.

Prohibited Practices

Junior (secondary loan) lenders in Maryland are prohibited from certain practices, including the following:

- Attempting to have debtors waive their legal rights
- Requiring accelerated payments for any reason other than default
- Having debtors execute assignments of wages for payment of loans
- Charging a fee to execute a release after a loan is paid

Balloon Payments

Maryland Secondary Mortgage Law requires that lenders, including private sellers, who take back a second mortgage containing a balloon clause (a clause that makes the final payment significantly larger than previous payments) grant—upon the borrower's request—an automatic, one-time, six-month extension beyond the maturity date. This provision applies to second mortgage loans made for buying residential property for owner occupancy.

■ RESIDENTIAL PROPERTY LOAN NOTICES

Lenders who make loans on residential property are required to provide prospective borrowers with a written notice informing them of their right to choose an attorney or a title insurance company. This notice must be provided within three days of their application for the loan. Lenders are also required to notify applicants that by completing their loan applications, they are terminating any right they might have had to rescind the contract for lack of a Property Disclosure and Disclaimer Statement, discussed in Chapter 4 of this book. The Secondary Mortgage Loan Law is Title 12 of the *Commercial Law* Article.

CHAPTER 12 QUIZ

1. Which statement about mortgages on Maryland real property is *TRUE*?
   1. They must be recorded to be valid between lender and borrower.
   2. They may not be refused to any persons because of their religion.
   3. By law, they must be for a minimum 10-year term.
   4. If in default, they are subject to strict foreclosure.

2. Hugh McDonald purchased his home with the aid of a balloon second mortgage that is reaching the end of its term. What are McDonald's rights now that the balloon payment is coming due?
   1. He must pay the final (balloon) payment immediately or risk foreclosure.
   2. He is entitled to automatic refinancing of the remaining balance.
   3. He automatically receives a six-month extension.
   4. He must be granted a six-month extension if he now requests it from the lender.

3. When Thomas Lowell obtained a loan to purchase a new home from BNN Savings Bank, BNN failed to record the mortgage document. The mortgage does not give BNN the power of sale in case of default. Which of the following is *TRUE?*
   1. As things stand, BNN Savings Bank will be able to enforce the mortgage in a court of law if Lowell defaults on his loan.
   2. If Lowell defaults on the loan, BNN cannot foreclose on the mortgage until the instrument is recorded.
   3. As mortgagor, it is Lowell's obligation to record the mortgage for his own protection.
   4. If Lowell defaults on the loan, BNN could sell the property without foreclosure action.

4. Bonita Harrison needs $365,000 to purchase a new home from a builder. She borrows it from First Maryland Savings Bank. Which of the following security arrangements can First Maryland Savings Bank use?
   1. Mortgage or deed of trust
   2. Real estate trust
   3. Installment contract
   4. Deed of release

5. Alpha Spurlin obtains a 30-year loan from Liberty Savings Association to purchase a Baltimore condominium unit. Along with monthly payments of principal and interest, the lender requires that she pay amounts for them to escrow for later payment of taxes and property insurance. Which of the following is *TRUE?*
   1. Liberty Savings must pay Spurlin interest on these escrow deposits when the loan is paid off.
   2. Spurlin may require the lender to maintain her escrow account in an interest-bearing depository.
   3. Liberty Savings must credit Spurlin's account with passbook-rate interest—but not less than 3%—annually on her average escrow balance.
   4. Spurlin must pay the lender a minimum of 3% interest for maintaining such an account for her.

CHAPTER 13

Leases

■ KEY TERMS

cognovit clause
common-law estates
confess judgment clause
constructive eviction
constructive notice
damages
dispossess
dispossession
  proceedings

distraint
exculpatory clause
holding over
inception of a lease
leased fee
leasehold
lease with option to
  purchase

memorandum of lease
periodic tenancies
possession
recorded
security deposits
tenant rights
warranty of habitability

■ OVERVIEW

Leaseholds in Maryland are the four familiar common-law types: (1) leases for a specified time period ("for years"), (2) leases from period to period ("from year to year" or "periodic"), (3) tenancies at will, and (4) tenancies at sufferance. Long-term ground leases, an example of the first type, are also common in certain areas.

■ MARYLAND GROUND RENTS

Ground leases exist in many areas in the State. Some of them may be redeemed (freed from ground rent) after specified periods, while others are irredeemable. The ground lease tenant typically owns the improvements located on the rented ground. One reason developers might establish a ground rent would be to keep the selling price of houses they have built within the financial reach of more purchasers. The purchaser of a house subject to ground rent merely rents the lot without purchasing it. If the purchaser/tenant does not pay the rent, however, the owner of the ground can record, and then foreclose, a lien on the property and, thus, take title to it in fee, together with the improvements (buildings) on it. This would leave the original purchaser with nothing—neither the house nor the land.

Ground rental is money paid to the landowner (landlord) by a tenant who possesses the landlord's land by virtue of a lease. Such leases usually give tenants possession of land for a specific term not to exceed 99 years. Possession of the land reverts (goes back) to the fee simple landlord when the lease finally expires, if it is terminated by the tenant's default or it is not renewed. Some ground leases have options for renewal for additional terms, either at predetermined, graduated rentals, or at rentals to be based on reappraisal of the land and improvements at the time of renewal.

It is apparently the intention of the Maryland legislature to end as many ground leases on residential property in Maryland as possible. Residential is defined as "property with four or fewer residential units."

Legislation passed in 2007 made all previously irredeemable residential ground leaseholds subject to redemption on September 30, 2010, unless the ground landlords (the "holders" of ground leases) recorded their intention to preserve their irredeemable status. For those that met this deadline, the leases are extended 10 years. At the end of the extension, the owners will again have to record such intentions every 10 years. If notice of intention to preserve irredeemability is not filed before each 10-year renewal term expires, the land becomes subject to redemption by the tenant by capitalizing the annual ground rent at 6%. For example, an annual ground rent of $2,160 would be capitalized by dividing it by the percentage stated in this law, 6%. $2,160 divided by 0.06 = $36,000. By paying $36,000 to the ground landlord, the tenant would become fee simple owner of the lot.

The law states that any residential ground lease for a term of 15 years or longer—that is not an irredeemable ground lease—may be redeemed at any time at the option of the tenant upon 30 days' notice to the landlord. A lease created between April 6, 1888, and July 1, 1982, may be redeemed at 6%; if created on or after July 2, 1982, at 12%. (Redemption at 12% costs half as much as redemption at 6%.) Properties may be redeemed for lesser sums if stipulated in the leases, or they may be redeemed for any sum to which the parties agree at the time of redemption.

Anyone who becomes holder of a ground lease—by some means, such as purchase or inheritance—is required (1) to notify the leasehold tenants within 30 days of their right to redeem the property and (2) to invite them to contact the new holder for details of such procedure.

Settlement agents must inform purchasers who borrow money to purchase a residential property that is under redeemable ground rent that the property is redeemable for a specified cost and that the cost can be rolled into the amount of the (purchase) loan being made.

Creation of a Ground Rent

Owners of a fee simple or leasehold estate in residential property that is suitable for, or being used for, four or fewer dwelling units may not subject them to ground leases or ground subleases. Some properties may still be subjected to ground leases: commercial property, mobile home sites, condos, co-ops, and residential uses involving more than four dwellings.

Ground Rent Disclosure

When property subject to ground rent is sold, the contract of sale must inform the buyer that nonpayment of the ground rental may result in:

■ loss of the entire property, in fee, to the ground landlord; and
■ termination of the buyer's leasehold.

Owners, or licensees representing them, when posting signs on ground rent property for sale, are required to show on the sign the amount of annual ground rental and cost of capitalization in numbers as large and clear as the numbers showing the price of the property.

Land subject to ground rent is not held in fee simple. The holder (ground landlord) has a leased fee, and the tenant/occupant has a leasehold. Therefore, if a contract of sale for property subject to ground rent does not disclose existence of the ground rent, yet the agreement calls for delivery of fee simple title to the purchaser, the seller must redeem the property before settlement. If the property is irredeemable, the seller cannot deliver fee simple title and will be in breach of contract.

Recent "Reform" Laws and Court Decisions Affecting Ground Lease Holders' and Tenants' Rights

In 2007, the General Assembly adopted several changes that substantially affected the legal framework for ground rent leases:

1. Effective September 30, 2010, all ground rent leases must be registered. Failing to register allows the Maryland State Department of Assessments and Taxation to extinguish the ground lease, and fee title to the real estate could be transferred to the ground tenant.
2. No longer may the ground tenant be threatened with ejectment as a remedy for failure to pay ground rent.
3. A 60-day notice and cure period was imposed.
4. Regarding previously irredeemable ground rent leases, a notice of intent to preserve irredeemability must be filed by a certain date (and every 10 years thereafter). Failing to do so will cause ground leases to become redeemable.
5. A three-year limitation period was imposed for collectability of ground rent payments in arrears.

Since the 2007 law was passed, Maryland high court decisions have caused the following changes:

1. Parts of the previous changes have been found unconstitutional by Maryland's high courts.
2. All ground rent leases are still required to be registered by their ground leaseholders, but there is presently no penalty for failure to register. Ground leaseholders who had failed to register their leases by September 2010, and had their ownership rights extinguished, have had those actions reversed; all such extinguishments have been declared null and void and will occur no more.
3. The 60-day notice prior to ejectment remains.
4. Handling of irredeemability remains the same.
5. This three-year limitation period for collectability of ground in arrears remains.

■ MARYLAND RESIDENTIAL LEASES

The Maryland Statute of Frauds found in the *Real Property* Article provides that to be enforceable, leases that end in less than one year from the date of agreement need not be in writing. However, all longer leases must be in writing. The one-year time period is measured from the signing of a lease—the date the lease agreement is made—until the end of its term.

Leases longer than seven years must be recorded. Recordation of a document requires acknowledgment before a notary public or similar official. Note, however, that even when such leases have not been properly recorded, they are still valid and binding between the original parties, against their creditors, and against their successors and assignees who have actual notice of the lease or who acquire the property while a tenant is in actual occupancy. Possession (occupancy) of property by a tenant under a lease for seven years or less gives constructive notice of the tenant's rights. However, occupancy at any time under an unrecorded lease that is for longer than seven years does not constitute such notice. It is clear that recording the longer lease serves to protect the tenant, while mere occupancy under a shorter lease (seven years or less) would provide protection by being accepted as notice. Although the law requires that any lease for a term longer than seven years be recorded, a recorded memorandum of lease satisfies this requirement.

Postsettlement Occupancy An Exception

No portions of the landlord and tenant statute dealing with residential leases apply when, after the sale of an owner-occupied residence, the sellers and purchasers agree that sellers may remain in possession for 60 days or less. This is called a postsettlement occupancy agreement.

Disclosure of Representation

Licensees must provide written disclosure of agency representation—the Understanding Whom form—to both lessors and lessees when negotiating any residential lease for longer than 125 days. This disclosure must be made no later than the first scheduled face-to-face meeting between the licensees and any prospective tenant or landlord. Please review the discussion on disclosure of representation in Chapter 2.

Residential Security Deposits and Surety Bonds

Landlords may not require security deposits of more than two months' rental, and they must give tenants receipts for these deposits. Failure to do so makes them liable to tenants for the sum of $25. More importantly, landlords are liable to tenants for up to three times any security deposit taken in excess of this limit, plus reasonable attorney fees.

Within 30 days of their receipt, deposit monies must be placed and maintained by landlords or their agents in accounts—used for this sole purpose—in a branch of a federally insured bank or a savings institution licensed to do business in Maryland.

In lieu of such accounts, a landlord may hold security deposits in insured certificates of deposit issued by banks, as previously described, or in securities issued by the federal government or the State of Maryland. The total of all these deposit accounts, certificates, and securities must be sufficient in amount to equal all the security deposits for which a landlord or landlord's broker is liable. Broker licensees' records of these funds must be available for inspection by members of the Commission or its agents during normal business hours.

A further statutory protection of residential tenants is that their security deposits held by landlords, as prescribed, are protected against attachment by creditors of either the landlord or the tenant.

Residential tenants, when their landlords agree, may now purchase a surety bond to protect their landlords against losses usually covered by a rental security deposit. In this way, tenants may meet security deposit requirements of their landlords by making an all-cash deposit, paying part in cash and providing the other part with a surety bond, or covering it all with a surety bond. The use of such bonds needs the agreement of both landlords and tenants. Tenants may not be required to protect the landlord in an aggregate amount greater than the sum of two months' rental, no matter what the composition of the coverage is. Landlords may not require the use of a surety bond.

A tenant pays the cost of the bond, which protects the landlord for an amount up to two months' rental. The cost of this bond is not returnable to the tenant. Unlike a cash security deposit, the bond earns the tenants no interest. Landlords, in turn, have no interest to pay when surety bonding is used rather than cash security deposits.

The law imposes—for the protection of tenants—many protective requirements for landlords' use of such bonds. Tenants have similar protections from the bonding company, if those companies violate detailed requirements imposed on them. The usual penalty against a landlord or a bonding company involves loss of the right to keep any of the security deposit or to claim any payment under the bond or an award to the tenants of three times the amount of money improperly withheld from them plus reasonable attorney fees. If tenants apply for and purchase bonds and landlords then refuse to accept bonds, the insurer must return the premiums paid and any other charges associated with applications.

At the time leases are written, landlords must give tenants written notice of various tenant rights. One example is the right to demand from landlords, at the beginning of leases, written reports of property condition inspections made in the presence of the new tenants. They must request these property-condition inspections by certified mail within 15 days of taking occupancy. Landlords who fail to provide these reports to tenants who make the proper request become liable to the tenants for as much as three times the amount of any security deposit taken. This amount could be offset (reduced) by amounts due in unpaid rent and tenant damages to the premises.

Tenants also have the right to request by certified mail—sent at least 15 days before their intended move-out—to be present at the final inspection. Landlords must set dates between five days before and five days after intended move-outs and notify the tenants in writing of these dates.

When leases are terminated, landlords must return tenants' security deposits within 45 days, together with simple interest at the statutory rate—presently 3% per annum (if the deposit if more than $50). Interest accrues at six-month intervals from the day the tenant gives the security deposit and does not compound.

Security deposits may be withheld by landlords at the end of leases to cover:

- unpaid rent;
- losses due to breach or violation of lease terms (the landlord is entitled only to the actual financial loss, damages, caused by the breach); and
- cost of repairs to leased premises because of damage to the leased premises by the tenants or their families, guests, agents, invitees, or employees in excess of ordinary wear and tear.

Landlords who wish to withhold deposits to compensate them for damages must present to their tenants, within 45 days of the termination of the tenancy, written statements of amounts actually expended in the repair of damages. Estimates without paid receipts do not satisfy this requirement. Landlords may not recover any money for their time in personally repairing or restoring the rental premises. They may, however, recover the cost of materials used in the repair work. Once again, failure to comply with this requirement to account makes landlords liable to tenants for three times the amount of security deposits wrongfully withheld, plus reasonable attorney fees. In addition, landlords may lose their right to recover from the security deposit any unpaid rent or rental income lost due to breach of lease. A legal action concerning security deposits may be brought by tenants any time during tenancy or within two years after its termination. Tenants may not waive any of the protections provided in this section of the law. Any provision purporting to do so in a lease agreement would be of no force and effect. Regrettably, there is no prohibition against printing such a "waiver" in a lease, even when its purpose appears to be intimidation of the tenants and the waiver is of no effect.

State law requires that landlords maintain systems of orderly records showing dates of payment and amounts of rent paid by tenants. Landlords must also retain copies of receipts given to tenants for cash rental payments.

■ MISCELLANEOUS REQUIREMENTS

Note that Baltimore County and City landlords must give tenants of multifamily dwellings notice when they are located in floodplain areas.

Owners of residential rental units in Baltimore City must file an annual registration statement with the Baltimore City Commissioner of Housing and Community Development, whether the units are occupied or not, and pay a registration fee. Other jurisdictions also may have registration requirements and conduct periodic inspections.

Owners of multifamily residential rental property (property having five or more residential units) are required by State law to post in a conspicuous place a sign listing the name, address, and telephone number of the property owner or managing agent. The information may instead be included in the lease or shown on rental receipts.

■ SALE OF LEASED PREMISES

Unless specified to the contrary in the lease, the purchaser of a property occupied by a tenant under a lease is bound by the conditions and terms of that lease, just as the original landlord was. A purchaser of rented property not wishing to become a landlord should include a clause in the property purchase contract requiring that the premises be delivered unoccupied and vacant at the time of settlement. Baltimore City and several other jurisdictions require that a landlord give residential tenants the right of first refusal before leased premises can be sold to someone else.

■ TERMINATION OF PERIODIC TENANCIES

The requirements to terminate periodic tenancies differ throughout the State. In all counties except Montgomery County and Baltimore City, the landlord must give the tenant written notice to terminate, as follows:

- One week for a week-to-week tenancy
- One month for a month-to-month tenancy
- Three months for a year-to-year tenancy

By contrast, a tenant's parol (oral) notice is sufficient to terminate such tenancies. If landlords can prove that the tenants gave such notice, they do not need to give their own notice to those tenants.

In Montgomery County, the parties may agree in writing to longer or shorter notice periods. However, the local laws of Baltimore City generally require that a landlord give the following written notices to terminate:

- 60 days for a tenancy of less than one year, or at sufferance
- 90 days for a periodic tenancy
- 30 days in all other cases

A tenant may terminate any of these tenancies by giving the landlord 30 days' notice.

Holding Over

When a landlord consents to a tenant's holding over (remaining on the premises after the end of the lease term), the tenant becomes a week-to-week tenant if the lease status was week-to-week prior to the holding over. In all other cases, the tenant becomes a month-to-month tenant, unless the lease provides otherwise and this lease provision (stating otherwise) is initialed by the tenant.

A tenant under a lease who unlawfully holds over beyond the termination of the lease is liable to the landlord for actual damages that may be caused by the holding over.

Landlords' Rights to Summary Dispossession

Landlords who give the required notice or have court orders for termination of tenancy may dispossess tenants and repossess property by simple court suit before a district court judge. The length of notice landlords must give tenants before beginning dispossession proceedings is generally one month in renewable monthly tenancies or in tenancies with a fixed term and no provision for renewal. For automatically renewable yearly tenancies, this notice (with certain exceptions) is three months; for renewable monthly or weekly tenancies, it is one month or one week.

Tenant Refusal to Comply

If the tenant or person in possession refuses to comply with the written request to remove from the property, the landlord may make a complaint in writing to the district court of the county where the property is located. The court issues a summons, served by the sheriff to the tenant, to appear before the court, and an attested copy is affixed to the property in a conspicuous place. This is considered sufficient notice.

Back Rent on Renewal of Lease

Tenants or assignees who apply to their landlords for renewal under a covenant in their leases giving them the right to renew must produce vouchers or evidence showing payment of rent accrued for three years preceding this demand and application. If tenants do not provide such proof, landlords, before executing the renewal of the lease, are entitled to demand and recover not more than three years' back rent in addition to any renewal fine that may be provided for in the lease. This commonly occurs in situations involving ground rent.

Failure to Demand Rent

If there is no demand for payment of rent for more than 20 consecutive years, landlords lose not only the unpaid rental but also the reversion of the property. Therefore, a landlord's failure to demand rent for 20 years could result in the tenant's receiving fee simple title. Landlords under any legal disability when the 20-year period expires have two years after the removal of the disability to assert their rights.

Receipts for Tenants' Rental

In Anne Arundel County, unless the tenant makes payment by check or rents the property for commercial or business purposes, the landlord is required to give the tenant a receipt showing the amount of payment and the time it covers. If convicted of violating this section of the law, any person or agent forfeits the rent for the period in question.

In other counties, when the tenant makes payment other than by check, the landlord or the landlord's agent must simply give the tenant a receipt.

Surrender of Premises

When a lease contains a covenant or promise by the tenant to leave, restore, surrender, or yield the leased premises in good repair, this does not bind the tenant to erect any similar building or pay for any building destroyed by fire or otherwise if the damage was not due to the negligence or fault of the tenant.

Landlords may ask the district court to seize and sell tenants' personal property for unpaid rent by filing a petition. Landlords may do this only if tenancy has continued for longer than three months (by written lease or periodic tenancy) or was at will. *Distraint* is the term used for a landlord's right both to seize and sell such property and for the court's action in awarding this right.

A rental agreement must clearly state information such as when tenancy expires, when rent accrues, or whether rent is to be paid in advance or in arrears. If it does not, a court may find the agreement's terms too vague and deny the landlord's request for distraint. If total annual rent is stated in the lease, and no requirement is stated for its partial advance payment in monthly installments, the entire yearly rental becomes due at the end of the annual lease term.

■ PROHIBITED RESIDENTIAL LEASE PROVISIONS

In Maryland, the following provisions are prohibited in residential leases:

- A provision (cognovit clause) that authorizes an attorney for the landlord to plead the tenant guilty (confess judgment clause) on a claim arising from the lease, especially failure to pay rental
- A provision under which the tenant agrees to waive or forgo any rights or remedies against the landlord as provided by law
- A provision allowing the landlord to charge a penalty for late payment of rent that is more than 5% of the amount of rent due for the period in which the rent is delinquent (In weekly rentals, this late charge may not exceed $3 per week or $12 per month.)
- Any provision under which the tenant waives the right to a jury trial
- Any provision under which the tenant agrees to a period for the landlord's notice to quit (in the event that the tenant breaches the lease terms) that is less than the period prescribed by law (Both parties, however, are free to agree to a period that is longer than that prescribed by law.)
- Any provision authorizing the landlord to take possession of the leased premises or any of the tenant's personal property, unless the lease has been terminated by operation of law and such personal property has been abandoned by the tenant
- Any exculpatory clause—that is, language in the lease intended to exempt or hold the landlord harmless from liability to the tenant or any other person for any injury, loss, damage, or liability arising from the landlord's omission, fault, negligence, or other misconduct on or about the leased premises in areas that are not under the tenant's control (e.g., stairways, elevators, hallways, and so forth)
- A provision (not specifically signed or initialed by the tenant) allowing the automatic renewal of the lease term for a period longer than one month
- A requirement that the tenant give the landlord a longer period of notice to terminate the tenancy than the period granted the landlord to similarly notify the tenant

All of the preceding provisions, if included in a Maryland lease, are considered unenforceable. Landlords who threaten or attempt to enforce one or more of these provisions may be liable to a tenant for actual damages and attorney's fees incurred as a result. Unfortunately for tenants, there is no penalty for a landlord's merely including these clauses in a lease.

▪ WITHHOLDING RENT

Maryland law requires that a landlord provide and maintain premises for residential tenants that are free of defects and do not present substantial and serious threats of danger to the life, health, and safety of the tenants. Where hazardous conditions exist on leased property, a tenant may give the landlord written notice by certified mail of the conditions and then wait as long as 30 days. If the hazardous conditions are not corrected within that period, a tenant may withhold rent from the landlord or pay it into an escrow account for necessary repairs. Such conditions include fire or health hazards or other defects that may threaten the safety or occupancy of renters, such as

- lack of adequate sewage disposal facilities;
- infestation of rodents in two or more dwelling units; or
- failure to meet the standards set in the *Environment* Article at §6-815 or §6-819 for dealing with lead-based paint hazards. (See Figure 13.1 and Chapter 14 in this book.)

Such a situation is not constructive eviction because in constructive eviction, tenants find any continued occupancy impossible and so move out.

The Baltimore City Code holds that there is an implied warranty of habitability by a landlord that the premises are fit for human habitation. It also provides for remedies for tenants if the premises are unsafe and dirty to the extent that the tenants' health is threatened. The warranty of habitability differs from rent escrow laws in that tenants already have the use of their rent money to make those repairs the landlord has failed to complete. Under the rent escrow law, rent must be paid into an account, where it is held until the repairs are made.

The district court can order tenants to pay rents into a rent escrow account of the court or administrative agency of the county. If the tenant fails to pay rent accrued or as it becomes due, the court, on certification of the account, can give judgment in favor of the landlord and issue a warrant for possession. On final disposition of the action, the rent escrow account is distributed in accordance with a judgment or hearing.

Note that minor, not dangerous, defects or housing code violations that go uncorrected are not considered just cause for nonpayment of rent.

Tenants' Rights to End Leases and Receive Relocation Expenses

If owners of affected properties fail to comply with applicable risk reduction standards to make their properties lead-safe, tenants may make formal, documented written requests to be released from their leases and receive up to $2,400 relocation expense awards for moving to properties that meet risk-reduction standards. Landlords have three days to produce valid risk-reduction satisfaction certificates, lead-free certificates, or certification that required work has been completed. If owners fail to provide such information in accordance with this request within three business days, tenants may bring actions in District Court for the relief requested: termination of lease, relocation expenses, and reasonable attorney fees.

LEASE AGREEMENT FORMS

A number of lease forms are available from local realty boards or associations, property owner associations, and tenant organizations. Any landlord who offers more than four dwelling units for rent on one parcel of property or at one location and who rents by means of written leases substantially increases the requirements concerning the form of written leases.

RETALIATORY EVICTIONS

A landlord may not evict tenants, increase rent, or decrease any services to which they are entitled for tenants' doing any of the following:

- Filing written complaints with the landlord or with a public agency against the landlord
- Filing a lawsuit against the landlord
- Joining a tenant organization

PEACEABLE AND QUIET ENTRY

Landlords are required by law to ensure that tenants may peaceably and quietly enter the leased premises at the beginning of the lease. Failure to do so allows the tenant, on written notice to the landlord before possession is delivered, to rescission of the lease, abatement of rent, or actual damages.

SAFETY REQUIREMENTS

Tenant safety is an ongoing concern of landlords and their agents and property managers.

Compliance with Risk Reduction Laws

Licensees helping to rent older properties must be prepared to protect their clients by conforming to the lead-based paint hazard disclosure-to-tenant requirements outlined in Figure 13.1.

FIGURE   13.1

Lead-Based Paint Disclosure and Registration Requirements

Dates Property Built	Federal Compliance Requirements
Before 1/1/1978 "Targeted Property"	Both of the following must be given to all lessees at the beginning of every tenancy and again every two years. Tenants' receipt of these is to be verified by their signature. 1. EPA booklet, *Protect Your Family From Lead in Your Home*, to be given to all lessees at the beginning and renewal of every lease or at least every two years. 2. Lead-Based Paint (Rental) Disclosure form, with signed copies to be kept by the landlord.
	Maryland Compliance Requirements
Before 1/1/1950 "Affected Property"	1. The property must be registered with the Maryland Department of the Environment and then reregistered annually. 2. Before a property is rented, it must be inspected by state-approved inspectors and any necessary abatement performed. 3. Maryland Department of the Environment Pamphlet, *Notice of Tenants' Rights*, and the EPA booklet, *Protect Your Family From Lead in Your Home*, are to be given to tenants at the beginning of every tenancy, every two years thereafter, and whenever the rental changes.

See Chapter 14 for more details on lead-based paint hazards.

Sprinkler Systems

Sprinkler systems must be installed in every newly constructed dormitory, hotel, lodging or rooming house, town house, and multifamily residential dwelling. Sprinkler systems are not required, however, if a dwelling unit is not serviced by a public water supply system.

Smoke Detectors

Smoke detectors must be installed in all multifamily buildings and hotels constructed before 1975 and having four to nine units. Also, they must be installed in all buildings having more than nine units—regardless of when they were built. The landlord is responsible for the installation, repair, or replacement of the detectors. The occupant of a one-family, two-family, or three-family residential dwelling constructed before July 1975 is required to equip the apartment with at least one approved smoke detector and to maintain the smoke detector. A smoke detector operated both by battery and by alternating current (AC) must be installed in every newly constructed residential dwelling unit. At least one smoke detector must be installed on each level, including basements but not attics.

Carbon Monoxide Alarms

All residential housing—including apartments and condos as well as commercial properties that contain sleeping quarters—that uses fossil-based fuel for any heating, cooling, cooking, or lighting purpose must be equipped with hard-wired carbon monoxide alarms within specified distances of sleeping areas and connected to a central system. Systems must conform to various national and State building technical specifications. This requirement applies to structures with building permits issued after January 1, 2009.

■ LEASE OPTION AGREEMENTS

A lease with option to purchase includes any lease that contains a clause giving the tenant the right until a specified date to purchase the landlord's interest in the property. No lease option on improved residential property in Maryland, with or without a ground rent interest, is valid unless it contains the statement "THIS IS NOT A CONTRACT TO BUY" in capital letters. It must also contain a clear statement of the option's purpose and effect with respect to the ultimate purchase of the property. The purchase price of the property as well as a consideration for the option privilege itself—even if only a nominal (token) amount—must both be recited. Note that the price of the option privilege is distinct and different from the consideration to be paid if the option is exercised.

■ MOBILE HOME PARKS

Title 8A of the *Real Property* Article sets forth the rights and responsibilities of mobile home park tenants and owners. It addresses such matters as park rules, maintenance, and tenancy.

■ SOURCES OF ASSISTANCE

Baltimore Neighborhoods Inc., a private nonprofit civil rights agency working on behalf of fair housing and tenants' rights in the Baltimore area, publishes guides to laws covering tenant-landlord relations in Baltimore City, the counties, and the State. These guides, revised annually to incorporate new laws, may be purchased from the organization at 2217 St. Paul St., Baltimore, MD 21218. The organization's website is www.bni-maryland.org.

CHAPTER 13 QUIZ

1. Sampson sold a house he owned that was occupied by Rawlins under a one-year lease having six months to run. What is Rawlins' position in view of this sale?
   1. Rawlins must vacate at the closing of the sale.
   2. Rawlins' lease continues until its expiration.
   3. The lease terminates at closing.
   4. The lease is not binding on the new owner.

2. What is a landlord who holds a tenant's security deposit of $2,400 required to do?
   1. Credit the tenant's deposit with $72 interest after one year.
   2. Allow the tenant 5% simple interest per year.
   3. Return the deposit within 30 days after termination of the lease.
   4. Give the tenant a receipt or be liable to the tenant for a sum of $1,200.

3. In Maryland, which of the following leases does NOT need to be acknowledged and recorded?
   1. 7-year apartment lease
   2. 8-year residential lease
   3. 9-year commercial lease
   4. 10-year residential lease

4. Jane Builder has just completed a new house, which she is offering for sale at $240,000 with fee simple title. If, to satisfy an immediate buyer, she creates a ground lease requiring $720 a year ground rent at a 6% redemption rate, which of the following situations would be created?
   1. The property may not be redeemed for at least 50 years.
   2. She can reduce the sale price to $228,000.
   3. She can reduce the sale price to $225,600.
   4. The in-fee price would be $235,680.

5. Arthur Buyer is interested in purchasing a residence for $325,000 with a ground rent of $1,250. When the deal is done, what will Arthur receive?
   1. A deed conveying to him a fee simple interest
   2. A leasehold estate subject to an annual ground rent of $1,250
   3. A deed subject to his redeeming the ground rent
   4. A fee simple deed after paying ground rent for five years

6. What kind of estate does a woman get who buys and occupies a house but has to pay a semiannual ground rent?
   1. A fee simple estate
   2. A leasehold estate
   3. An estate at will
   4. An estate at sufferance

7. Why are ground rents often originated?
   1. To reduce the amount of cash required to purchase a property
   2. To force the tenant to keep the property in good repair
   3. To provide further assurances to a mortgagee
   4. To prevent a lender from foreclosing

8. What will it cost to redeem a parcel when its ground rent is $600 a year?
   1. Five percent will require $6,000.
   2. Six percent will require $10,000.
   3. Ten percent will require $7,500.
   4. Twelve percent will require $15,000.

9. What is the process by which a residential landlord has a court seize and sell a tenant's personal property for unpaid rent called?
   1. Ejectment
   2. Abandonment
   3. Dispossession
   4. Distraint

10. Which of the following provisions, if included in residential leases in Maryland, is enforceable?

1. Tenants agree to pay the landlord a 5% penalty for late rent payments.
2. Tenants agree to let landlords use their passkeys to take possession of tenants' property if tenants fall more than one month behind in rent payments.
3. Tenants agree to waive or forgo any rights or remedies against landlords provided by law.
4. All the above

Environmental Issues and Real Estate Transactions

■ KEY TERMS

affected properties   jointly and severally   mold

asbestos   methyl tertiary-butyl ether   storage tanks

carcinogenic   (MTBE)

■ OVERVIEW

Maryland, like most states, faces complex environmental challenges. Almost all of them call for balancing economic vitality with environmental concerns, human safety, and quality of life. These tensions can pit the rights of property owners against the wishes of others for preservation or restoration of natural resources. Nationwide, literally hundreds of statutes, ordinances, and regulations are written each year to address these matters. Maryland legislation in this matter is influenced by federal statutes, which often compel stricter enforcement than Maryland originally envisioned.

Maryland, along with other states, struggles to coordinate its laws and regulations with advances in environmental science that often outrun them.

Various resources dealing with Maryland environmental concerns and programs are available at www.mde.state.md.us, the Maryland Department of the Environment (MDE) website.

■ MULTIPLE CHALLENGES

Environmental concerns include the loss of woodlands, farmlands, and tidal and nontidal wetlands. These concerns overlap other ecological issues such as endangered species, clean air, clean water, fisheries, and other wildlife. Recreation and camping needs are also part of the puzzle.

Hazards to human health include auto emissions and other air and/or water pollution from ozone, asbestos, radon, radium, lead-based paint, wastewater sewage, industrial waste, leakage from underground storage tanks, and acid rain.

■ MULTILEVEL APPROACHES

The State reaches upward, outward, and inward in its efforts: upward toward federal agencies, outward toward neighboring states, and inward to subdivisions and municipalities. To this last group, the State typically grants enabling powers to authorize their participation through zoning and other environmentally related activities. Various subdivisions are authorized to set standards even more rigorous than those set by the State. If they are less strict than the State's, the more rigorous State laws prevail.

Cooperative Approaches

It is rare that an environmental issue can be handled effectively by the Maryland State government acting alone. Its activities and interests overlap and interact with those of the federal government, neighboring states, State subdivisions and municipalities, and private and corporate citizens.

■ ENFORCEMENT

Enforcement of standards set forth in statutes, regulations, and ordinances is carried out by the MDE except in cases where county enforcement capabilities and resources are comparable to those of that department. The Secretary of MDE may delegate enforcement powers to such counties for a two-year period.

■ THE CHESAPEAKE BAY

The Chesapeake Bay, nearly 200 miles long and fed by 48 major rivers, 100 smaller rivers, and thousands of other tributaries, is the largest and most productive estuary in the United States. It covers 64,000 square miles and provides habitat for myriad species of plants and animals. Its 15-million-person population is expected to swell to 18 million by 2020.

Chesapeake Bay Critical Area Act

This law identifies the critical area as all land within 1,000 feet of the average high-water line of tidal waters or the landward edge of tidal wetlands and all waters of and lands under the Chesapeake Bay and its tributaries.

The General Assembly has strengthened this act and supporting laws by

■ giving the Critical Area Commission authority to update and enforce the law,
■ allowing the State to revoke the licenses of builders who knowingly violate the law,

- increasing the no-build buffer zone for new subdivisions in rural areas from 100 feet to 200 feet, and
- tightening the rules about where new housing can be located.

The Buffer

Earlier legislation had designated as the buffer a 100-foot, natural vegetation, forested zone extending from the mean high-water line landward from tidal waters and tidal wetlands. That buffer is now 200 feet. The vegetation required for the first 100 feet is different from the second 100, where grasses are generally acceptable.

The buffer's trees filter runoff water returning to streams and reduce sediments, fertilizers, and toxic substances. Human activities in the area are sharply reduced because of their adverse impact on the nearby waterways and wildlife. No disturbance of the buffer may be permitted by local jurisdictions unless an applicant can meet strict provisions for a variance.

A wealth of interesting and useful information on this matter is found at the Critical Area Commission for the Chesapeake and Atlantic Coastal Bays website: www.dnr.state.md.us/criticalarea.

■ FILLING OF WETLANDS RESISTED

Filling wetlands, for whatever purpose, is regarded as one of the most environmentally pernicious of actions. It may be permitted only when no alternative course of action is available or when the person seeking a permit will create new areas of wetland to compensate for those being filled. The replacement area ratios (new-to-lost) range from 1:1 to 4.5:1.

■ IMPACT ON RESIDENTIAL REAL ESTATE

Many of these environmental issues directly and indirectly affect availability of residential housing. Preserving agricultural space and wetlands reduces the amount of land available for development. Indeed, the present policy of Maryland is not just to maintain but to increase the total area of all State wetlands.

In seeking to achieve environmental and public safety goals, the State and its subdivisions impose regulatory and impact fees and increasingly require costly safety measures and techniques that protect both people and the environment. By slowing development and imposing fees on developers—fees that are then passed along to consumers—governments can make it more costly for people to buy homes in less developed areas. This is intended to encourage renewal of older, developed areas and more intense use of that land rather than "sprawling" into rural and semirural areas. This encouragement has not been strongly supported by enforcement activities at the local level so that, statewide, sprawling actually increased, rather than abated, during the life of the Smart Growth program, which began in 1992. A recent effort took the form of the Smart, Green, and Growing legislative package—passed in 2009—which requires local jurisdictions to set their own Smart Growth goals and report on their progress according to a range of indicators.

One statutory requirement that affects every licensee is that all contracts for sale of property suitable for one or two single-family units contain the "Notice to Buyer Concerning the Chesapeake and Atlantic Coastal Bays Critical Area," quoted in full in Chapter 9.

■ MARYLAND DEPARTMENT OF THE ENVIRONMENT

Targeting Asbestos

Within the MDE, the Air and Radiation Management Administration, among its other duties, sets and enforces standards for asbestos removal and encapsulation projects. It also licenses people who work in that field. Much attention of the department is directed toward asbestos identification and its containment in or removal from public buildings such as schools, colleges, and universities.

However, asbestos is found in varying amounts in single-family homes, with older homes often having greater amounts. Until the 1970s, asbestos, because of its insulating properties, was a popular component of siding, kitchen floor tiles, and heating and cooling insulation. Licensees should not attempt to answer questions about asbestos and should neither minimize nor exaggerate its effects. Refer questions to companies that are licensed to deal with asbestos.

Waste Management Administration

Also within the MDE is the Waste Management Administration, which deals with environmental restoration and land redevelopment, oil control, lead poisoning, solid waste, scrap tires, sewage sludge, and hazardous materials. It oversees aboveground storage tanks for oil and gas and underground storage tanks (USTs) for regulated substances. It seeks to identify, prioritize, and abate contaminated sites.

Owners of certain underground storage tanks containing petroleum products must remove or pay for the removal of tanks that leak. MDE regulations set standards for evidence of the financial responsibility of property owners for costs of cleanup, corrective action, and liability.

Of ongoing concern is the presence of methyl tertiary-butyl ether (MTBE) in the air and in groundwater. This substance has been increasingly used to replace tetraethyl lead in gasoline as an agent to reduce knocking in gasoline motors. As federal requirements for clean air get stricter, more MTBE is used. The increased use of such reformulated gasoline (RFG) produces less carbon monoxide (CO) from automobile operation, but, inevitably, some of the MTBE additive gets into the ground and the air—some from spills, some from leaking underground storage tanks (LUSTs), and some from simple evaporation.

MTBE is suspected of being carcinogenic (cancer causing), although this characteristic has not yet been proven. Yet, even before MTBE reaches suspected unsafe levels, drinking water infiltrated by it has an unpleasant taste and odor. This problem is especially bothersome in areas where there is no public water supply and citizens use individual wells. Moreover, once MTBE is released into the environment, it breaks down into tertiary butyl alcohol (TBA), which cannot be detected by taste and odor at similar levels of concentration. Enforcement of remediation is most active in areas that do not have public water and where levels from 20 to 40 parts per billion have been detected. Where wells have been affected, property transfers by sale have often been halted. Proper filtration can abate the problem but imposes considerable cost on the party responsible for installation of filtration equipment.

The MDE is required to provide notice to the local health department upon a finding by the Department of specified oil contaminants, including MTBE, in groundwater samples. The local health department then provides owners of property located within one-half mile of a site found to be contaminated with a notice of that fact. The person responsible for an oil discharge is liable for the costs of providing the notice.

Water Management Administration

Among the most important functions within the MDE are those given to the Water Management Administration, which seeks to protect drinking water. With its team of inspectors, it also oversees tidal and nontidal wetlands, floodplains, water appropriations, waterway and floodplain construction, sediment control, stormwater management, coal mining, and oil and gas exploration.

Mold

There are a great many varieties of mold, some toxic, some irritating, some mildly annoying, and some (such as penicillin) very useful. Mold identification and removal—and the training of technicians to do those things—has become an industry in itself. It is a complex subject about which there is considerable interest, modest knowledge, and quite a bit of fear. There are 50 websites—offering legal help for people who have found mold in their houses—for every one website giving information about the problem itself. The presence of mold has inspired dramatic litigation, with some celebrity homeowners suing builders and others for millions of dollars in damages and medical costs.

It is physically difficult to remove toxic mold from a home once it is identified. However, even greater human and financial costs threaten persons who have physical reactions to the presence of mold. Licensees are urged not to disturb mold by such actions as pulling out bathroom drywall or peeling off wallpaper. Even dead mold triggers severe allergic reactions in some persons. Licensees are never to assure buyers or tenants that a home is mold-free or even mold-safe. Give no reassurances but do not generate unnecessary fears. Refer all questions to attorneys and certified, licensed experts.

Mold formation can be reduced by proper ventilation of areas where water may condense or drip. Household relative humidity greater than 40% encourages mold growth. It thrives on moisture, wood, paper, and darkness. A house with improperly installed roof "flashing" or poorly maintained soffits, drains, and downspouts allows water to find its way into wall spaces, where it joins all the other factors that foster mold growth. Engineering inspections of houses will often reveal situations that can produce mold, even if they do not find the mold itself. Much of Maryland has favorable conditions for mold growth year-round, so proper home construction and maintenance are the leading methods of reducing mold infestation, related respiratory diseases, and possible consequent litigation.

■ REDUCTION OF LEAD RISK IN HOUSING ACT

Maryland's Reduction of Lead Risk in Housing Act seeks "to reduce the incidence of childhood lead poisoning, while maintaining the stock of available affordable rental housing." This act, the environmental law that affects more existing Maryland residential properties than any other law, undergirds Maryland's Lead Paint Poisoning Prevention Program.

There is broad-based scientific agreement that exposure to lead-based paint can produce devastating results in young children, newborns, and fetuses. This law is an earnest attempt to reduce the exposure of children under age six and of pregnant women to the effects of lead-based paint in residential rental properties built before 1978.

Lead Paint Poisoning Abatement

State and federal legislation concerning lead levels in certain rental properties impose substantial responsibilities and burdens on investor-owners of many income properties and on their agents. At the same time, these laws allow investors to limit their liability for lead poisoning by following certain procedures.

The elevated blood lead (EBL) level that triggers notification of local health departments is now 10 (rather than the previous 15 or 20) micrograms per deciliter. The law applies also to exterior structures, such as playground equipment and benches. It requires that an inspection report state that all interior and exterior surfaces are lead-free or that the interior is lead-free and the exterior surfaces that were chipping, peeling, or flaking have been restored with non-lead-based paint.

Seeking to Protect Children and Mothers

Maryland's Lead Paint Poisoning Prevention Plan makes children under age six and pregnant women with elevated blood lead (EBL) levels eligible for specific financial relief for medical treatment ($7,500) and for relocation to lead-safe housing ($9,500). The portion of the law that prevented victims from going to court for further relief if they accepted the specific amounts has been declared null and void; other provisions of the law remain in place. Landlord's responsibility can no longer be limited to $17,000, and that much insurance will provide negligible protection. Previously, investors wishing to limit their liability for lead poisoning of tenants only had to bring their properties into compliance with lead-safe standards and keep them that way.

That Part of Plan Encouraging Modest Settlements Struck Down

In 2011, the Maryland Court of Special Appeals declared that the $17,000 ($7,500 + $9,500) limit on landlord liability granted by the law to be unconstitutional because it took away an injured party's right to sue for appropriate damages if the landlord only complied with the modest requirements of the plan. The plan didn't limit, or cap, the liability of landlords. Rather, it made them eligible to present qualified offers of amounts up to $7,500 for medical expenses and up to $9,500 for relocation and rent supplement expenses to their tenants found to have EBL levels. If tenants with EBL levels accept the "qualified offer," they give up the right to sue the landlord for larger sums. In exchange, they get their money when they need it and don't have to face the prolonged uncertainty of initiating a lawsuit that may be particularly difficult to win. The downside pointed out by the high court is that the medical and other amounts are miniscule and do not balance the injured party's loss of the right to the courts in later tort action. Such access had been extinguished when a qualified offer was either rejected or never made.

In view of the former loss limits, companies insuring residential properties that were or had been made lead-free or lead-safe had been required to provide liability coverage for lead paint poisoning up to $17,000 (the total of $7,500 and $9,500).

The part of the law establishing such modest amounts for the injured party in return for loss of right to sue was declared contrary to Maryland's Declaration of Rights, Article 19. The rest of the statute was left intact after the offending provisions were severed.

Active Enforcement

The law is vigorously enforced. Moreover, its requirements increase periodically. Note that affected properties (see Chapter 13) are those constructed before 1950 that contain at least one rental dwelling unit; the term also refers to an individual unit within such a multiunit building, as well as residential rental properties built between 1950 and 1977, for which the owner has opted to comply with this law.

Properties to Be Registered

One statute, in effect since October 1994, divides residential rental properties into two significant groups, based on dates of construction:

- Before 1950
- From 1950 through 1977

Based on those classifications, tens of thousands of rental dwelling properties are registered with the MDE. Owners must register every residential rental built before 1950 for a $15 fee and then pay annual renewal fees, also $15, for each. For example, an owner with a home built before 1950, divided into four apartments, must register each unit for $15 and then pay $60/year renewal fees as long as the properties remain in rental use. The annual renewal amount is also $15 per rental unit for post 1950 units whose owners may opt to join the program. The "opt-in" program makes such owners eligible to make qualified offers in the event children are found to be poisoned by lead in properties.

Licensees' Responsibilities

Licensees acting as management agents for landlords who have affected residential rental properties share their clients' legal responsibilities. Consequently, they must become familiar with aspects of inspection, lead reduction procedures, property registration, and periodic renewal of registration, insurance, and limitation of liability with respect to lead-paint issues. The State—through its leadership and agencies—is manifesting its determination to pursue the goal of a lead-safe rental environment for the children of Maryland.

■ FEDERAL LAW ALSO APPLIES

The requirements of Maryland law are in addition to, and do not take the place of, the requirements set forth in federal law concerning lead in residential properties built prior to 1978. The federal law requires distribution of information in the form of the booklet *Protect Your Family From Lead in Your Home* both to potential tenants and to potential purchasers of properties built before 1978. This 17-page booklet can be seen at and downloaded from http://www2.epa.gov/lead/protect-your-family-lead-your-home.

Additional HUD/EPA provisions require giving purchasers a form, Disclosure of Lead-Based Paint and Lead-Based Paint Hazards. The form becomes a part of the contract to purchase. It allows purchasers to demand as much as a 10-day interval to secure a lead assessment inspection of the property and to rescind the contract if sellers will not correct any deficiencies that are found. The inspection or risk assessment period can be lengthened, shortened, or waived by mutual written consent between the purchaser and the seller.

Effective in April 2010, workers involved in lead paint hazard abatement, removal, and testing are now required by EPA to complete training for these activities. There are three levels of certification for graduates of this training. For the safety of tenants and purchaser, and to protect landlord and seller clients from criminal or civil liability, licensees are reminded to always employ—or have their clients employ—testing and abatement firms whose employees are certified for the level of work undertaken.

The form also contains the sellers' disclosure of all known lead-paint hazards in the property and a lead warning statement. It requires the purchasers' signatures regarding receipt of this information, receipt of the EPA/HUD pamphlet, and their decision as to whether they will make use of the maximum 10-day contingency period.

Even owners who sell or rent their own property without the aid of real estate licensees are required to provide the form and the pamphlet. The rental form makes no provision for an inspection period but otherwise contains essentially the same information as the form for sales. It refers, of course, to lessors and lessees rather than to purchasers and sellers. Figure 14.1 presents a typical form for sales. The student should remember that a different form is used for rental transactions, which does not contain a 10-day period for lead inspection and subsequent cancellation.

The form contains many blanks that require a response—either an initial or a check mark. Licensees should make certain that there is such a response in every blank. In the situation there is one blank that is not responded to, it is treated as failure to meet the federal requirement. Using the form intended for rental situations for a sale, and vice versa, also fails to satisfy the law.

When a licensed agent makes any of these mistakes, both the licensee and the principal—whether homeseller or landlord—are held responsible. Fines of up to $11,000 may be imposed, and an assessment of treble damages can be levied for deliberate failure. Fines are assessed jointly and severally (that is, not proportionately). Therefore, the licensee should scrutinize every form for appropriateness and completeness before delivering it to its recipient.

There is actually no official federal form for either a rent or a sale situation. Nonetheless, any form used is required to have substantially the same language as the wording prescribed in HUD regulations. Many associations of brokers, therefore, provide HUD's language in both forms, word for word.

Unlike the federal law, Maryland statutes require inspection and, if necessary, remediation by owners of "affected residential rental property" (as defined in 6-801[b] of the *Environment* Article) in addition to delivery of the MDE *Notice of Tenants' Rights* every time such properties have change of occupancy or an increase in rent. The six-page MDE booklet, *Notice of Tenants' Rights*, is available for download at www.mde.state.md.us/assets/document/LeadCoordination/tenants_rights.pdf.

The requirements for distribution of lead-based paint literature by both the federal government and Maryland are presented in Figure 14.2.

FIGURE 14.1

Lead-Based Paint Disclosure Form

Disclosure of Information on Lead-Based Paint and/or Lead-Based Paint Hazards

Lead Warning Statement

Every purchaser of any interest in residential real property on which a residential dwelling was built prior to 1978 is notified that such property may present exposure to lead from lead-based paint that may place young children at risk of developing lead poisoning. Lead poisoning in young children may produce permanent neurological damage, including learning disabilities, reduced intelligence quotient, behavioral problems, and impaired memory. Lead poisoning also poses a particular risk to pregnant women. The seller of any interest in residential real property is required to provide the buyer with any information on lead-based paint hazards from risk assessments or inspections in the seller's possession and notify the buyer of any known lead-based paint hazards. A risk assessment or inspection for possible lead-based paint hazards is recommended prior to purchase.

Seller's Disclosure

(a) Presence of lead-based paint and/or lead-based paint hazards (check (i) or (ii) below):

    (i) _____ Known lead-based paint and/or lead-based paint hazards are present in the housing (explain).

    _____

    (ii) _____ Seller has no knowledge of lead-based paint and/or lead-based paint hazards in the housing.

(b) Records and reports available to the seller (check (i) or (ii) below):

    (i) _____ Seller has provided the purchaser with all available records and reports pertaining to lead-based paint and/or lead-based paint hazards in the housing (list documents below).

    _____

    (ii) _____ Seller has no reports or records pertaining to lead-based paint and/or lead-based paint hazards in the housing.

Purchaser's Acknowledgment (initial)

(c) _____ Purchaser has received copies of all information listed above.

(d) _____ Purchaser has received the pamphlet *Protect Your Family from Lead in Your Home.*

(e) Purchaser has (check (i) or (ii) below):

    (i) _____ received a 10-day opportunity (or mutually agreed upon period) to conduct a risk assessment or inspection for the presence of lead-based paint and/or lead-based paint hazards; or

    (ii) _____ waived the opportunity to conduct a risk assessment or inspection for the presence of lead-based paint and/or lead-based paint hazards.

Agent's Acknowledgment (initial)

(f) _____ Agent has informed the seller of the seller's obligations under 42 U.S.C. 4852d and is aware of his/her responsibility to ensure compliance.

Certification of Accuracy

The following parties have reviewed the information above and certify, to the best of their knowledge, that the information they have provided is true and accurate.

_____ _____   _____ _____
Seller   Date   Seller   Date

_____ _____   _____ _____
Purchaser   Date   Purchaser   Date

_____ _____   _____ _____
Agent   Date   Agent   Date

Note: This is the form given by sellers to purchasers. The form to be given by landlords to tenants is different.

FIGURE 14.2

Federal and Maryland Requirements for Residential Structure Lead-Paint Poisoning Disclosure Literature

Built Dates Are Inclusive	Lease	Sale	Federal Requirements	MD Requirements
1/1/1979 and forward (Fed) and 1/1/1978 and forward (MD)	Yes	Yes	n/a	None
1950–1978 (Fed) 1950–1977 (MD)	Yes	Yes	EPA booklet and rental disclosure form	None
Before 1/1/1950	Yes	No	EPA booklet and rental disclosure form	MDE notice
Before 1/1/1950	No	Yes	EPA booklet and sale disclosure form	None

CHAPTER 14 QUIZ

1. Which of the following is *NOT* a direct source of Maryland air pollution?
   1. Radon
   2. Leakage from underground storage tanks
   3. Asbestos
   4. Automobile emissions

2. Which of the following is *TRUE* both of open space preservation and of ecological challenges?
   1. They are concerns that must be addressed separately.
   2. They are not appropriate issues for State government to address.
   3. They overlap in many ways.
   4. They can best be dealt with by individual municipalities.

3. Which of the following is *TRUE* of the Maryland Smart Growth Initiative?
   1. It is a disguised "no-growth" plan.
   2. The plan seeks to develop new areas in a systematic and orderly fashion.
   3. One of its goals is to revitalize older neighborhoods.
   4. It seeks to reduce density in housing.

4. What is the guideline for environmental regulations imposed by local jurisdictions within the State?
   1. They must not be stricter than those imposed by the State itself.
   2. They may be stricter than those imposed by the State.
   3. Such regulations must be authorized by federal mandate.
   4. Local environmental regulations do not require State enabling acts.

5. What can be accurately stated about most environmental issues?
   1. They can usually be handled by the State alone.
   2. Such issues require cooperation between the State and local municipalities.
   3. They require cooperation among local municipalities, the State, and other states.
   4. They often involve local, State, regional (interstate), and federal cooperation.

6. Which of the following is *TRUE* of the Chesapeake Bay Critical Area Act?
   1. The act does not clearly define what a critical area is.
   2. It establishes buffer zone size at 1,000 feet.
   3. The act keeps local governments from approving virtually any disturbance of the land in a buffer zone.
   4. It defines critical area buffer as all land within 100 feet of high-water line of tidal bodies and within 100 feet of the dry edge of tidal wetlands.

7. Which statement about the Chesapeake Bay Critical Area Act's buffer zone is accurate?
   1. It preserves and protects trees and other natural vegetation, mainly to help purify the air.
   2. The buffer zone is the first 200 feet landward from tidal waters, tidal wetlands, and tributary streams.
   3. It is meant to provide wildlife a safe habitat.
   4. It provides a pleasant area for fishing and hunting.

8. In what way is filling of wetlands addressed by Maryland's environmental laws?
   1. Such filling is regarded as mildly hurtful to the environment.
   2. It is allowed only as a last resort.
   3. Filling is subject to multiple levels of regulation.
   4. It is no longer allowed under any circumstance.

9. Which of the following will *NOT* increase as a result of State and local government environmental actions?
   1. The amount of land available for real estate development
   2. The size of the State's wetland areas
   3. The cost of housing in less-developed areas
   4. The intensity of land use in older, developed areas

10. Which statement is *TRUE* concerning the "Notice to Buyer Concerning the Chesapeake and Atlantic Coastal Bays Critical Area"?

    1. This notice is required in all contracts for the sale of real property in the State.
    2. It is required in all contracts for the sale of Maryland residential property.
    3. This notice is not required in certain Maryland counties.
    4. The notice informs purchasers whether the property they are purchasing is located in the critical area of the Chesapeake and Atlantic Coastal Bays.

CHAPTER

15

Fair Housing

■ KEY TERMS

complainant	natural person	respondent
conciliation agreement		

■ OVERVIEW

Competent real estate licensees realize that fair housing compliance is very demanding. Licensees must have knowledge of applicable federal, State, and local laws, each of which often has its own list of protected groups and of prohibited and required activities. In this chapter, you may notice some similarities and some differences among State, federal, and local laws regarding fair housing.

In this chapter, the term *Commission* refers to the State of Maryland Commission on Human Relations, not the Maryland Real Estate Commission.

■ COMMISSION ON HUMAN RELATIONS

Nine members, appointed by the Governor for staggered six-year terms, comprise the Human Relations Commission. The members choose their own chairperson and are served by an Executive Director and a Deputy Director. The Executive Director selects an attorney to serve as the Commission's General Counsel. The body meets monthly with additional special meetings after five days' notice to the members.

In addition to its work with fair housing, the Commission works to reduce discrimination in employment and in public accommodations. It not only follows up on complaints from the public but may also take the initiative and generate complaints when at least three of its members agree to do so. The Commission is also subject to the very law from which it receives its authority in that it must not show partiality or favoritism in its own staffing and personnel policies. All State agencies, departments, boards, and their employees are similarly subject to the *State Government* Article, Title 20, *Human Relations* (formerly Article 49B, *Human Relations Commission*).

Processing Complaints

Complaints to the Commission must be made within one year of the alleged discriminatory action or the end of such action, whichever is later. Complaints must be in writing and under oath. When a complaint is received, the Executive Director considers it and refers it to staff for investigation. Copies of the written staff report submitted to the Executive Director are then sent both to the complainant (the aggrieved party making the complaint) and to the respondent (the party accused of discriminatory behavior). If the respondent is also a real estate licensee, a copy of the report is sent to the state Real Estate Commission.

If the report concludes that a discriminatory act probably has been committed, staff members seek to deal with the matter by conference, conciliation, and persuasion. If no agreement is reached between complainant and respondent, a report of that fact is sent to all parties.

If the initial conclusion of staff is that there is no probable cause, the report is considered a "final order," which can then be appealed by the complainant to a circuit court in the county where the alleged violation occurred.

When there is found to be probable cause and no agreement is reached, all findings are certified by staff. A written notice is then sent in the name of the Commission to the respondent, requiring an answer to the charges at a public hearing before a hearing examiner to be held in the county of the alleged violation.

If conciliation is productive, a written conciliation agreement is signed by the parties. Its terms are made public, unless the parties request they not be and the Commission determines such disclosure would not serve the purposes of the statute.

Up to this point, all proceedings are nonpublic and held in strict confidence. Indeed, a Commission member or one of its staff members who violates this confidentiality can be punished by a fine of not more than $1,000 and imprisonment of not more than one year.

At a public hearing, the General Counsel makes the case in support of the complaint. The respondent may give written answer, be heard in person, call and examine witnesses, and be represented by counsel.

When hearing examiners find (conclude) that respondents have engaged in a discriminatory practice, they may order them to

- cease and desist,
- take positive action to remedy the situation,
- reinstate or rehire (in an employment dispute), or
- provide any other appropriate equitable relief.

If the finding is that there was no discriminatory practice, the examiner shall issue and file an order of dismissal. False and/or malicious complaints are punishable by a fine of not more than $500 and/or one year in prison. [SG §20-1104(c)]

If a respondent fails to do what is ordered, the Commission may sue to enforce compliance with any order within its authority.

Alternative Complaint Procedure

Whereas complaints to the Human Relations Commission must be made within one year, the complainant may apply to a court for relief at any time up to two years from the time of the alleged discriminatory event or breach of a conciliation agreement.

A civil action (suit) may be initiated against the respondent in a circuit court in the appropriate county before or even during the early stages of the processing of a complaint by the Commission. However, when this happens, the administrative hearing process on the same alleged discriminatory practice must stop immediately. The complainant is required to notify all parties of initiating civil action.

■ FAIR HOUSING LAWS

Persons who believe they are being discriminated against in a Maryland property transaction—whether it involves real property or personal property—because of their race may, by virtue of the Civil Rights Act of 1866, petition a federal court to order an end to the discrimination. Alternatively, they may choose to file a complaint with the Maryland Human Relations Commission if they experience discrimination in a residential real estate–related transaction. Aspects of a real estate–related transaction that would be covered include not only selling and brokerage but also appraisal, insuring, and lending, either for rental, purchase, or improvement and repair of a home.

Because Maryland has laws and enforcement mechanisms that have been adjudged substantially equivalent to the federal Fair Housing Act of 1968, as amended, residential discrimination complaints are handled by State agencies and by State courts. Complaints made to HUD are referred by HUD to the Commission.

The Fair Housing Act may be found on the internet at www.justice.gov/crt/about/hce/title8.php.

Those seeking help under the Maryland law—*State Government* Article, Title 20 *Human Relations*, §19 and following—will find that the protected categories are similar to, but go beyond, those in the federal law. In addition to the federal categories of race, color, religion, sex, familial status, national origin, and disability,

Maryland includes marital status and sexual orientation. The act defines *sexual orientation* as "identification of an individual as to male or female homosexuality, heterosexuality, or bisexuality."

Note that Maryland statutes are using the phrase "individual with a disability" to replace "handicapped person." Federal statutes currently use "mental disability" in place of the previous term "retarded."

Exceptions

The Maryland law has exceptions to its antidiscrimination requirements that parallel those in the 1968/1988 Fair Housing Act.

In both, an individual is permitted to discriminate in the sale or rental of a single-family dwelling if the property is sold or rented without the help of any broker, of any person in the business of selling or renting dwellings, or of any agent of either of these. The seller must use no discriminatory advertising in marketing the property. Unlike the federal law, Maryland's *State Government* Article, Title 20, *Human Relations* makes no requirement about the number of properties such seller may own or how many may be sold within a specified time period. Racial discrimination, however, is not permitted in any of these situations because of the Civil Rights Act of 1866, which is still the law of the land.

The law allows an owner-occupant of a single-family principal residence to reject tenant applicants for rooms based on sex, marital status, and/or sexual orientation.

Also, the owner of a building of five or fewer rental units who occupies one of those units may also reject applicants in the three previously listed categories. This contrasts with the federal law's standard of a total of four or fewer units.

Maryland's other exceptions closely follow those in the federal Fair Housing Act by permitting exclusion of certain protected groups under specific circumstances:

- Religious organizations may limit rental accommodations to one sex and to members of the organization's religious denomination, if their denomination doesn't discriminate on the basis of race, color, national origin, and familial status.
- Private clubs may refuse nonmembers who seek accommodations, if they do not discriminate in admission of members.
- Owners may refuse to rent or sell to persons convicted of manufacture or distribution of illegal drugs.
- Operators of housing for the elderly may reject occupancy (not ownership) by families with young children. Either of two situations permits such exclusion.
  - All residents of the community are required to be age 62 and above.
  - At least one person age 55 or more resides in 80% of the units.
- Owners need not rent to families larger in number than the limits set for occupancy by local government units. Such reasonable occupancy standards are typically based on adequacy of number of rooms and square footage of units for safe occupancy.

Counties, municipalities, and other local governments are also empowered to enact ordinances and extend protection to additional groups. Such ordinances may not be less strict than the statewide requirements.

All jurisdictions recognize the federal core of protected categories: race, color, religion, national origin, sex, physical or mental impairment, and familial status. The State has added marital status and sexual orientation, while some counties have added one or more of the following: occupation, personal appearance, source of income, creed, and political opinion.

Sources of law relating to enforcement include the Civil Rights Act of 1866; the Civil Rights Act of 1964; the Fair Housing Act of 1968, as amended; Title 20 of the State Government Article of the Maryland Code; §17-526 of the *Business Occupations and Professions* Article of the Maryland Code; Chapter 27 of the Montgomery County Code; Title 12, Subtitle 2 of the Howard County Code; Division 12, Subdivision I of the Prince George's County Code; and Chapter 13 of the Laws of Rockville. Although not comprehensive, this list is suggestive of the number of laws governing and protecting the people of Maryland in the area of fair housing.

■ PROTECTED GROUPS AND CATEGORIES

The basic list of protected categories is found in the federal fair housing law, which extends protection on the basis of race, color, religion, sex, national origin, physical or mental impairment, and familial status. To that list the State of Maryland adds sexual orientation and marital status. In addition, various counties add one or more of the following: age, ancestry, gender identity, family responsibility, occupation/source of income, political opinion, personal appearance, presence of children, and creed. In addition to knowing the federal and state-protected groups, a licensee doing business in multiple counties is advised to know the protections extended in each.

Maryland's recognition of same-sex marriage, although not directly related to fair housing, could be regarded as an aspect of marital status, a statewide protected category. Firms and their licensees must become and stay familiar with such implications of the new law.

■ DISCRIMINATION IN HOUSING

Examples listed in the Maryland statute of unlawful discriminatory housing practices against protected groups include:

- refusing to sell, rent, or negotiate after a bona fide offer;
- making unavailable or denying a dwelling or representing that a property is not available for inspection, sale, or rent when it is, in fact, available;
- discriminating in terms, conditions, or privileges of sale or rental of a dwelling;
- discriminating in the provision of related services or facilities;
- making (or ordering to be made) any publication, notice, or statement concerning properties for sale or rent that indicate any preference, limitation, or discrimination; and
- seeking, for profit, to induce any person to sell or rent a dwelling by making representations regarding the entry of a protected group into an area. (The federal law ignores the profit motive.)

Special Provisions for Individuals with Disabilities

The terms describing physical impairments have evolved from *handicap* to *disability* to *impairment* in recent years.

In addition to the protections in the previous list, the following prohibited acts are added on behalf of persons with physical or mental impairments:

- Discrimination against an applicant with such impairment or against nonimpaired applicants who will have a person with an impairment residing with them in the dwelling after it is sold, rented, or made available
- Discrimination in sale, rental, or availability of a property
- Discrimination in terms, conditions, or privileges of sale or rental or in connection with the dwelling after sale or rental
- Refusal to permit reasonable modifications of existing premises occupied or to be occupied by individuals with impairments, as needed to give them full enjoyment of the dwelling and made at the tenant's expense and with the tenant's agreement to restore the premises to their condition before the modification (This right also applies to unit owners and residents in condominiums.)
- Refusal to make reasonable accommodations in rules, policies, practices, or services when such accommodations are necessary to give persons with impairments equal opportunity to use and enjoy a dwelling
- Failure to design or construct a multifamily dwelling for first occupancy so that the public use and common areas are readily accessible to and usable by persons with impairments. All doors for passage into and within all premises within the dwelling must be wide enough to accommodate wheelchairs, and all premises must have suitable adaptive design features (for example, an accessible route into and through the dwelling; light switches, electrical outlets, thermostats, and other environmental controls in accessible locations; reinforcements in bathroom walls to allow later installation of grab bars; and kitchens and bathrooms designed so that individuals in wheelchairs can maneuver about the space).

For helpful information on the rights of people with disabilities and the responsibilities of housing providers, go to the HUD website (http://hud.gov), scroll over "Topic Areas," and select "Information for Disabled Persons" from the dropdown menu.

Discrimination in Real Estate Services

The law forbids any person or business entity that engages in real estate–related transactions to:

- discriminate against any person in making a transaction available or in the terms or conditions of a transaction because of membership in a protected group; or
- deny access to, membership in, or participation in a multiple listing service, brokers' organization, or other service, organization, or facility relating to the business of selling or renting dwellings, or to discriminate in the terms or conditions of membership or of participation based on protected group status.

Maryland statute makes it unlawful to coerce, intimidate, threaten, interfere with, or retaliate against persons who seek to exercise the rights granted by this law or against persons who encourage others to exercise their rights. Persons guilty of such actions may be fined not more than $1,000, suffer imprisonment for not more than one year, or both. If the violation results in bodily injury, penalties may range up to $10,000 and 10 years in prison; if it results in death, imprisonment may be for any term of years or for life. [*State Government* Article Title 20 § 1103(c)]

Enforcement

The Commission may sue to enforce an agreement that a respondent in a case has breached.

At the time a complaint is first received, the Commission itself may also initiate a civil action, in the circuit court of the county where the property is located, for relief of the complaining party. Having done this, the Commission may still proceed with its administrative proceedings. However, if an aggrieved party initiates a civil action under federal or State law seeking relief for a discriminatory housing practice, the Commission may review the complaint and refer the matter to the State Attorney General but then may not continue to hear the same charges.

Anyone who deliberately submits false information to the Commission as it investigates or who fails to make full disclosure—or who changes previous records, reports, or accounts—shall be fined no more than $100,000 or imprisoned for no more than one year, or both. [*State Government* Article, Title 20 § 1102(c)]

Aggrieved persons may begin civil actions in an appropriate State court not later than two years after the discriminatory action. They may file no civil action based on the same discrimination, though, after the Commission or a State or local agency has succeeded in producing a conciliation agreement except to enforce that agreement.

Relief granted in a civil action may not set aside any lease or sales contract to other bona fide purchasers or tenants who did not have actual notice of the filing of a complaint with the Commission or of the civil action.

Pattern of Discrimination

When the Commission believes there is a pattern of discrimination or resistance to the rights granted by this law, it may commence a civil action in circuit court. The court may award preventive relief or grant temporary or permanent injunctions and restraining orders against those responsible for violations. The court may also award, in addition to attorney fees, monetary damages to aggrieved persons in amounts not to exceed $50,000 for a first violation and $100,000 for subsequent violations.

■ COMMERCIAL PROPERTY

Neither the owners or the operators of commercial property, their agents and employees, nor any persons licensed or regulated by the State may discriminate against an individual in the terms, conditions, or privileges of property leased for commercial usage or in the provision of services or facilities in connection with the property, because of the individual's race, color, religion, sex, age, physical or mental impairment, marital status, or national origin.

■ THE REAL ESTATE BROKERS ACT

The Brokers Act also addresses discrimination against protected groups.

Whether or not acting for monetary gain, a person may not knowingly induce or attempt to induce another person to sell or rent a dwelling or otherwise transfer real estate or knowingly discourage or attempt to discourage another person from purchasing real estate by:

- making representations regarding the entry or prospective entry into a neighborhood of individuals of a particular race, color, sex, religion, or national origin;
- making representations regarding the existing or potential proximity of real property owned or used by individuals of a particular race, color, sex, religion, or national origin; or
- representing that the existing or potential proximity of real property owned or used by individuals of a particular race, color, sex, religion, or national origin will or may result in the lowering of property values; a change in the racial, religious, or ethnic character of the block, neighborhood, or area; an increase in criminal or antisocial behavior in the area; or a decline in the quality of schools serving the area.

This contrasts with both Human Relations Commission Law and the federal Fair Housing Act, which require the profit motive for such blockbusting.

A person may not provide financial assistance by loan, gift, or otherwise to another person if the person has actual knowledge that the financial assistance will be used in a transaction that results from a violation of these prohibitions.

Solicitation of Residential Listings

If one of the purposes of the solicitation or attempted solicitation is to change the racial composition of a neighborhood, a person may not solicit or attempt to solicit the listing of residential properties for sale or lease by in-person, door-to-door solicitation, telephone solicitation, or mass distribution of circulars.

Baltimore County law generally forbids canvassing by any person—licensee or not—to generate listings or simply to confer with owners or tenants about real estate. By canvassing, the law means door-to-door solicitation or solicitation by use of circulars, visitations, or telephone. However, solicitations when the solicitor, or the employer of the solicitor, has been invited or requested by the owner or tenant are permitted.

Baltimore County law provides several methods of canvassing that are not considered solicitation. These include advertisements in bona fide newspapers of general circulation or on radio or television, literature distributed through the U.S. mail, legitimate personal referrals, contacts with property owners resulting from the owners' having personally advertised the property for sale, and solicitation for the purpose of obtaining information for appraisals or similar collection of general sales or market data.

Violation of either the Baltimore City or Baltimore County law is punishable as a misdemeanor, with possible penalties upon conviction of a fine, imprisonment, or both.

Laws concerning solicitation vary from jurisdiction to jurisdiction. It is the responsibility of licensees to be familiar with the local laws where they perform acts of real estate brokerage. In preparation for the licensing exam, students are advised to learn the information given about Baltimore, Baltimore County, and Montgomery County, even though they may plan to work elsewhere.

Conservation Areas

The Brokers Act empowers the Real Estate Commission to identify and designate certain localities as conservation areas. In these areas and for limited time periods, all advertising of properties for sale and the use of For Sale signs is suspended. Brokerage firms may not solicit listings from owners of such properties but may list them when approached by their owners. This is done for the purpose of preserving racial stability in the affected locality in the event of a threatening volume of real estate transactions. Requirements for establishing such areas are presently so cumbersome that not one such area has been designated for almost a quarter century.

■ ENFORCEMENT

A person aggrieved by a fair housing violation may have to decide the avenue through which to seek redress—whether through a local, county, State, or federal agency.

Federal Laws

In the area of race, aggrieved persons may go directly to federal district court for injunctive relief. For race and other matters, they may sue in local courts for damages. If complaint of an alleged Maryland violation is reported to HUD, that agency will refer the matter to the Maryland Human Relations Commission because Maryland laws are substantially equivalent to the federal fair housing laws.

State Enforcement

Complaints made or referred to the Maryland Human Relations Commission are investigated, mediated, and resolved by agreements enforceable in the courts. The Commission may also initiate civil proceedings.

Financial Penalties

If the Maryland Human Relations Commission, after proper investigation and hearing, concludes that a respondent—the person against whom the charge was brought—has engaged in any of the unlawful practices previously listed, it may seek an order assessing a civil penalty against the respondent not exceeding $500 for a first offense. If it is the second offense within five years, the penalty can be in an amount not more than $1,000. If there were two prior offenses within the last seven years, the maximum penalty would be $2,500.

If the respondent is a natural person—an individual rather than a firm or organization, the penalty may be imposed without regard to the time periods between previous violations.

Fair housing provisions of the Brokers Act may be enforced administratively by the State Real Estate Commission or judicially by the Office of the Attorney General. Courts and other government agencies finding licensees guilty of discrimination are required to report their findings to the Real Estate Commission.

Local Laws and Their Enforcement

Chartered counties are empowered to enforce fair housing law violations with fines or penalties not to exceed those provided in the federal Fair Housing Act Amendments of 1988 and 1993. Many counties use their own Human Rights or Human Relations Commissions instead of, or in addition to, possible court enforcement.

■ DISCRIMINATION IN FINANCING

It is unlawful for any bank, savings association, credit union, insurance company, or other creditor to deny a housing loan or credit to persons who apply or to discriminate against them in the fixing of the down payment, interest rate, duration, or other terms or conditions of a loan because of the race, color, religion, creed, marital status, familial status, sex, national origin, the physical or mental disability of such person or of any member, stockholder, director, officer, or employee of such person or of the prospective occupants, lessees, or tenants of the dwelling for which the loan application is made.

■ HUD FAIR HOUSING ADVERTISING GUIDELINES

Section 804(c) of the federal Fair Housing Act (FHA) makes it unlawful to make, print, or publish or cause to be made, printed, or published any notice, statement, or advertisement with respect to the sale or rental of a dwelling that indicates any preference, limitation, or discrimination based on race, color, religion, sex, handicap, familial status, or national origin or an intention to make any such preference, limitation, or discrimination. In January 1995, a HUD memorandum listed, among other things, some words and phrases that will not create advertiser liability under Section 804(c). The list is found in Figure 15.1. Note that these phrases relate to characteristics of property rather than those of persons.

FIGURE 15.1

Fair Housing Advertising Guidelines

In January 1995, the HUD Office of the Assistant Secretary for Fair Housing and Equal Opportunity issued a memorandum that includes specific phrases that would not be considered in violation of fair housing advertising laws.

Protected class	Acceptable phrases in advertisements
Race, color, and national origin	Master bedroom Rare find Desirable neighborhood
Religion	Merry Christmas Happy Easter Images of Santa Claus or Easter Bunny Valentine's Day graphic Kosher kitchen in the building Chapel on site
Sex	Mother-in-law suite Bachelor apartment
Handicap/disability/impairment	Great view Walk-up apartment Walk-in closets Jogging trails Walking distance to bus stop
Familial status	Two-bedroom Cozy family room No bicycles allowed Quiet streets

Ads should focus on the property advertised rather than on potential tenants or purchasers. It is better to say "swimming pool on site" than "great place for swimmers." Care should be taken not to advertise in media that are directed solely toward a racially or religiously segmented geographic or economic market. If more than one local publication or electronic medium is used, the same phraseology should be used in all of them.

Advertisements may describe the behavior expected of prospective residents (e.g., "nonsmoking" or "sober").

Multiple listing services often have restrictions on terms and phrases that can be used in the comments sections of listings. These limits may be more restrictive than published lists used by other trade groups or by the government. Members the National Association of REALTORS® are subject to the REALTOR® Code of Ethics, which mentions additional protected classes.

■ THE MARYLAND STATUTE

Maryland's fair housing law, the *State Government* Article, Title 20 *Human Relations*, has been found to be substantially equivalent to the Fair Housing Act of 1968 as amended. It is of central importance and is the source of much of the material in this chapter.

■ EDUCATION REQUIREMENTS

Real Estate Commission General Regulations 11, 14, and 17 require that all license applicants, as a part of their prelicensure educational requirements, be instructed in the human relations aspects of the practice of real estate, including study of fair housing laws and the effects of such undesirable practices as exploitation, steering, blockbusting, prejudicial solicitation, discriminatory practices, misleading advertising, and other related activities. All licensees (except those who exclusively perform commercial brokerage) are required to take 1.5 hours of continuing education in fair housing before each biennial license renewal.

CHAPTER 15 QUIZ

1. James and Frances Wong, who are of Chinese descent, tell their licensed real estate salesperson that they need a three-bedroom house in the $320,000 to $330,000 price range that is within walking distance of an elementary school. The salesperson, after identifying the Wongs as genuine prospects, finds a house on Judson Street that meets all the Wongs' requirements, but the salesperson knows that the residents of the neighborhood are unhappy about Asians moving into the area. What should the licensee do?
   1. Refrain from bringing this particular house to the Wongs' attention
   2. Tell them about the house but suggest that they would be happier in another neighborhood
   3. File a complaint with the Human Relations Commission
   4. Inform the Wongs about the availability of the house and arrange to show them the listing

2. With respect to fair housing, which of the following is *TRUE* of all persons engaged in real estate transactions?
   1. It is their responsibility to know all applicable federal, State, and local antidiscrimination statutes and ordinances.
   2. Errors and omissions (E&O) insurance will protect them if they violate fair housing laws.
   3. They may refuse to be held liable.
   4. They have the responsibility to decide what is best for their customers and clients.

3. When salespersons of different races are trying to sell a residential property listed in a neighborhood that is predominantly Caucasian, which statement is *TRUE*?
   1. They are acting properly by not showing this listing to white prospects.
   2. They violate Maryland and federal laws when they decide whether to show a listing based on a prospect's race.
   3. They need not introduce into the neighborhood anyone not of the predominant race of the neighborhood.
   4. They should have a salesperson of the same race as the prospect show the property.

4. A broker approaches homeowners seeking to list their property for sale. They had not been thinking of selling, but the broker tells them, "The time to sell is now" because the neighborhood is experiencing a large minority group influx and that the value of their property "is sure to drop" if they wait any longer. What is this behavior called?
   1. Blockbusting
   2. Steering
   3. Blind advertising
   4. Redlining

5. What act or law does a private club that does not discriminate on the basis of race, color, or national origin, and is not operated as a commercial hotel violate fair housing by limiting tenancy to members?
   1. The Fair Housing Act of 1968
   2. The Maryland Fair Housing Law
   3. The Real Estate License Law
   4. No State or federal laws

CHAPTER 16

Closing the Real Estate Transaction

■ KEY TERMS

binder	settlement officer	title search
homeowner	title insurance	total payment
mortgagee		

■ OVERVIEW

Whether it is called settlement, closing, going to escrow, or by some other name, this event is the culmination of real estate brokerage activities because it is when legal title to Maryland real property passes from sellers to purchasers and then to the mortgage lender. Typically, as a result of the closing, purchasers take on long-term debt, and sellers get funds from the sale of their property from which they are able to satisfy outstanding mortgages and other liens against the property sold and to pay commissions to their listing broker.

Listing brokers may divide their commissions with in-house affiliates who assisted purchasers, intra-company agents who represented buyers and sellers, or co-brokers who either assisted buyers as subagents or represented them as buyers' agents.

■ EVIDENCE OF TITLE

In Maryland, it is customary, when buyers enter into an agreement to purchase, for them to authorize the title (settlement) company to order the title search required for mortgagee title insurance. An abstract of title is produced based on the results of this title search. If the information in the abstract indicates marketable title, a settlement company will issue a binder that commits a title insurance company to provide a permanent title insurance policy at the time of settlement.

Instead of a policy of title insurance, some attorneys may issue their own certificate of title. Others simply indicate their opinion of title based on the abstract, without insuring the title. The issuance of either title insurance or of a certificate depends on a favorable abstract of title.

Lenders almost always require mortgagee (lender) title insurance for their protection. In addition, State law requires that purchasers be offered homeowner (buyer) title insurance by the settlement officer at every residential closing. Buyers who decline homeowner title insurance are asked to confirm their refusal in writing. For the different characteristics and functions of mortgagee and homeowner title policies, the student should consult the principles text.

■ SETTLEMENTS

Most purchase contracts and sale agreements are closed in the office of a title company, the buyer's or seller's attorney, the mortgage lender, or the real estate broker. Closing in Maryland is usually performed at a face-to-face meeting involving buyers, sellers, agents, and a settlement officer. Closing in escrow, as described in the principles text, is generally not practiced in Maryland.

Real estate brokers or their salespersons normally are present at settlement, although the interaction is—and should be—principally among the officer conducting the settlement, the parties to the agreement, and any attorneys present. Licensees are present for whatever nonlegal services they may be asked to render; to provide personal support for their clients; and, of course, to receive commission checks for their brokers.

■ CLOSING AND TAX STATEMENTS

The buyers' or sellers' attorney or a settlement company officer will prepare the necessary closing statement. Licensees should know how these statements are calculated so they can accurately estimate sellers' expenses of sale and net proceeds from the transaction. They should also be able to estimate the amount of additional cash purchasers will need at closing. They should be able to understand and explain to customers and clients every entry on the settlement sheet almost always used: HUD-1.

Closing costs are apportioned according to statute, where applicable, and/or by contractual agreement. Typically, the seller is responsible for such property charges for the day of closing as ad valorem taxes, special assessments, and utilities. By federal law, all owners/sellers must provide the closing agent with their forwarding addresses and Social Security numbers. Corporate sellers must provide their corporate tax identification numbers.

If Maryland property is being sold by individual out-of-state owners, Maryland statute requires that 7.5% of the total payment to the sellers be withheld. Total payment is defined as the consideration for the property, reduced by mortgages paid and other costs of the sale; essentially, it means the sellers' bottom line: "cash to seller," on the settlement sheet. The amount withheld is credited to other amounts of the sellers' prepaid Maryland income tax. The taxpayers may have any or all of it refunded by claiming overpayment on their annual State income tax return. If the out-of-state seller is not a natural person but an entity, such as a corporation, partnership, LLC, or trust, 8.25% is to be withheld. Sellers claiming to be Maryland residents are required to sign affidavits to that effect at closing. Since it is easier to collect taxes from owners who live within the State, sellers who have their permanent residence within the State at the time of closing will not have these amounts withheld.

Buyers and sellers must affirm (sign an affidavit as to the accuracy of) information they have given that will be reported to the IRS. Typically, the person conducting settlement will request photo IDs of the principals. Copies of these IDs are maintained in the title company's records. Licensees should make sure that their sellers are prepared to provide all the required information at the time of settlement. The closing agent or title company can answer any questions that may arise.

■ EVIDENCE OF RELEASE

Within 30 days after closing, settlement (title) company officers, who are responsible for disbursement of funds, must mail or deliver to the sellers evidence of having recorded the release of mortgage. If the recording of release is delayed beyond the 30-day period for causes beyond their control, settlement officers must mail or deliver to the sellers a letter explaining the delay. They must send another letter for each additional delay of 30 days. Failure to follow these rules may subject them to an audit of all their accounts by the court.

However, if persons conducting closing properly disburse all funds entrusted to them in the closing procedure within five days, no such evidence is required unless specifically requested by purchasers or vendors. Vendors (sellers) and purchasers are to be informed in writing of these requirements before the delivery of a deed.

Settlements in Maryland must be performed by, or under the supervision of, an attorney. This does not mean that an attorney is present or has even seen the paperwork. It does mean that there must be an attorney responsible for the preparation and execution of closing and the proper disbursement of funds. To be recorded, deeds on Maryland realty, as mentioned in Chapter 10, must be prepared by an attorney or by either the deed's grantor or grantee. "Prepared by an attorney" may well mean "prepared by personnel trained and supervised" by the attorney who is responsible for their performance. Supervision does not always have to be done in person. The student is reminded of the "evidences of reasonable and adequate supervision" required of real estate brokers mentioned in Chapter 3.

Representation

Who do settlement officers represent? They usually owe certain fiduciary duties to several parties but exclusive loyalty to none. When they order and evaluate the abstract of title, they owe the purchaser due care. When they issue title insurance, they are acting as agents of the title insurance company. In collecting taxes for the state and federal tax information for the IRS, they have responsibility to gather and handle those funds and that information with due care. They owe the duty of paying off old liens and recording releases of those liens satisfied by those payoffs. They owe buyers the duty of recording their new deed. They must also record any mortgages that were given to lenders at settlement. In addition to their obligations to all these parties, settlement officers represent themselves and their title company.

CHAPTER 16 QUIZ

1. Which of the following is *TRUE* of residential closings in Maryland?
   1. They are always to be performed by an escrowee.
   2. They are always to be performed by real estate brokers.
   3. They are always to be performed by title company clerks.
   4. They are always to be performed under an attorney's supervision.

2. What is the requirement for handling evidence of the release of debt after a closing?
   1. It must be sent to the county courthouse within 30 days of closing.
   2. It must be sent to the purchaser within 5 days of closing.
   3. It must be sent to the seller within 30 days of closing.
   4. It must be sent to the former mortgagee within 5 days of closing.

3. Which statement is *TRUE* of attorneys who personally conduct settlements?
   1. They owe all parties due care in the execution of closing duties.
   2. They represent the seller.
   3. They represent the buyer.
   4. They may represent both the buyer and the seller.

4. Which of the following is *TRUE* about the ordering of title searches in Maryland residential transactions?
   1. They are ordered at the direction and expense of the seller.
   2. They are ordered at the direction and expense of the purchaser.
   3. They are ordered by the salesperson who prepares the contract.
   4. They are ordered by the broker of the listing client.

5. When a Maryland property is sold by an out-of-state corporation, which of the following is *TRUE*?
   1. The buyer is no longer protected by the Maryland Guaranty Fund.
   2. The buyer must set aside 7% of the consideration.
   3. The closing officer must withhold 8.25% of the seller's proceeds.
   4. The closing officer must withhold 6% of the consideration.

Maryland Real Estate License Examinations

■ OVERVIEW

Passing the State licensing examination is a major requirement for persons seeking a real estate license. Every applicant would like to pass on the first try, not only to speed up the licensing process, but also to reduce the cost incurred by retaking the test, to minimize inconvenience, and to avoid embarrassment.

The salesperson license examination can be taken only after successful completion of 60 hours of prelicense instruction given by an approved provider. An additional 135 hours is required before taking the broker examination. Before scheduling examinations for applicants, the testing service requires proof that all education requirements have been met for the tests they applied for.

Figure A.1 shows a summary of the key features of the exam.

FIGURE A.1

Summary of Facts about Examinations

Exam	Portion	Number of Questions	Total Time Allowed	Minimum Number Correct Required to Pass (70%)	Fee Regular	Fee Express for Retake
Salesperson	National	80		56		
	State	30	120 minutes	21	$66	$76
	Both	110				
Broker	National	80		56		
	State	40	120 minutes	28	$66	$76
	Both	120				

■ THE REAL ESTATE LICENSE EXAMINATION

PSI Examination Services Inc. (PSI), Las Vegas, Nevada, an independent testing service under contract with the Commission, prepares and administers the licensing examinations. PSI's testing program is adapted to each state's real estate license laws and practices and to the priorities of its licensing agency.

Candidates receive two scores for their examination: the state score and the national score. The passing grade set by the Commission is currently 70% on each. This means the salesperson candidate must answer at least 56 out of 80 questions on the national portion correctly and 21 out of 30 on the state portion. Broker candidates must correctly answer 56 out of 80 on the national and 28 out of 40 questions on the state portion. Salesperson and broker candidates each have 120 minutes to complete the entire exam. In 2011 and 2013, between 40% and 56% of all candidates for salesperson licensure exam passed both portions of the test when taking it for the first time.

The national section of the examinations for both broker and salesperson contains questions based on general real estate information. Subjects include Property Ownership, Land Use Control and Regulation, Valuation and Market Analysis, Financing, Laws of Agency, Mandated Disclosures, Contracts, Transfer of Property, Practice of Real Estate Brokerage, Mathematics, and Specialty Areas.

The Maryland (State) section contains questions based on Title 17 of the Maryland Annotated Code (the Brokers Act), as well as questions relating to the General Regulations and the Code of Ethics established by the Maryland Real Estate Commission. Test questions deal with duties and powers of the Commission, licensing requirements, and business conduct. Questions relating to Environmental Issues, Water Rights, Listing and Buyer Agreements, and Common Interest Ownership Properties are also found in the State portion. There are four questions for salesperson (five for broker) applicants on Property Management and Landlord/Tenant; Common Interest Ownership Properties; Subdivisions; and Commercial, Industrial, and Income Property. The testing service (PSI) *Candidate Information Bulletin* contains a very helpful listing of the topics and subtopics on each exam and the number of questions on each. This bulletin can be downloaded from their website: http://candidate.psiexams.com/.

Practice exams for 14 states can be purchased through that site. Unfortunately, Maryland is not one of those states. The other exams could, nevertheless, provide valuable practice and insights.

Tests presented at testing centers are not preprinted but are generated daily from a computer database. Thus, they can be continually updated and the order of items rearranged.

■ APPLICATION PROCEDURES

The *Candidate Information Bulletin* also contains directions to the six testing centers in the State: Baltimore Center:

The Rotunda, 711 W. 40th Street, Suite 352, Baltimore, MD 21211; College Park Center: The Sterling Building, 4920 Niagara Road, Suite 211, College Park, MD 20740; Crofton Center: Morauer III Building, 2137 Espey Court, Suite 3, Crofton, MD 21114; Hagerstown Center: Westshire Professional Center, 920 West Washington Street #204, Hagerstown, MD 21740; Lanham Center: 5900 Princess Garden Pkwy., Suite 240, Lanham, MD 20706; and Salisbury Center: 1323 Mt. Hermon Road, Beaglin Park Plaza Suite 2A, Salisbury, MD 21804. Those who have passed the required prelicensing course and are ready to take the examination should mail completed application forms, with evidence of passing the prelicense course, as well as the $65 testing fee for each exam, plus any other required documents, to

PSI Examination Services
ATTN: Examination Registration MD RE
3210 East Tropicana
Las Vegas, NV 89121

Failure to follow the instructions on the registration form carefully may result in students not being scheduled promptly for the examinations they request.

The basic registration fee for taking (and retaking) a Maryland Real Estate Licensing Examination (broker or salesperson) is $65. Payment can be made to PSI by personal check, money order, company check, or cashier's check.

Candidates who have previously provided complete certification of eligibility to PSI may register by mail or through Express Registration on the telephone, by fax, or on the internet. Such applicants will be persons who failed all or part of a previous exam or whose initial application form was incomplete, although accompanied by proper proof of their completion of the education requirement. An additional $10 fee is charged for Express Registration. A valid Visa® or MasterCard® is needed.

First-time applicants are to send their registration forms, other necessary documents, and the registration fee directly to PSI. In return, PSI will mail them (usually within two weeks) a Registration Confirmation Notice. This notice explains how to make an examination appointment. Once this appointment, including place, date, and time for examination, has been made, an applicant may still request changes by calling 1-800-733-9267 two or more days before the scheduled testing date. All examinations, even if delayed, must still be completed within 90 days of original registration, or the candidates must reapply and pay another registration fee. This expiration date is shown on each student's confirmation notice.

The registration form asks for information that will be relayed to the Commission so it can process the license applications when candidates pass their tests. It also asks for certification that the candidate has successfully completed the mandatory educational hours. In addition, it contains a statement of irrevocable consent, which is required from applicants who live outside Maryland. Applicants must answer the Registration Form questions to the best of their ability. The form is then signed as an affidavit, subject to the penalties of perjury.

■ TESTING PROCEDURES

Candidates may take an examination at any of the several testing centers located in Maryland. All candidates must bring positive identification to the testing site. This identification must include at least one government-issued picture ID with the candidate's signature on it—such as a driver's license, state ID, or passport. The second (additional) form of ID could be a credit card with the candidate's signature and preprinted legal name. All IDs must have exactly the same name as the document certifying completion of the required prelicense education and the registration form, including the same middle initial and same use of generation (Jr., Sr., II, III, etc.).

PSI uses a computerized testing system approved by the Commission. On conclusion of the testing session, the computer will show candidates whether they passed or failed. Official, hardcopy notification of examination results will be mailed to candidates. The real estate examinations are administered every business day during the week at most locations. There is no walk-in testing.

Candidates take their examinations seated at specially designed, semiprivate computer work stations. On-screen instructions provide a 15-minute tutorial in the use of the keyboard. About as many keys are used as are found on a touch-tone telephone. Taking the test requires no computer skills. Instructions appear on the screen to guide the candidate through each step of the test. Both the salesperson and the broker test allow a total of 120 minutes—90 for the national, 30 for the state. Note that for brokers, there are 40 state-related questions, not 30, for the 30-minute period. There is an optional on-screen clock for candidates to watch.

No notes, books, cell phones, pagers, or children are allowed in the examination center. Silent, nonprinting, nonprogrammable, battery-operated calculators may be permitted, but they must not have alphabet keys. There is no smoking, eating, or drinking at the center. A candidate who tries to copy a question or an answer or to communicate examination content to another person may be disqualified and possibly subject to legal action for violation of copyright laws.

When candidates first take the real estate exam, they are given the state section, then the national. Candidates who have already taken the exam but passed only one of its two sections are permitted to reregister and retake the group of questions—state or general—that they need to pass. Candidates must pass both sets of questions to be eligible for a Maryland real estate license. A part failed must be retaken and passed within one year of the other portion or the candidate must start over by taking and passing both. There is no limit (other than their financial resources) to the number of retakes applicants may take.

■ TYPES OF QUESTIONS ON EXAM

The tests use multiple-choice answer format. An incomplete statement or a question is presented and is followed by four possible numbered choices. Applicants are sometimes asked to find the one correct answer. At other times, they must find the one wrong answer. Here are examples of each:

■ FOR EXAMPLE

Which one of the following cities is the capital of the state in which it is located?

1. New York City, NY
2. New Orleans, LA
3. Lincoln, NE
4. Scranton, PA

■ FOR EXAMPLE

All the following are even numbers EXCEPT

1. 118.
2. 230.
3. 734.
4. 437.

The questions given here are not representative of those on the examination. Examples of more difficult questions and problems have been included in the chapters of this book so that you will become familiar with them and be better prepared for the examination.

The PSI testing approach is designed to assess reasoning processes as well as factual real estate knowledge. In answering examination-type questions, consider all answer choices carefully and eliminate the least likely ones instead of randomly selecting an answer. However, it is better to guess than to give no answer at all. The purpose of the examination is to provide a measure of your knowledge of real estate and, thereby, allow you to demonstrate your qualification for licensure. You should try to answer all questions without spending too much time on any one question. The fourth answer choice for each math test item is often *None of the above*. Do not be surprised by it.

Here are the answers to the example questions:

1.   1   2   3   4
        [ ]   [ ]   [x]   [ ]

2.   1   2   3   4
        [ ]   [ ]   [ ]   [x]

For an online tutorial about taking the computer-administered exam, go to http://candidate.psiexams.com/tutorial.jsp.

■ MORE HELP IN PREPARING FOR THE LICENSE EXAMINATION

The author has tried to prepare you for the Maryland Real Estate License Examination by including in this book the kinds of items usually found on the test. Familiarity with the test items, however, will not in itself ensure a passing score. Your most important preparation for this examination involves thoughtfully studying real estate principles and practices and brokerage laws and regulations.

Concentrate on learning the material by studying the principles text and this book. When using the tests and exercises in these books, understanding the correct answers on practice exams is far more important than merely recognizing them.

Consider carefully the rationales (explanations) of answers provided in the answer keys.

Dearborn™ Real Estate Education publishes other instructional materials in addition to *Modern Real Estate Practice* and *Maryland Real Estate Practice & Law* that are especially designed to aid you in passing the licensing exam: *Mastering Real Estate Math*, *Study Guide for Modern Real Estate Practice*, and *Guide to Passing the PSI Real Estate Exam*.

■ MARYLAND-SPECIFIC TEST ITEMS

The Maryland-related questions throughout this volume are in the format found on the real estate licensing exam. Use them to identify strengths and weaknesses in your knowledge.

List the items you miss and use that list as a guide for further intensive study of the text. Sometimes, you may want to test yourself on an entire list of questions. Other times, you may wish to attempt the items one by one, checking your answers as you go. Decide why every correct answer is correct. In items that ask you to find the wrong answer, do so, but then try to learn all you can from the three correct answers to the same questions. Make intelligent use of all practice questions and the answer keys.

APPENDIX B Practice Exam

1. When a salesperson whose license has not been renewed negotiates a sale of real property, who is the commission payable to?
   1. The broker only
   2. No one
   3. The salesperson only
   4. The broker and the salesperson according to prior agreement

2. If a salesperson license is issued on January 2, 2014, when will it expire?
   1. January 2, 2016
   2. September 2, 2016
   3. April 1, 2016
   4. March 31, 2016

3. When prospective purchasers first arrive at a brokerage office to find a house to buy, how does the Brokers Act require them to be treated?
   1. As customers
   2. As clients
   3. As agents
   4. As factors

4. Which of the following is *TRUE* of salespersons' real estate licenses?
   1. They must be placed and kept in a safe place chosen by the salespersons.
   2. They are to be carried by the salespersons when performing acts of real estate brokerage.
   3. They must be retained in their brokers' offices.
   4. They must be maintained in personnel files by their brokers.

5. What is the maximum amount that a claimant may receive from the Guaranty Fund on losses from one transaction?
   1. An unlimited amount
   2. $250,000
   3. $50,000
   4. $25,000

6. Under the Junk Fax Prevention Act, which of the following is *TRUE* of persons who send faxes?
   1. They need not provide a way for the recipients to opt out of getting more faxes.
   2. They may use recipient addresses they receive from a fax-spamming company.
   3. They may send faxes only between 9:00 am and 5:00 pm.
   4. They must have an established business relationship with the recipients.

7. Who may be members of the State Real Estate Commission?
   1. Only licensed salespersons
   2. Only licensed brokers
   3. Unlicensed persons and licensed brokers and salespersons
   4. Persons appointed by the Attorney General

8. Who issues Maryland real estate salesperson and broker licenses?
   1. Local Board of REALTORS®
   2. Providers of required real estate courses when applicants pass them
   3. The Maryland Association of REALTORS®
   4. The Real Estate Commission

9. What body sets ethical standards that must be observed by all Maryland real estate licensees?
   1. National Association of REALTORS®
   2. State Real Estate Commission
   3. Maryland Association of REALTORS®
   4. Local boards and associations

10. When a partnership owns a real estate brokerage firm, which statement is *FALSE?*
    1. The broker is responsible for the real estate brokerage activities of the partnership.
    2. The broker must be one of the partners.
    3. The broker must be designated by the partnership as its broker of record.
    4. The broker must have a contractual or employment agreement with the partnership.

11. When builders sell houses they have built and own, which of the following is *TRUE*?
    1. They need not hold real estate licenses.
    2. They must be licensed if they sell more than six per calendar year.
    3. They must be licensed brokers.
    4. They may be licensed as salespersons but not affiliated with brokers.

12. What advance notice must developers give to those who desire to convert apartment buildings more than five years old into time-share projects?
    1. 180 days' notice to each tenant
    2. 120 days' notice to each tenant
    3. No prior notice
    4. Notice to each tenant within 10 days from filing the Public Offering Statement

13. Which of the following is *NOT* the responsibility of Maryland real estate licensees?
    1. Fair treatment of third parties
    2. Competence in performance of duties
    3. Giving of legal guidance
    4. Loyalty to their principals

14. In which states do lenders receive defeasible fee interests in mortgaged land?
    1. Title theory states
    2. Lien theory states
    3. Modified lien theory states
    4. Trust theory states

15. What is the maximum penalty that the Maryland Real Estate Brokers Act authorizes the Commission to impose on a licensee?
    1. $25,000
    2. $15,000
    3. $5,000
    4. $1,000 and/or one year's imprisonment

16. What determines the amount of commission set in a listing agreement?
    1. Maryland statute
    2. The local Board or Association of REALTORS®
    3. Mutual agreement between the parties to the agreement
    4. The Real Estate Commission sitting in executive session

17. What is done with earnest money deposits received by salespersons of a firm?
    1. They deposit them in their trust accounts.
    2. They give them to the sellers of the property.
    3. They place them in their broker's safe.
    4. They give them to their broker for prompt deposit in the firm's trust account.

18. Which of the following statements about tenancy by the entirety in Maryland is *FALSE*?
    1. If husband and wife divorce, the tenancy is terminated.
    2. Both spouses' signatures are required to sell such property if both are living.
    3. Upon death of either spouse, the form of ownership converts to tenancy in common.
    4. Only a legally married husband and wife can own property as tenants by the entirety.

19. When a broker receives a full-price offer from a prospect and, at the same time, a less-than-full-price offer through a cooperating agent, what must the broker do?
    1. Submit only the full-price offer
    2. Submit only the offer from the other broker's customer
    3. Submit both offers
    4. Submit the first offer received and then, if it is rejected, the other offer

20. What law requires certain contracts for the transfer of an interest in realty to be in writing to be enforceable?
    1. The Written Instrument Law
    2. The Parol Evidence Law
    3. The Statute of Limitations
    4. The Statute of Frauds

21. Which of the following is *NOT* a Maryland requirement for a residential land installment contract?
    1. It must be recorded by the vendor within 15 days after it has been signed.
    2. It must include all terms of the transaction.
    3. It must be signed by the vendor and vendee.
    4. It must be filed with the Real Estate Commission.

22. What is the effect of a licensee presenting the Understanding Whom Real Estate Agents Represent form?
    1. It informs prospective purchasers and lessees of the various ways they can be served by real estate brokerage firms.
    2. It creates a representation agreement between the agent who presents the form and the prospect to which it is presented.
    3. It gives a licensee the prospect's permission to engage in a transaction involving dual agency.
    4. It ends a licensee's presumed buyer representation of a prospect.

23. How long must confidential matters learned from a client remain confidential?
    1. Until the client dies and the estate is probated
    2. Until the agency relationship (either presumed or contractual) is terminated
    3. Until the Statute of Limitations has expired
    4. Until those matters become common knowledge from other sources

24. When does Title 17 require the Commission's form, Understanding Whom Real Estate Agents Represent, to be presented?
    1. At first contact with a prospective purchaser or lessee
    2. At the first face-to-face contact between the licensee and a prospect
    3. No later than the moment a prospect expresses the desire to look at a property listed with the licensee's company
    4. No later than the first scheduled face-to-face meeting between the licensee and the prospect

25. From which of the following may agency relationships be legally inferred?
    1. Ministerial actions of a licensee
    2. Magisterial guidance from a licensee
    3. Payment or promise of payment to a licensee
    4. A prospect's expectations of a licensee

26. Which of the following statements regarding rental security deposits is *FALSE*?
    1. The landlord must credit the tenant with 3% per annum simple interest on these funds at the end of the lease.
    2. Interest on security deposits is computed and compounded at six-month intervals.
    3. The portion of the deposit not withheld must be returned to the tenant within 45 days of end of occupancy together with an accounting of how any withheld portion was spent.
    4. Tenants may recover three times the amount of security deposit improperly withheld by the landlord, plus reasonable attorney fees.

27. Which of the following is *NOT* something for which licenses may be suspended or revoked by the Commission?
    1. Drunken driving convictions
    2. Accepting net listings
    3. Performing acts of brokerage on an expired license
    4. Failure to be current in court-ordered child support payments

28. Which is *TRUE* of licensees representing client buyers?
    1. They owe certain statutory duties to sellers.
    2. They cannot be compensated by sellers.
    3. They can be regarded as cooperating agents and, therefore, the subagents of the seller.
    4. They may tell the seller's agent that their client is highly motivated.

29. In purchasing a condominium, the most important document given to the buyer is the declaration. Which of the following does the declaration *NOT* do?
    1. Authorize a board of directors to administer the condominium affairs pursuant to the bylaws and to assess the owners so as to maintain the condominium adequately
    2. Describe the condominium units and the common areas and any restrictions on their use
    3. Establish the undivided interest percentages
    4. Set forth rules for behavior of unit occupants

30. Which is *TRUE* of a Maryland condominium declaration?
    1. It must be recorded before the property can be placed under a condominium regime.
    2. It cannot be rescinded once it is recorded.
    3. It can be changed only with the unanimous approval of the council of unit owners.
    4. It must be printed in a daily newspaper before changes may be made.

31. In which of the following situations is deficiency judgment permitted when a property sells at foreclosure for less than the mortgage debt?
    1. Judicial foreclosure
    2. Nonjudicial foreclosure
    3. FHA loans
    4. All of the above

32. What may brokers *NOT* do in dealing with contested earnest money deposits?
    1. Put their clients' interests ahead of the other parties' because of their fiduciary duties
    2. Let the money remain in their trust accounts
    3. Notify both buyers and sellers how they intend to distribute the contested funds
    4. Distribute the money as they proposed in their notice if neither of the parties gives proper notice of protest

33. What may be done with rental security deposits?
    1. They may not be withheld by the landlord for unpaid rent.
    2. They may be kept during the lease in the landlord's personal savings account to earn interest.
    3. They may be withheld by the landlord to cover estimated damages at the end of the lease.
    4. They may be withheld by a landlord for the actual amount expended to repair damages caused by tenants.

34. Which of the following is *NOT* one of the evidences of reasonable and adequate supervision by a broker listed in the Brokers Act?
    1. A proven pattern of the broker's physical presence in the broker's office, 9:00 am to 5:00 pm , seven days per week
    2. Availability of company policy and procedure manual in each office containing, among other things, rules for handling funds of others and the requirements of fair housing laws
    3. Existing records of every-other-month training meetings provided for all the broker's affiliates together with a record of those attending and a list of topics presented
    4. A paper trail showing that all contracts are approved by an experienced supervisor before being presented

35. Which is *TRUE* of an agency agreement listing a Maryland property for sale?
    1. It may contain a provision for the broker to keep all the sale proceeds above a certain amount as the brokerage commission.
    2. It is binding if signed by the owner of the largest share in a property that is owned by several owners.
    3. It may indicate that the amount of brokerage commission to be paid will be negotiated between owner and broker after an offer is presented.
    4. It may not require notice from either party to activate its termination date.

36. Which of the following statements about usury in Maryland mortgage loans is *TRUE*?
    1. There is no interest limit on first mortgages involving Maryland real estate.
    2. There is no interest limit on second mortgages involving Maryland real estate.
    3. There is no interest limit on land (installment) contracts involving Maryland real estate.
    4. Interest limits imposed on mortgages are not imposed on deeds of trust.

37. Which of the following is *TRUE* of a pair of prospects who enter a Maryland brokerage office and ask help in finding a house to rent?

1. They are considered by Maryland statute to be represented by that brokerage firm.
2. They are considered customers by Maryland statute.
3. They will owe a reasonable and customary brokerage fee if the firm finds them a property that they lease.
4. They must be given the Commission's form, Understanding Whom Real Estate Agents Represent, immediately upon their arrival.

38. What is required for most Maryland real estate licensees to renew their licenses?

1. Completion of at least 3 hours of continuing education in fair housing.
2. Completion of at least 1.5 hours of continuing education in ethics.
3. Completion of a total of at least 15 hours of approved continuing education courses.
4. Completion of at least 6 hours of continuing education on changes in federal, State, and local laws.

39. Maryland's requirements for a real estate broker licensee's office include all the following *EXCEPT*

1. it must be a place where the firm regularly conducts insurance sales.
2. it must have a sign visible to the public that includes the words *Real Estate*, *REALTORS®*, or *Realtist*, whichever is applicable.
3. records of all trust monies must be kept there in a secured area and available to the Commission's inspectors on demand.
4. it must have available the license of the broker and every affiliate who works out of that office.

40. Associate Broker John Buonasera, known as Mr. B, has published a flier to attract business. This is the entire ad:

> Come to me, Mr. B, for all your real estate needs: Buying, Selling, or Renting.
>
> Use my services and you will be pleased. Results guaranteed!
>
> I charge 2% less than most other REALTORS® for my excellent service.
>
> My personal assistants and I are available to you 24/7 to answer your real estate questions and meet your brokerage needs.
>
> Call my cell phone, toll free: 1-888-555-5555.

Which of the following statements about the advertisement is *FALSE*?

1. The ad makes it clear that Mr. B is not the broker of a firm.
2. The ad is improper because Mr. B doesn't mention the designated name of the broker whose firm he works for.
3. The ad is improper because Mr. B gives his own phone number and not that of the firm.
4. The ad is improper because, although a nickname may be used if it is registered with the Real Estate Commission, his full name, John Buonasera, must also be shown as it appears on his license.

41. When must all licensees take the three-hour required course in agency?

1. Before becoming licensees, as part of their 60-hour required prelicense course
2. As continuing education for renewing their licenses every two years
3. In addition to the 15 hours of continuing education required for each license renewal
4. At alternate license renewals as part of the 15 hours of required continuing education

42. Which of the following is *FALSE* concerning the required three-hour continuing education course in supervision?
    1. It must be taken by all licensees for every alternate license renewal on or after January 1, 2012.
    2. It must be taken by all brokers for every alternate license renewal on or after January 1, 2012.
    3. It must be taken by team leaders beginning with their first renewal on or after January 1, 2012.
    4. It must be taken by branch managers at alternate renewals on or after January 1, 2012.

43. Which statement is *TRUE* about the mandated Supervision and Agency courses for license renewal?
    1. Both must be taught by attorneys.
    2. Both must be presented by teachers identified by the Commission.
    3. Each is in addition to the basic 15 hours of continuing education required of most licensees.
    4. Unlike other continuing education courses, both will have a final exam.

44. In which of the following situations must the licensee present the Commission's disclosure of agency representation form?
    1. Purchase prospect refuses presumed buyer representation.
    2. Transaction involves unimproved property zoned commercial.
    3. Brokerage services are for a residential leasehold of three months (90 days).
    4. Prospect wants to lease a property improved by five single-family units.

45. Which statement about State of Maryland fair housing law is *TRUE*?
    1. State law permits local governments to pass fair housing laws more permissive than the State's.
    2. In a multifamily community that is advertised for, and occupied exclusively by, persons 62 years of age or older, sellers may refuse to sell a unit for occupancy to a family with minor children.
    3. In a multifamily community that is advertised for, and occupied exclusively by, persons 62 years of age or older, sellers may refuse to sell a unit to a family with minor children to hold as investment property.
    4. In a multifamily community that is advertised for adults and in which 80% of the units are occupied by at least one person aged 50 or older, sellers may refuse to sell (or rent) for occupancy to a family with minor children.

46. Which of the following does *NOT* define the term *team*?
    1. A team must have at least two licensee members, one of whom may be the firm's broker.
    2. Members of a team hold themselves out (present themselves) to the public as a being part of one entity.
    3. Members of a team designate themselves by a term such as "group" or "team" and work together on a regular basis to provide brokerage services.
    4. At least two members of a team must be licensees, whose license certificates are retained in the same office or branch office.

47. Which statement about team leaders is *TRUE*?
    1. The team leader is appointed (designated) by the firm's broker.
    2. The team leader may be an office manager.
    3. The team leader has an additional continuing education requirement at each renewal because of being a team leader.
    4. A team leader may select which team members will serve as intra-company agents in delivery of dual agency services.

48. Which statement about teams is incorrect?
    1. Members select their own team leader.
    2. Persons licensed under different brokers may be members of one team.
    3. The team leader may be a salesperson.
    4. Team advertising must show the name of at least one licensee team member.

49. Which is *NOT* a duty of the team leader?
    1. Maintain an up-to-date list of team members
    2. Provide an up-to-date list of team members to the firm (manager or broker)
    3. Supervise members of the team
    4. Keep any trust funds received during team activity in an account totally separate from the team leader's or any other team member's funds

50. Which statement about advertising by a team is *FALSE*?
    1. Advertisements for the team must not even give the impression that the team is itself a brokerage firm.
    2. Advertisements for a team must give the name of at least one member of the team.
    3. Advertisements for a team must include the phone number of the team leader.
    4. Advertisements for a team must clearly show the designated name of the brokerage firm and indicate that the team is part of the firm and not a separate unit.

APPENDIX C Complaint Procedure

■ POSSIBLE STEPS IN HANDLING COMPLAINTS AGAINST A LICENSEE

1.	Complaint is received by Real Estate Commission (REC).
2.	Complaint is reviewed by REC designee, usually the Executive Director.
2.1.a	OR: If complaint is deficient in form (i.e., unsigned or not made under oath), it is returned to complainant as rejected with explanation for the rejection.
2.1.b	OR: If complaint lacks facts alleging prima facie case, it is returned to Complainant as rejected with that reason given.
3.	Complaint is adjudged by REC designee to be in good form and to contain facts that suggest a violation of Brokers Act or REC Regulations has taken place.
4.	REC designee refers complaint to a hearing panel of the REC.
4.1	REC informs Complainant that the complaint is being processed.
5.	Hearing panel examines the complaint, and if the panel finds it is worthy of action, refers the matter to Investigative Services for investigation.
5.1	OR: Panel concludes that the facts do not warrant further pursuit of the complaint. Complainant is notified of this finding of insufficient grounds and that the complaint is rejected. There is no right to appeal this finding.
6.	Licensee who is being complained about (the Respondent) and Respondent's broker are informed of the complaint and asked by the panel for written comment.
7.	Investigative Services investigates and reports its findings to the hearing panel.
8.	Hearing panel examines the report from Investigative Services and the responses from the Respondent and Respondent's broker. Panel concludes that Respondent has violated law or regulation and **sets the matter in for** (schedules) a hearing.
8.1	OR: Panel concludes that the facts do not warrant further pursuit of the complaint and that the complaint is rejected. Complainant is notified of this decision. There is no right to appeal this finding.
9.	Panel notifies Respondent and Respondent's broker of the scheduled hearing and informs them of their rights to be present, to respond, to be represented by counsel, and to have witnesses subpoenaed (at Respondent's expense). They are also informed what the charges are and the possible penalties that could be imposed. Respondent must have 10-days' notice prior to the hearing. Complainant is also notified.
10.	In almost every case, the hearing is held before an administrative law judge (ALJ). It is open to the public. Written and/or oral testimony is given. An assistant attorney general (AAG) presents the Commission's case. Respondent has opportunity to be heard in defense or mitigation. ALJs base their conclusion on **preponderance of evidence**. **Hearsay evidence** is admitted but weighed with discretion. The AAG and the respondent's attorney may both rebut testimony and give summations. No decision is announced at the hearing. Hearing is conducted according to the Rules of Procedure of the Maryland Office of Administrative Hearings. [COMAR 28, Subtitle 02.01—C, a 16-page document.] Some days after the conclusion of the hearing, the **proposed decision** of the ALJ is sent to the REC.
11.	A *new* hearing panel is given the proposed decision to review along with the case record. Panel adopts (or modifies) the proposed decision and sends it to the Respondent and the Complainant, giving each one notice of the right to file an exception within 10 days.
12.	If either Complainant or Respondent takes exception within 10 days, the panel sets a date for a hearing at which the parties can present arguments against the decision and rebut each other's argument. Parties must have 14 days advance notice of this hearing.
13.	The panel that sent out the proposed decision hears the arguments taking exception to the decision. The panel reaches a decision.
14.	Some days later, the panel notifies parties of its decision rejecting the exception and issues a **final written order**.

15.	Parties submit to the decision contained in the final written order.
15.1	OR: A party **appeals** to the **circuit court.** (The appeal alone does not create a **stay** of the decision for a licensee.)
15.1.a	AND: Appellant (one who is appealing), if a licensee, petitions the circuit court for a stay of the decision (perhaps delaying the suspension or revocation of appellant's license). Court usually grants this request and seeks a bond not exceeding $50,000.
15.1.b	AND: Circuit court denies the appeal and lets final order stand.
15.2	BUT: Appellant carries appeal to Court of Special Appeals.
15.2.a	AND: Court of Special Appeals affirms the final order.
15.3	BUT: Appellant carries appeal to Court of Appeals.
15.3.a	AND: Court of Appeals sustains the final order.
15.1.2 or 3	OR: Any of the three courts could have granted the appeal and set aside the final order.
16.	Appeals are exhausted; final order will be executed by the REC.
	End of case

Note: These steps address a violation of the statute or the regulations in which no financial reimbursement was sought from the Guaranty Fund.

APPENDIX D

Maryland Real Estate–Related Websites

■ KEEPING UP-TO-DATE

Print materials like this volume are up-to-date when written and printed. However, changes in laws, regulations, and the business environment are constant. In various chapters of this book, websites (URLs) have been given for specific topics. Here, in Appendix D, several "master" websites of great value are listed. They can aid students who become licensees in meeting their responsibility to remain current on all real estate matters. These sites are veritable springboards into a wealth of information for the student of Maryland real estate brokerage. Most are listed according to the entity that maintains them.

A discussion follows each weblink.

The Maryland General Assembly

http://mgaleg.maryland.gov/

This is the main source of information for everything that happens in the legislative branch of Maryland government. It gives the dates for the annual sessions and the number of senators, delegates, and districts. It enables its readers to identify their legislators by giving their own zip codes and to contact any State legislator by email.

The site lists all bills that have been introduced in the State legislature since 1996. It gives the status of current bills and the ultimate disposition of all bills from previous sessions. Bills are indexed by subject, statute affected, sponsor, and bill number.

The site also sets forth the order of business for both the senate and house, their current agendas, and hearing schedules. It lists all the bills either signed or vetoed in the most recent session. In the case of a veto, a link is given to the letter in which the State governor explains the veto.

In every instance, the actual texts of bills can be brought to the screen and then printed out or saved.

State of Maryland Home Page

www.maryland.gov

On this home page, select "Online Services" in the upper right-hand corner. Here are links to almost 100 State agencies. The home page also gives links that connect the student with the executive branch, the Maryland judiciary, the Maryland State Law Library, Maryland State departments, agencies, boards and commissions, and important agencies of the federal government. It also links to each Maryland county for local government information and business developments.

Office of the Secretary of State Division of State Documents

www.dsd.state.md.us

This website provides links to the Code of Maryland Regulations (COMAR), which offers the entire text of every State agency regulation together with suggestions on how to search; *The Maryland Register,* the official publication of the State government where changes to COMAR are published; and the *Annotated Code of Maryland,* where the Brokers Act can be found in the *Business Occupations and Professions* Article, at Title 17. Any of this information can easily be downloaded and saved.

The Maryland Real Estate Commission

www.dllr.state.md.us/license/mrec/

Here, the student will find the names of Commission members, their terms, and the area of the state each licensee-member represents. At this site, the Commission makes available forms for complaints against licensees and forms for license renewal. It provides a means of inquiring about licensees by name. It contains information about licensing requirements, examinations required, license reciprocity, continuing education, and requirements for reinstatement of expired licenses. It also gives direct access to the current year's new laws and administrative changes that impact real estate licensees. It also links to COMAR and to the *Annotated Code.*

Maryland Statutes Text

www.lexisnexis.com/hottopics/mdcode/

This site gives ready access to the text of every Maryland statute. It does not, however, provide the commentary and explanations found in the *Annotated Code of Maryland.* Parts of any statute can be downloaded but only one segment at a time.

Maryland Association of REALTORS®

www.mdrealtor.org

After each annual session of the Maryland General Assembly, the association publishes a review of legislation important to the real estate practitioner. This document is also available to nonmembers of MAR. Copies of reviews from previous years are also available at that site.

The State Department of Assessments and Taxation

www.dat.state.md.us

Billed as "Maryland's Largest Source of Real Estate Data," this site not only gives information about Homeowners' Tax Credit, Homestead Tax Credit, and Renters' Tax Credit but also the assessment of every parcel of real estate in Maryland. It also explains the semiannual property tax payment schedule.

The site provides average sale prices of residential properties sold by county and by quarter for the last several years. Rates for the transfer tax, recordation tax, and tax stamps are also provided county by county.

PSI Examination Services Information and Tutorial

www.psiexams.com

At this site, see "View the Examination Tutorial" (found at the bottom right corner of the screen) to see a tutorial about taking a licensing examination. It is a preview of the tutorial given to the applicant, on screen, at the time of taking the examination and pictures the keyboard used and the function of the most important command keys. The site also has a link to the locations of all the testing centers used for taking Maryland real estate licensing exams. Students who register can download the "Candidate Information" booklet, which contains the application to take an exam.

Various Forms Required in Many Maryland Residential Real Estate Sales Transactions

Understanding Whom Real Estate Agents Represent form (1) Sometimes called the "Understanding Whom" form	The Commission's agency relationship information form, Understanding Whom Real Estate Agents Represent, must be presented not later than the first scheduled face-to-face meeting with a buyer (lessee) or a seller (lessor). This is a disclosure form, not a contract to represent any party. Merely presenting the form, no matter what boxes are checked, and whether or not it is signed, does not end presumed buyer representation or create or end any other agency relationship.
Understanding Whom Real Estate Agents Represent form (2) Presumed Buyer Representation and the "Understanding Whom" form	When prospects first seek assistance from a licensee in locating property to purchase or lease, the Brokers Act presumes that the licensee represents prospective purchasers (or tenants) and owes them fiduciary duties, such as confidentiality and loyalty. Licensees dealing with such prospects must, at their first contact, orally inform them of this representation and give them a completed Understanding Whom Real Estate Agents Represent form. Although the agent is not required to get prospects' signatures on the form during the period of presumed agency representation, the agent should keep a copy of the form as given to the prospects.
Understanding Whom Real Estate Agents Represent form (3) In regards to the written representation agreement	When a written agency agreement to represent either buyer (or lessee) or seller (or lessor) is completed, the licensee may be required to complete a new Understanding Whom Real Estate Agents Represent form. (This would be true in a situation where buyer representation and/or dual agency are now being undertaken and had not been checked in an earlier form.)
Consent for Dual Agency form	The Commission's Consent for Dual Agency form is signed by buyers (or lessees) and sellers (or lessors). One must have been signed by the buyer and one by the seller before a licensee can show a buyer client one of his firm's listings. Showing properties listed by other firms does not require the use of this consent form. This notification form is to be given to the seller no later than when the seller signs the listing agreement. It must be given to the buyer no later than the initial scheduled showing of the subject property. The signed forms provide proof that notifications were made. An additional separate Consent for Dual Agency form is required for each property to be shown under dual agency because the forms are both property-specific and owner-specific. Before an offer involving dual agency is presented, both parties—who have already signed the form—must also sign the Affirmation at the bottom of page two of the form. This form is most often needed when the prospective buyer is a client. It is not needed when the prospect is a customer and the licensee is acting as cooperating agent (the subagent of a seller). The latter case does not involve dual agency since the firm represents only one side of the transaction.
Notification of Dual Agency Within a Team form	When members of the same team are representing opposing parties in a dual agency transaction, the law requires that the buyer and seller each be notified in writing that (1) the two intra-company agents in that transaction are members of the same team, and that (2) the team itself could have a financial interest in the outcome of the transaction and in addition to any financial benefit obtained by selling one of their broker's own listings.
Property Condition Disclosure/ Disclaimer form	Purchasers are to be given a Property Condition Disclosure/Disclaimer form before an offer to purchase is submitted. It must have been properly completed and signed by sellers. Although this is a duty of sellers, responsibility to get it done falls upon the licensee representing the seller, the cooperating agent assisting the buyer, or the licensee representing the buyer. A buyer not receiving this form prior to ratification of contract may rescind the contract at any time prior to applying for financing. All agents should ensure that the form is presented to the purchaser before the purchaser submits an offer.

Lead-Based Paint Disclosure Statement

Booklet:
Protecting Your Family From Lead-Based Paint Hazards
Prior to submitting a written offer

Purchasers are to be given the following before an offer to purchase is signed:

- The Property Condition Disclosure/Disclaimer form must be properly completed and signed by sellers. This is a duty of all sellers, but responsibility rests with licensee representing the seller, by a cooperating agent assisting the buyer, or by the licensee representing the buyer. A buyer not receiving this form prior to ratification of contract may rescind the contract at any time prior to applying for financing. All agents should ensure that the form is presented to the purchaser before the purchaser submits an offer.
- The Lead-Based Paint Disclosure Statement and the booklet *Protecting Your Family From Lead-Based Paint Hazards* are to be given to purchasers of residential property built before 1978. This form is to accompany the contract of sale from this point forward. Licensees should get receipts from persons to whom they give this statement and booklet.

All forms

At time of contract presentation

At the time of contract presentation, copies of, or receipts for, disclosures given to all parties are to be in hand. When relevant, these include: Understanding Whom Real Estate Agents Represent forms; Consent for Dual Agency with Completed Affirmations; Property Condition Disclosure-Disclaimer; Disclosure of Dual Agency Within a Team; and, if applicable, the federally mandated Lead-Based Paint Disclosure Statement together with receipts for the information booklet *Protecting Your Family From Lead-Based Paint Hazards*.

ANSWER KEYS

CHAPTER 1: MARYLAND REAL ESTATE LICENSE LAW AND RELATED REGULATIONS

1. **(3)** Salespersons are not employed by owners but by brokers. They must work not only for brokers who are duly licensed but for brokers under whom they themselves are licensed.

2. **(2)** An affiliate's license certificate must be retained in the office out of which the affiliate works. Affiliates' licenses are rarely if ever in their own hands. All licensees carry pocket cards, not licenses.

3. **(4)** Changes in office location, company names, or employment of an affiliate must be communicated to the Commission. Sharing of a commission, whether between brokers and their affiliates or between and among brokers, is not the domain of the Commission.

4. **(1)** Salespersons must not split or otherwise have commissions divided with anyone. Brokers pay commissions but never, in whole or in part, to a nonlicensee.

5. **(2)** Freedom from broker control is not an IRS requirement for an IRS-recognized qualified agent. On the contrary, broker control is vital for reasonable and adequate supervision required by license law. The other requirements are accurately stated.

6. **(3)** Only license renewal fees are paid every two years (biennially). Initial fees, as the name implies, are paid only at the beginning of licensure. This is also true of fees for the Guaranty Fund.

7. **(3)** It is a misdemeanor for which the penalty is not more than $25,000 and imprisonment for not more than three years. It is unethical, not a felony, and not a legitimate listing technique.

8. **(2)** The Commission has this authority over nonlicensees who perform acts of real estate brokerage. The same violation may also result in a fine and also imprisonment if prosecuted by a state's attorney in a court of law.

9. **(3)** Unlicensed practice of real estate brokerage is a misdemeanor.

10. **(3)** Puffing, intemperance, and slander of competitors are ill-advised, but Title 17 does not mention them. It does, however, forbid acts of bad faith.

11. **(4)** Title 17 regards a deliberately false statement to the Commission in a matter involving a Guaranty Fund claim a misdemeanor with a fine by the Commission of not more than $25,000 for a third offense; or a $25,000 fine and imprisonment for not more than three years for a third offense when prosecuted in court by a state's attorney.

12. **(4)** While out-of-state businesses such as corporations, LLCs, and partnerships may be licensed under special conditions to perform commercial brokerage, standard Maryland brokerage licenses are granted only to individuals.

13. **(2)** Neither the House of Delegates nor the Executive Director is involved. The State Senate provides "advice and consent" and the Secretary (of DLLR) provides "advice" to the Governor who actually appoints members to the Commission.

14. **(2)** All brokerage licenses now expire two years from their date of issue. Previously, salesperson licenses had expired on April 30 of the next even-numbered year. Broker licenses previously expired on March 1 of the next even-numbered year.

15. **(2)** The Brokers Act is an exercise of the police power that protects the public interest. The public includes both consumers and providers of brokerage services.

16. **(3)** The Executive Director is chosen by the Secretary of Labor, Licensing, and Regulation from a list of three nominees submitted by the Commission. The Governor, the Senate, and the classified system are not involved.

17. **(3)** Ads placed by affiliates, or by their broker, for the sale of listed property must all clearly reveal the designated (official) name of the brokerage firm. Showing the affiliates' names, phone numbers, email addresses, and/or website URLs is permitted only if the name and phone number of the brokerage are also meaningfully and conspicuously displayed.

18. **(1)** The Guaranty Fund must be maintained at not less than $250,000. If it falls below that amount, an assessment for all new licenses and renewals is authorized.

19. **(2)** The three parts of the Code of Ethics refer to licensees' relations with the public, the client, and fellow licensees.

20. **(2)** The Commission has five licensee members and four consumer (nonlicensee) members.

21. **(1)** When the Commission is hesitant to issue a license to an applicant, they deny the request and offer the applicant a chance to be heard. Depending on the outcome of the hearing, the Commission either maintains its original position or grants the license.

22. **(1)** The Commission has statutory authority to set license and certain other fees associated with its operation. This authority, before being granted to the Commission, previously belonged to the General Assembly.

23. **(2)** In return for a fee, helping someone buy or sell Maryland real estate is an act of brokerage that requires licensure. The other three situations are specifically exempted from requiring a license.

24. **(4)** After being submitted to the Comptroller of the State, license fees are forwarded to the State Real Estate Commission Fund. This is an accumulating fund retained for the use of the Commission year after year.

25. **(1)** The law forbids that individuals who hold real estate licenses be employed by the Commission. Moreover, while employed by the Commission, employees shall not perform acts of brokerage for which licenses are required. The Executive Director and field inspectors are examples of employees.

26. **(1)** It is the broker's responsibility to return such license certificates to the Commission whenever any salesperson or associate broker leaves the firm for any reason.

27. **(2)** Maximum recovery from the Guaranty Fund is $~~25,000~~ per transaction. Only actual losses are covered.

28. **(4)** The first three statements are true, but not every person needs a license to perform acts of brokerage. There are a number of categories exempt from the requirement.

29. **(2)** Sales associates may deliver brokerage services only through and under a broker whom they are licensed, not an associate broker, and not just any broker. Salespersons may never operate brokerage businesses under their own names, unless they happen also to hold broker licenses.

30. **(1)** Attorneys who advertise publicly that they are in the business of providing brokerage services must hold broker licenses. A power of attorney given to an individual (by a buyer or by a seller) allows that individual to perform a single act of real estate brokerage. Salespersons for home builders need not hold real estate licenses; however, they must be registered with the Home Builder and Home Builder Sales Representative Registration Unit of the Consumer Protection Division of the Maryland Attorney General's Office. Trustees conducting a trustee's sale of foreclosed properties are specifically exempt from the license requirement.

CHAPTER 2: REAL ESTATE AGENCY

1. **(2)** Real estate brokers' principals are their clients. Brokers are agents of their principals.

2. **(3)** Such dual agency can be performed in Maryland real estate only when a broker appoints two such intra-company agents (ICAs). Brokers may be agents of either buyers or sellers but may not represent both personally. However, the broker's firm may represent both buyer and seller if the broker designates two intra-company agents: one for the seller, and one for the buyer. The person who appoints the two ICAs cannot serve as one of them.

3. **(4)** The players are properly identified in choice (4). Bettina is not a single-agency broker because she is performing dual agency here through her company.

4. **(2)** A broker who represents a client-buyer must disclose that fact to any seller or the agent of any seller he encounters.

5. **(4)** Presumed buyer representation (PBR) begins when a prospect seeks assistance to rent or buy residential property. PBR ends when a buyer asks to make a contract offer on a property. PBR also ends when the licensee shows the prospect a property listed with the licensee's firm. [Although this fact is ignored in the practice of many agents, 17-533(d) states, "A licensee who is acting as a presumed buyer's or lessee's agent may show and assist the buyer or lessee only on *real estate that is not listed by the broker of that licensee.* (Emphasis added)] PBR does not end when a prospect is shown the property of another firm.

6. **(4)** The only way a firm may represent both buyer and seller in the same transaction is for its broker (or branch manager) to appoint two intra-company agents—one to represent the buyer, the other the seller. Neither a salesperson nor a broker can personally represent both buyer and seller in a transaction, even with the parties' permission. "No harm" is no excuse for a broker's improperly conducting dual agency.

7. **(4)** It is a violation of privacy under the Americans with Disabilities Act to state that a present or former occupant of a property under consideration by a purchaser had or is said to have had HIV, AIDS, or AIDS-Related Complex (ARC). No fiduciary duty is breached by withholding such information or opinion.

8. **(3)** Title 17, the Brokers Act, requires disclosure not later than the first scheduled face-to-face meeting with buyer or seller prospects. The rule for REALTORS®, by contrast, is disclosure of representation at the first contact. To wait until an offer is made—or until a party requests disclosure of representation—is to violate the law and also risk possible collapse of a settlement, with consequent litigation, and costly disciplinary action by the Commission.

9. **(3)** Agents must obey their clients, not their customers. The other three duties are owed to customers as well as to clients.

10. **(2)** Only firms with a minimum of three licensees may engage in dual agency under Maryland law because there must be two intra-company agents appointed by a broker. The broker may not self-appoint to be an intra-company agent. Ministerial duties do not support a charge by either party of disloyalty or undisclosed dual agency.

11. **(3)** Whether or not the licensee presents the agency disclosure form, the prospect is still presumed by law to have presumed buyer representation (PBR) until either the prospect or the licensee refuses PBR, prospect is shown a property listed by the licensee's firm[1], prospect wants to prepare an offer on any property, or prospect enters into as formal representation (buyer broker) agreement.

12. **(3)** Lawful dual agency requires that the firm designate two licensees as intra-company agents (ICAs), one for each party. Agreement by the parties to dual agency is required but not, by itself, sufficient. A firm with only a broker and one agent cannot meet this requirement because the broker may not serve as an ICA. The Commission does not certify for dual agency; it merely enforces statutory requirements for its performance.

13. **(1)** In § 17-533(i)(1), the Brokers Act requires this disclosure, orally, at a licensee's first meeting (not first, scheduled, face-to-face meeting) with a prospect. Licensee must also then disclose that the prospect can decline the presumed representation. The prospect's signing a representation agreement would not reveal PBR; it would end it. If dual agency has arisen because prospect has been shown an in-house property, PBR has already ended.

14. **(1)** A cooperating agent is the subagent of the listing broker who represents the sellers; therefore, the cooperating agent cannot represent buyers, only assist them by bringing them to the listing company. Cooperating agents' fiduciary duties are to sellers.

15. **(3)** The Brokers Act requires licensees to present the disclosure of representation form (Understanding Whom Real Estate Agents Represent) at the first scheduled, face-to-face meeting with buyer prospects. When licensees represent buyers, they must also present properly completed Understanding Whom forms to sellers at first contact. The disclosure of agency representation form, when delivered—whether signed by the prospect or not—never creates or ends a contract or a relationship.

---

1   General Assembly of Maryland, "Article – Business Occupations and Professions: § 17-533(d)," General Assembly of Maryland, http://mgaleg.maryland.gov/2014rs/statute _google/gbo/17-533.pdf (accessed May 16, 2014).

CHAPTER 3: REAL ESTATE BROKERAGE

1. **(2)** If price is shown, so must be the amount of the annual ground rent and the cost to redeem the lot.

2. **(1)** An ad may show the name of the listing salesperson but must show the broker's designated name. Showing the asking price is optional. One MLS member may not advertise properties listed by other members.

3. **(4)** The statute calls for brokers to have a definite place of business and to maintain there an office for regular conduct of business and maintenance of records. Commission regulations state that a mail drop, answering service, or mechanical answering device, together or separately, will not meet this requirement.

4. **(4)** Only a licensed real estate broker may operate a Maryland real estate brokerage firm.

5. **(1)** All ads must contain the designated name of the broker. It may or may not be the broker's legal individual name, but it must be the name shown on the broker's license as issued by the Commission.

6. **(2)** Licensed brokers of firms, the persons primarily responsible for actions of the firms and their affiliates, are not required or forbidden to perform any of the other three functions.

7. **(1)** If a salesperson's name appears in an ad, the designated name of the broker must also be clearly and conspicuously displayed. If the salesperson's phone number is given, the clearly identified phone number of the firm must also be shown.

8. **(2)** Unless there are instructions to the contrary, earnest money deposits held by a broker must be placed—and kept until properly disbursed—in a non-interest-bearing account in an insured, approved Maryland depository institution. The other choices describe forbidden actions.

9. **(4)** The broker's signature is sufficient by itself, although other combinations of other licensees and nonlicensees are permitted, providing that at least one is a licensee.

10. **(3)** Unlicensed persons, such as personal assistants, may assist in the holding of open houses by providing security for the licensee conducting them or handing out printed materials, but they may not conduct open houses. They are permitted to do the other listed functions.

11. **(1)** The use of the forbidden terms *Realty*, *Real Estate*, and *Associate*(s) leaves only one acceptable choice because it does not suggest that the team is a separate brokerage firm.

12. **(3)** The Brokers Act specifies that intra-company agents for dual agency situations be designated by the firm's broker. The other three statements are correct as written.

13. **(2)** The name of at least one team member is required in team advertising but not necessarily the team leader's name. The other three choices correctly state requirements.

14. **(1)** The Broker's Act states, "[T]he team name must be directly connected with the name of the brokerage." The other choices are not in the law.

15. **(4)** A salesperson who has had at least three years of license activity and is chosen by the members of the team may be its leader. The other three statements are true.

CHAPTER 4: LISTING AGREEMENTS AND BUYER REPRESENTATION AGREEMENTS

1. **(1)** A net listing is forbidden in Maryland real estate brokerage. The other three are permitted.

2. **(3)** Chapter 7 of the Regulations of the Commission, entitled *Residential Property Disclosure/Disclaimer Statement*, requires that the Residential Property Condition Disclosure and Disclaimer Statement be completed at the time a licensee lists the property. It is to be completed by the client, not the licensee. Later completion is a violation of the regulation.

3. **(2)** A buyer may rescind the contract before application for a loan is made. If no loan is needed, and no loan application is made, the right of rescission could last until settlement. A buyer who receives the statement after the contract is fully signed has five days to rescind. However, when a buyer makes a loan application, and is informed by the lender that by applying, the buyer will lose the right to rescind, the right is ended. However, if the lender fails to so inform the buyer, the right continues. If the lender later speaks up and informs the buyer sometime after a loan application is made, buyer has another five days. Obviously, it is important to get the statement to the buyer before the buyer submits the offer.

4. **(2)** Before the firm may offer a property for sale, a completed copy of the listing must be given to the seller. Advertising the property is one way of offering a property for sale.

5. **(1)** A Maryland affiliate must hold a Virginia license and be working for a Maryland broker who is also licensed as a broker in Virginia. The other choices do not qualify. The broker for whom a salesperson is working on a Virginia property must hold a Virginia broker license.

6. **(3)** Forms published by a multiple listing service are copyrighted and may be used only by its members who subscribe to that service. A person using such a listing agreement would, of course, also have to be a licensee.

7. **(3)** To be valid and to conform to the Brokers Act, listing agreements for Maryland real estate must be written (not parol), signed by all owners and by an authorized representative of the brokerage firm, and state the compensation to be earned either as a percentage of the selling price or as a dollar amount. Automatic renewal provisions are forbidden.

8. **(4)** Buyers who receive the form prior to submitting their offer may not rescind the contract based on that offer because of something revealed in that form. The three rights of rescission, shown in the other choices, do not exist.

9. **(1)** The rate or amount of commission is established by negotiation between broker and client and must be clearly stated in the listing contract. There is no established rate imposed, or even suggested, by government or by the real estate industry.

10. **(3)** The General Regulations of the Commission, supported by the Brokers Act, require listings on Maryland residential property to be written. Listings create agency relationships and must contain definite termination dates requiring no notice from either party.

CHAPTER 5: INTERESTS IN REAL ESTATE

1. **(3)** These easements are for the purpose of keeping the land on which they are purchased in agricultural use. This, in turn, benefits the environment by slowing suburban sprawl.

2. **(4)** A minimum of 20 years' continuous use is required by Maryland statute. Twenty-five years' continuous use meets and exceeds that requirement, but 25 years' intermittent use does not.

3. **(4)** Prescriptive easement is recognized. The other three choices, which are examples of legal life estates, are not recognized in Maryland.

4. **(1)** An owner whose land is bordered by a navigable river owns to the average high-water mark but may construct a pier that reaches farther out. This riparian owner owns the pier but not the water or land beneath it. Although the owner has the right to use water from the stream, he may not prevent the water from passing through by a dam or other means of diversion. No wharf is to be constructed without approval of the governmental agencies that have authority to grant or withhold such permits.

5. **(4)** State real estate transfer taxes help fund the purchase of agricultural easements.

CHAPTER 6: HOW OWNERSHIP IS HELD

1. **(2)** Maryland is not a community property state.

2. **(3)** It will be construed to create a tenancy by the entirety.

3. **(2)** In tenancy by the entirety, when one spouse dies, the surviving spouse becomes owner in severalty because concurrent ownership of any kind requires more than one owner.

4. **(1)** Chapter 4 of the Regulations of the Maryland Real Estate Commission requires timeshare developers to register with that body.

5. **(2)** Unless a higher proportion is specified by the condominium's declaration, Maryland condominium bylaws require a two-thirds vote of the council of unit owners. Additionally, notice and quorum restrictions may apply.

6. **(3)** Rental conversion to condominium requires registration with the Maryland Secretary of State.

7. **(2)** Those who purchase a new condominium from its developer may void their contracts right up until settlement if they have not received the Public Offering Statement. If they proceed with settlement, they lose the right to void their agreements. Other choices are incorrect.

8. **(2)** They have a 10-day right of cancellation for any (or no) reason.

9. **(4)** All these documents must be delivered to the purchasers not later than 15 days before closing. When they have been delivered, condominium resale purchasers then have seven days to cancel without any announced reason.

10. **(3)** The Maryland Attorney General's office mediates most forms of condominium disputes among these parties.

CHAPTER 7: LEGAL DESCRIPTIONS

1. **(1)** References to the recorded plat of subdivision are sufficient to describe lots within that subdivision. They are used both in listings and in sales agreements.

2. **(2)** A location drawing shows that the improvement is actually on the lot and shows other basic facts. Placing fences, however, requires a boundary survey, which is usually more expensive.

3. **(3)** This description is dignified by reference to the recorded plat of subdivision for its details. The other choices lack material details such as adequate boundaries and other dimensions.

4. **(4)** This description makes use of distances, compass directions, and monuments to describe a parcel in outline—all characteristic of metes-and-bounds surveys.

5. **(3)** Most Maryland legal property descriptions use either the metes-and-bounds or the recorded plat of subdivision method. For convenience, street addresses and post office box numbers may appear, but they are not part of the actual legal description. Baltimore City, however, uses a system of parcels on numbered blocks.

CHAPTER 8: REAL ESTATE TAXES AND OTHER LIENS

1. **(4)** Some jurisdictions at each of those levels have been enabled to levy taxes on Maryland real estate. They are given this authority by state enabling acts.

2. **(2)** Each parcel of residential Maryland real estate is reassessed once every three years at full market value. An out-of-sequence reassessment may be performed when a property has undergone significant improvement.

3. **(3)** Contractors have six months from the completion of their work to record a notice of lien. Six months after March 15 would be September 15.

4. **(1)** Annual real estate taxes are due on July 1, but the two installment payments are not late until October 1 and the following January 1.

5. **(1)** For situations involving a first-time homebuyer, the State transfer tax is reduced from 0.5% to 0.25% and is charged to the seller. Therefore, the seller pays 0.25% of the consideration. ($0.0025 \times \$400,000 = \$1,000$.) The parties may not agree to shift this charge to the buyer.

CHAPTER 9: REAL ESTATE CONTRACTS

1. **(1)** The Maryland Statute of Frauds requires that all contracts for transfer of interests in property for more than one year be in writing and signed. The sales contract transfers equitable title to the buyer and, thus, meets this description. There are widely used industry contracts, but there is no standard contract. All parties must sign.

2. **(2)** *Parol* means oral. A licensee who fails to reduce agreements between parties to writing violates the Brokers Act. An oral agreement to purchase might be valid (enforceable in court) under very specific, limited circumstances.

3. **(1)** Licensees dealing on their own behalf must disclose their licensee status (the fact that they are licensees) to the other party. Typically such disclosure is written into the contract being used.

4. **(4)** The others are all required for the protection of the purchaser.

5. **(3)** Inclusion of the notice is required in all counties, even those excluded by the notice.

CHAPTER 10: TRANSFER OF TITLE

1. **(3)** Maryland requirements for adverse possession include open, hostile, continuous possession for 20 years under claim of right or color of title.

2. **(4)** All three are true. Even when a valid will is left, a widow or widower who receives less than their intestate share can contest the will under the Law of Descent and Distribution.

3. **(4)** Deeds are valid between the parties—the "party of the first part" and the "party of the second part"—even without recordation. That means they can be enforced by either one against the other. Recorded deeds, however, protect grantees against third parties.

4. **(3)** To be recorded, a deed to Maryland real estate must have been prepared by the grantor, grantee, or an attorney. It must show (or be accompanied by an affidavit showing) the full consideration. Only a typewritten will may be recorded.

5. **(4)** Although often witnessed by three, a will with only two witnesses satisfies Maryland law. The other three statements are false.

CHAPTER 11: TITLE RECORDS

1. **(4)** Instruments that affect land partially in each of two counties are recorded in both counties.

2. **(2)** Customarily, title search is ordered by the settlement company on behalf of the buyer and at the buyer's expense.

3. **(1)** Deeds and mortgages affecting Maryland land are recorded in the office of the county clerk of circuit court.

4. **(3)** These instruments are recorded in the grantee and the grantor index. They typically refer to previously recorded transactions. The selling (or the listing) broker's name is not a matter for recordation.

5. **(2)** Witnessing does not take the place of the required acknowledgment before a notary. A deed must be notarized to be recorded. A deed must have been drawn up either by an attorney or one of the parties.

CHAPTER 12: REAL ESTATE FINANCING

1. **(2)** The Federal Equal Credit Opportunity Act forbids refusal of credit to an applicant based on the applicant's religion.

2. **(4)** Maryland law requires that his lender grant James a six-month extension if he requests it.

3. **(2)** Under Maryland law, courts may not foreclose on an unrecorded mortgage. It is the lenders' (mortgagees') obligation to record their mortgages.

4. **(1)** Mortgages and deeds of trust are the two ways that lenders secure almost all Maryland residential loans. A bank would not be involved in an installment contract unless it was selling property it owned. Real estate trusts and deeds of release have no relation to the situation described.

5. **(3)** Banks, savings banks, and savings associations are required by state law to credit the borrower's escrow account with passbook rate (or 3%, whichever is greater) interest annually for first mortgage loans for which they hold servicing duties.

CHAPTER 13: LEASES

1. **(2)** If there is no provision in the lease to the contrary, common law provides that a tenant's right of possession is uninterrupted by transfer of ownership of the leased fee. Rollins' rights and responsibilities as a tenant continue until the original end of the lease.

2. **(1)** Maryland statutes require that landlords credit tenants' security deposit accounts with 3% per annum simple interest, computed in six-month intervals, but not compounded. Therefore, a deposit of $2,400 would earn $72.

3. **(1)** A lease for seven years or less need not be recorded, but a lease for more than seven years must be recorded. Acknowledgment before a notary would be required for recordation.

4. **(2)** An annual ground rent of $720, capitalized at the rate of 6%, suggests that the value of the land alone is $12,000 (720 divided by 0.06). By not selling the land to the buyer, the builder can lower his price for the property by $12,000, to $228,000.

5. **(2)** Arthur will receive a leasehold on an improved lot with ground rent as stated.

6. **(2)** One who pays rent for the land she possesses holds a leasehold estate.

7. **(1)** One purpose for which ground rents are created is to make the purchase of a developer-built house more affordable. The buyer buys the house but rents the lot rather than buying the land outright.

8. **(2)** The annual ground rent divided by the capitalization rate gives the cost of redemption. Example 2 is the only one of the four that satisfies this formula. ($600 divided by 0.06 = $10,000.)

9. **(4)** Court seizure and sale of a residential tenant's personal property for unpaid rent is called distraint.

10. **(1)** Five percent of one month's rent is a penalty for late payment allowed by Maryland statute. The other provisions may appear in a lease, but they are unenforceable in court and any attempt to enforce them is itself a violation of the law.

CHAPTER 14: ENVIRONMENTAL ISSUES AND REAL ESTATE TRANSACTIONS

1. **(2)** Leakage from USTs (underground storage tanks) pollutes the ground and groundwater rather than directly entering the air.

2. **(3)** The two objectives are interrelated because preservation of open space is, itself, an important method of preserving ecological balance.

3. **(3)** Revitalization of older neighborhoods is intended to slow sprawl into the open countryside. The plan seeks to increase housing density and does not encourage development of new areas.

4. **(2)** State law enables local jurisdictions to impose environmental regulations that are even stricter than those of the State. To take effect, however, the local regulations may not be less strict.

5. **(4)** Addressing environmental issues involves multiple levels of government as well as overlapping geographic jurisdictions.

6. **(3)** State agencies seldom allow local governments to approve any disturbance of the land in a buffer zone. The buffer zone is 200 feet, and the critical area is 1,000 feet.

7. **(2)** Where a critical area ends, a 200-foot buffer zone begins.

8. **(2)** It must be shown that there is no other way to accomplish a worthy objective before filling of wetlands is permitted.

9. **(1)** Maryland's regulatory environmental actions seek to make less new land available for real estate development, a situation which increases costs of construction in rural areas and encourages more intense use of previously developed urban centers.

10. **(2)** Language in the notice excludes certain counties in its warnings. Nevertheless, the notice must appear in residential sales contracts in every county.

CHAPTER 15: FAIR HOUSING

1. **(4)** Any warning about hostile attitudes in the residents of the neighborhood would tend to discourage the purchasers and, therefore, amount to steering.

2. **(1)** Persons involved in real estate transactions are bound by all antidiscrimination laws. They are held to have constructive notice because ignorance of a law does not excuse its violation.

3. **(2)** To show the property to prospects based, either positively or negatively, on their race is a violation of fair housing laws. It is steering regardless of its motivation and no matter who does it.

4. **(1)** Blockbusting is attempting to frighten present owners into listing their properties for sale. Although it is typically done for financial gain, that is not a requirement for prosecution under the Brokers Act.

5. **(4)** The situation described is one of the exceptions built into the Fair Housing Act of 1968. Maryland has parallel exceptions in its fair housing laws. In addition, such a club may advertise tenancy "for members only."

CHAPTER 16: CLOSING THE REAL ESTATE TRANSACTION

1. **(4)** Closings in Maryland are performed under the supervision of an attorney. This does not mean the attorney has to be physically present.

2. **(3)** The settlement officer is required to account to the seller for the payoff no longer than 30 days after closing.

3. **(1)** No matter whom attorneys performing settlement represent, they owe all parties due care in conducting the closing, disbursing funds, and so forth.

4. **(2)** Title evidence is usually ordered on behalf of and paid for by the purchaser.

5. **(3)** The closing officer must withhold 8.25% of an out-of-state corporate seller's net proceeds. If the seller were an individual rather than an entity, the amount withheld would be 6.75%. In 2005, applying the law's formula changed the withholding rate for a nonresident individual from 7.5% to 6.75%. The previous 8.25% rate of withholding for nonresident entities did not change.

APPENDIX B: PRACTICE EXAM

1. **(2)** No commission can be claimed by a firm based on the activity of a person who should have been properly licensed but was not.

2. **(1)** Licenses are issued for a period of two years from their date of issuance.

3. **(2)** Based on presumed buyer/lessee representation, they are owed client-level duties.

4. **(3)** Salespersons' and associate brokers' licenses must be retained in the brokers' branch office out of which each works.

5. **(3)** The maximum loss that is covered is $25,000 per transaction.

6. **(4)** Since 2005, the amended law has allowed unsolicited fax advertising if the sender has an established business relationship (EBR) with the recipient and the recipient has given the fax number to the sender with permission to use it.

7. **(3)** Membership of the Maryland Real Estate Commission is composed of five licensee members (either salespersons or brokers) and four consumer (nonlicensee) members.

8. **(4)** Although passing the courses is required, not all who pass apply for a license and not all who apply are granted one by the Real Estate Commission. The Brokers Act (Title 17) empowers the State Real Estate Commission to issue salesperson, associate broker, and broker licenses.

9. **(2)** The State Real Estate Commission has authority over all Maryland licensees, while the Association of REALTORS® has authority only over its members. Not all licensees are REALTORS®.

10. **(3)** A partnership wishing to provide brokerage services must find a broker and designate that person as the broker of their firm. The broker could be one of the partners but need not be. No unlicensed partner, however, may participate in any act of brokerage.

11. **(1)** Although many builders use licensed brokers to sell their homes, the builders don't need to employ licensees or be licensees. Changes in the law in 2008, however, require builders and their salespeople to register with the Home Builder and Home Builder Sales Representative Registration Unit, an agency in the Attorney General's Office.

12. **(2)** The Maryland Time-Share Act requires that a developer converting a residential rental building into a time-share holding give its residents 120 days' advance notice and provide them with other assistance in certain circumstances.

13. **(3)** Unless they are also qualified to practice law in Maryland, real estate licensees are forbidden to give legal advice, although they often explain common contract provisions.

14. **(1)** In a title-theory state, the mortgagees (lenders) receive bare legal title to mortgaged property. However, they agree (in the mortgage defeasance clause) that their claims will be extinguished by borrowers' paying off the debts secured by their mortgages.

15. **(1)** The Commission may impose a fine as much as $25,000 for a third offense and/or suspend or revoke the license of the offender. Violations prosecuted by the Attorney General, on the other hand, may result in fines as much as $25,000 in addition to possible imprisonment for periods from one to three years.

16. **(3)** It is a cardinal principal of federal and state antitrust legislation that competing providers of a service such as real estate brokerage are not to establish, try to establish, or even discuss with one another, the fees they charge the public.

17. **(4)** Salespersons should never maintain trust accounts for customers' or clients' money. Earnest monies also should not be kept in the office safe. Such deposits must be promptly (and in no event, longer than seven business days after the last party has signed) deposited by the broker or the broker's designee in the firm's trust account.

18. **(3)** Tenancy by the entirety involves only two persons: a married couple. When one of the two dies, the one left is alone and has no one to be a tenant in common with. The survivor's ownership thus is in severalty.

19. **(3)** The fiduciary duty of brokers requires that they put the benefit of their clients (in this case, the sellers) ahead of their own. If the seller clients can see all available offers, they can choose the one that is best for them and not be maneuvered into accepting an offer that would most benefit the brokerage firm.

20. **(4)** Maryland's Statute of Frauds requires that, to take effect, transfers of any interest in real property for more than one year must be in writing and signed.

21. **(4)** No legal requirement about land (installment) contracts requires contact with the Commission. The other statements are true.

22. **(1)** Representation agreements are not created by delivery of this form. Presentation of the form doesn't end presumed buyer representation or give permission for dual agency either. Each of these requires a separate written agreement. The form in question merely tells the one to whom it is delivered whom the licensee presenting it is representing. It also explains the ways parties can be represented or served by licenses.

23. **(4)** Neither death of a client nor expiration of an agency agreement ends the requirement for agents to maintain confidentiality. That requirement ends by permission of the client or by the information becoming common knowledge from other sources. The Statute of Limitations does not address this matter.

24. **(4)** The Brokers Act, Title 17, specifies that the form be presented "not later than the first scheduled face-to-face meeting with a prospect." In contrast, the REALTOR® Code of Ethics requires that agency representation be disclosed even sooner—"at first contact."

25. **(2)** Neither payment or promise of payment of consideration, nor the delivery of ministerial (servant) acts, is a basis for inferring that an agency relationship exists. On the other hand, a customer who receives expert (magisterial) guidance from a licensee could properly infer an agency relationship.

26. **(2)** The interest is computed in six-month intervals but is not compounded. The other statements are accurate.

27. **(1)** Although heinous, drunken driving is not one of the offenses listed in Title 17 as warranting penalties. The other three offenses are bases for such disciplinary action by the Commission.

28. **(1)** Licensee duties to nonclients include honesty, reasonable care, and disclosure of material facts. A seller's brokerage fee may properly be shared with the agent of the buyer, even though that agent is not a subagent of the seller. Compensation for representing a buyer also requires a written agreement with the buyer.

29. **(4)** The declaration is a document separate and distinct from both a condominium's bylaws and from its rules. It does not contain either the bylaws or the rules. The other three statements are accurate.

30. **(1)** A property is placed under a condominium regime (governance) by recording its declaration.

31. **(1)** Deficiency judgments for a lender are possible when foreclosure has been court-supervised (as it is in judicial foreclosure). Such judgments are not available to lenders in cases of nonjudicial foreclosure and of foreclosure of FHA-insured loans.

32. **(1)** The good-faith duty of fairness to both parties prevents brokers from putting the interests of their clients ahead of those of the adverse party in deciding to whom contested earnest money will be paid. Title 17 makes the other three alternatives available to the broker in such situations.

33. **(4)** Security deposits may be withheld for actual costs of repair for tenant damage to the rented property over and above normal wear and tear as well as for unpaid rent.

34. **(1)** The mere physical presence of a broker, no matter how many hours are invested, is not one of the evidences of reasonable and adequate supervision listed in Title 17. No credit is given for attendance. The other three choices are each found in that statute.

35. **(4)** Maryland law requires that listing agreements contain (among other things) a termination date that is effective without further action by either broker or client. Automatic extension provisions are forbidden.

36. **(1)** There is no limit on the interest rate for first mortgages. Second mortgages and land contracts are limited to 24%. Deeds of trust, used in place of the traditional mortgage, are subject to the same limits as mortgages.

37. **(1)** Renters receive presumed representation (just like buyers) for which no fee may be claimed. The law no longer regards walk-ins as customers. Although the statute says, ". . . not later than the first scheduled face-to-face meeting," it is prudent to give unscheduled walk-ins the agency disclosure form immediately.

38. **(3)** Biennial renewal for a licensee requires a total of 15 clock hours of approved courses. Among these must be at least three hours of ethics, three hours of legislative update, and—except for exclusively commercial licensees—one and one-half hours of fair housing. In place of fair housing, commercial licensees may take one and one-half hours of class presenting the Americans with Disabilities Act.

39. **(1)** It must be the place where the firm regularly conducts real estate, not insurance, transactions. The other three requirements are stated accurately.

40. **(1)** On the contrary, the ad gives the impression that associate broker Buonasera is the head of a firm, its broker. The other statements about improper advertising are accurate.

41. **(4)** Beginning with all licensees' first renewals on or after January 1, 2012, their continuing education must include the three-hour Agency and Disclosure course at alternate renewals (i.e., every four years) as part of their required 15 hours.

42. **(1)** It must be taken—not by all licensees, but only by brokers, branch managers, and team leaders—for every alternate license renewal on or after January 1, 2012. It is taken as part of, and not in addition to, their required 15 required hours of instruction.

43. **(2)** To fulfill license renewal requirements, both the Agency and the Supervision courses must be taught by teachers identified by the Commission. Such teachers must have had specific Commission-sponsored training for presenting those courses.

44. **(1)** A prospect who declines presumed buyer representation—something orally disclosed by the licensee to the prospect early in any first interview—must still be given an agency representation disclosure (Understanding Whom) form before the end of the first scheduled face-to-face meeting with the licensee. The other three choices are situations to which the requirement does not apply. They are situations specifically exempted by §17529 of the Brokers Act.

45. **(2)** Maryland and federal fair housing laws allow exclusion of families with children from occupancy of housing for elderly who meet certain requirement. However, such families may not be denied ownership. In choice (4), the age stated (50) is incorrect; it must be 55 or older in order to be true.

46. **(1)** The firm's broker may not be a team member (or leader). The other three statements are correct.

47. **(2)** A branch manager is permitted to be a team member or its leader. A team leader is chosen by the members of the team, not the firm's broker. The leader's additional educational requirement is not imposed for each renewal, only for alternate renewals which take place on or after January 1, 2012. Only the firm's broker may designate intra-company agents (ICAs) for dual agency that occurs within a team.

48. **(2)** Team members exercising licensee status must be licensed under the broker of the firm and work out of the office where each team member's license certificate is retained. It is conceivable, but ill-advised, that a licensee whose only license is with another firm could be a team member. Such a person could only serve as an unlicensed personal assistant. The other answer choices are correct.

49. **(4)** Trust funds received by a member of a team must follow company policies and procedures and immediately be given to an officer of the firm responsible for handling such funds. They must then be deposited in the firm's escrow account promptly but not later than seven business days after the contract to which the funds apply has been signed by all parties. Team members and leaders are not authorized to have such trust accounts. The other three choices correctly state duties of team leaders.

50. **(3)** The team leader's phone number is not required but may appear. The clearly identified phone number of the firm, however, is required. The other choices are true statements.

Index

Notes

Notes